DISCARDED

Political Ascent

STATE, CULTURE, AND SOCIETY
IN ARAB NORTH AFRICA
Series Editors
John P. Entelis, Fordham University
Michael Suleiman, Kansas State University

The states and societies of Arab North Africa have long been neglected in the scholarly literature dealing with the Arab world, the Middle East, and Islam, except in the context of dramatic international events. Yet this region has a rich historical and cultural tradition that offers important insights into the evolution of society, the complexity of cultural life, forms of social interaction, strategies of economic development, and patterns of state formation throughout the developing world. In addition, as the region has assumed more importance in geopolitical terms, both the United States and Europe have become more directly involved in its economics and politics. Few books of a scholarly or policy nature, however, analyze and interpret recent trends and changes in the constellation of relations between regional and global powers. This new series—the first in English to focus exclusively on North Africa—will address important conceptual and policy issues from an interdisciplinary perspective, giving special emphasis to questions of political culture and political economy.

Books in This Series

Political Ascent: Contemporary Islamic Movements in North Africa, Emad Eldin Shahin

The North African Environment at Risk, edited by Will D. Swearingen and Abdellatif Bencherifa

Polity and Society in Contemporary North Africa, edited by I. William Zartman and William Mark Habeeb

Political Ascent

Contemporary Islamic Movements in North Africa

Emad Eldin Shahin

WestviewPress

A Division of HarperCollins*Publishers*

State, Culture, and Society in Arab North Africa

Copyright © 1997 by Westview Press, A Division of HarperCollins Publishers, Inc.

Published in 1997 in the United States of America by Westview Press, 5500 Central Avenue, Boulder,
Colorado 80301-2877, and in the United Kingdom by Westview Press, 12 Hid's Copse Road,
Cumnor Hill, Oxford OX2 9JJ

Library of Congress Cataloging-in-Publication Data
Shahin, Emad Eldin, 1957–
  Political ascent : contemporary Islamic movements in North Africa / Emad Eldin Shahin.
    p.   cm.—(State, culture, and society in Arab North Africa)
  Includes bibliographical references and index.
  ISBN 0-8133-2775-X (hc)
  1. Islam—Africa, North—History—20th century. 2. Islam and
politics—Africa, North. 3. Africa, North—Politics and government.
I. Title. II. Series: State, culture, and society in Arab North Africa.
BP64.A4N677 1997
3200.5'5'0961—dc21   96-46801
                                                                                                           CIP

The paper used in this publication meets the requirements of the American National Standard for
Permanence of Paper for Printed Library Materials Z39.48-1984.

10   9   8   7   6   5   4   3   2   1

*For Lilia Rezgui, Omar, Tarek,
and Farrah Shahin*

Contents

Acknowledgments

I owe a great deal of debt to many people for the completion and production of this book. I am most grateful to my teachers at the various stages of my education: James Piscatori, Senior Fellow at the Oxford Centre for Islamic Studies, a great mentor and a good friend; Walid Kazziha, Professor of Political Science at the American University in Cairo, who taught me how to belong; Enid Hill, Professor of Political Science at the American University in Cairo, a perceptive teacher of Western political theory; Raymond Hinnebusch, Professor of Political Science at the College of St. Catherine, who left a lasting impact on me; and I. William Zartman, Director of the African Studies Department at SAIS, Johns Hopkins University, a great scholar of North Africa. I am specially grateful to the late Galal Keshk, from whom I learned to always be proud of my culture.

I must also thank all the people who made my research in Tunisia and Morocco feasible. For the friends in Tunisia, it might be prudent not to mention their names. However, I will always remain grateful to everyone of them. In Morocco, I wish to thank Dr. Mohamed Guessous, Dr. Mohamed Tozy, Abdullah Saa`f, Rashid Medwer, and Mostapha al-Haya, who were all very generous with their time and granted me interviews. I must also thank the American Institute for Maghrib Studies (AIMS) for a short-term grant in the summer of 1985.

Many friends and colleagues have helped me with comments and editorial assistance on the manuscript. I should like to thank Sana Abed-Kotob, Paul Schemm, and Alice Umbarak. However, I remain responsible for any mistakes which I have inadvertently made. I wish to thank Dr. Ahmed Yousef, Director of the United Association for Studies and Research, for granting me access to the Association's rich archives. I should also like to thank those at Westview Press for their support and cooperation, and in particular Barbara Ellington and Patricia Heinicke. I am grateful to Professor John Entelis, who encouraged me to publish this work. I am equally indebted to the many people who have been of great support to me; particularly, my father, my family in Egypt, Said al-Hassan, and Abdullah Banakhar.

I adopted a simplified form of Arabic transliteration. The diacritical marks have been omitted. The ' has been used to indicate the *hamza* and has been used for the `*ayn*. Arabic names and words have been transcribed in a consistent way, except for those which have an accepted form in English or French. Arabic words and titles of works appear first in transliteration and then in English translation in brackets.

Emad Eldin Shahin

1

Introduction

The place of religion and politics in Middle Eastern society has immense importance not just in academic terms but in everyday affairs. And, despite the numerous studies focusing on contemporary Muslim politics, there is a perennial need to take a balanced perspective on the general role of Islam in political development and social change in Muslim societies. To date, most studies of the Islamic resurgence have expressed either sympathy towards or hostility against the increased role of Islam in political affairs. This study parts ways with previous analyses by examining political Islam without assuming a position in this ideological debate. This is an academic attempt to place Islamic resurgence in its historical context and view it as an integral part of the cultures within which it has evolved. In addition, it is important to state that attempts to devise a "theory" to forecast and explain the emergence and spread of active Islamic movements are facing serious problems. This should not come as a criticism of the many excellent studies currently available on political Islam. Several factors explain the difficulty in generating an objective and comprehensive theory of Islamic renewal.

First, the Islamic revival is still in flux, with almost all Islamic movements currently passing through a transitional phase, especially at the political level. This is evident in the transformation of several Islamic organizations from reform, protest, or revolutionary movements into political parties, as in Algeria, Yemen, Jordan, and Turkey, or into bureaucratized institutions exercising power, as in Iran and Sudan. In other locales, public Islamic movements have been harshly suppressed, have become clandestine, or have split under pressure. Egypt, Morocco, Tunisia, and Algeria after 1991 are cases in point. Such transformations affect the nature of the Islamic movements, their practices, and their relations with the other forces in society.

Second, Islamic movements operate in different environments and under dissimilar conditions. Some function in a multi-party system and in an atmosphere of relative political liberalization while others exist under authoritarian systems with a dominant single party. These conditions naturally affect the behavior of the movements and their responses to the ruling regimes. In some countries, Islamic activists have accepted their place within the existing political formula of their respective regimes, mainly republican, nationalist, and secular; in others they have rejected completely any participation in a secular system and advocate the overthrow of the regime. The diversity in conditions and responses thus makes generalization about political Islam a difficult task.

Third, a large number of Islamic movements are still evolving ideologically. Although Islam is their ideological reference, their interpretations of its injunctions may differ. Political, social, and economic issues that could in the past be overlooked by these movements are now becoming central, particularly as many of them have opted for active participation in the political process. Although many of these issues have been in discussion for over a century—reform and renewal, modernity and authenticity, democracy, nationalism, women, minorities, relations with the West—they are still topics of vigorous debate and often contention among Islamists.

Fourth, most studies monitoring the phenomenon of Islamic revival focus primarily on its "vertical" manifestations—movements attempting to oust incumbent regimes and install an Islamic government—while only briefly touching on the "horizontal" aspects of Islamic revival: increased societal piety that is not necessarily political in nature; individual Muslim thinkers linked to a broad historical current of Islamic reform; the issue of identity; and the struggle between secular and religio-political models in the area. Therefore, the suppression of a movement in a specific country does not necessarily mean the containment or failure of political Islam in general.

Fifth, the perception of Islamic revival through the secular framework of analysis misses significant dimensions of these movements. Most studies of political Islam share, sometimes unconsciously, a reluctance to accept the concept of the inseparability of religion and politics in the Muslim countries. This perspective often marginalizes the role and relevance of religion in social and political development and views the

rise of political Islamic movements in Muslim societies as being the
result of a process gone awry—economic crises, societal problems,
insecurity, or extremism—and not as a normal and genuine response of
communities that aspire to devise an indigenous model and to live their
Islam in a modern world, particularly at a time when their identity and
even existence are threatened. This approach led many analysts to
explain the victory of the Islamic Salvation Front (FIS) in Algeria, for
example, in terms of discontent with the National Liberation Front
(FLN) and not support of the FIS, despite the existence of over fifty
political parties that might have won these dissatisfied votes. It places
the burden of proof for democratic commitment on the Islamists rather
than on the incumbent secular regimes, whose dismal record of
dictatorship is only too evident. The former are denied and suppressed
for their intentions, as in the case of the FIS in Algeria, in order to
prevent a potential threat to democracy, while the latter, who actually
repress democracy yet consistently garner an astonishing 99.9 percent of
the votes, are accepted and supported. Many analysts seem to ignore the
fact that social movements can maintain a non-violent nature only in an
open and tolerant society.[1]

Finally, many of the declared objectives of the Islamic movements—
solidarity; even unity, of the Muslim nation; economic, political, and
cultural independence; control over natural resources; and resolution of
the issue of Palestine—have put them on a collision course with the
West. The apparent contradiction between these objectives and Western
interests in the region often clouds Western intellectual and political
perception of and response to these movements. Political Islam is
increasingly, and needlessly, being seen as a major threat to the West.
The two cultures are obviously different, as products of two unique
historical experiences, but this ought to be recognized in terms of
diversity and not enmity. The difference is over policies and interests
and not essentially ideological.[2]

The purpose of this work is to examine the role of Islam and the
Islamic movements in the post-independence Maghrib—Tunisia,
Algeria, and Morocco. It focuses on these movements as forces of
politically relevant change in modern Muslim societies by analyzing
their nature, organization, and direction. It is necessary to distinguish
these movements from pre-independence Islamic forces and to juxtapose
them with the contemporary pool of post-colonial, foreign-inspired
models of development. It is also important to go beyond viewing
modern Islam in what have become conventional terms—whether these

be "political" (hostage crises, the Islamic bomb, the Islamic threat, and terrorism), "economic" (international aid, mounting debts, oil, and dependency), or "social" (unrest, instability, and anomie).

This work does not view the contemporary Islamic movements as a new phenomenon. That Islamist-inspired politics has drawn the attention of Western observers only since the 1970s does not mean that this trend was nonexistent or dormant before. The movements of the 1970s were largely an expression and a continuation of a reform-protest trend that had appeared earlier, albeit under different circumstances. The main theme of this book, then, is that contemporary political Islam is a widespread response to the determination of the post-independence state to relegate Islam to a subordinate political and social position and to the perceived inadequacy of secular-oriented Western models of development in addressing the indigenous problems of society. The Islamic movements, with their ideas and values rooted in the cultural and historical matrix of Tunisia, Algeria, and Morocco, are challenging the legitimacy of their rulers and seek to reconstruct the religio-political base of society in response to the secular policies of the post-colonial incumbent elites.

The choice of the countries of the Maghrib is of particular significance. The politics of the Islamic movements in the Maghrib has been woefully neglected by the English-speaking academia.[3] Most studies of Islamic trends have focused on the Arab East (the Mashriq), and there is still a need for a comprehensive comparison and analysis of the Maghribi brand of Islamism. While the historical movements in countries like Egypt remain, of course, extremely relevant, too often it is assumed that what goes for Egypt or Syria can be extrapolated to cover the entire Middle East (or the Muslim world for that matter). Political Islam in North Africa is unique and is significant for the region as a whole for a number of reasons. The movements in the Maghrib have been distinguished from their eastern counterparts by a marked willingness to work within the system right from the beginning. This has led to some important intellectual contributions from various Maghribi Islamic thinkers about the relations between Islam and the state and Islam and democracy, as well as the feasibility of non-violent struggle. In many ways, the Islamist intellectual center of gravity has moved away from the Mashriq to North Africa. The region continues to produce fresh and innovative writings on the nature of contemporary Islamic thought. The key to the region's uniqueness is, of course, related to the particular role Islam has played and to its proximity to Europe and to French culture in particular. Since their inception, Islamic groups in North Africa have had to grapple with the very real and close presence of European languages and culture. Also of note is the fact that the Maghrib is one of the few places where Islamic groups have actually at times been officially recognized and allowed to compete in elections. It is hoped that this book will go a long way towards illuminating this especially vibrant aspect of contemporary political Islam that has for too long been relegated to the intellectual back burner of the discipline.

The comparison of Tunisia, Algeria, and Morocco is particularly apt. The three countries share, to a large extent, the same pre-colonial historical experience. Since the seventh century, Islam has been the dominant religion in North Africa. Over the centuries, Islam has performed various functions: it has played a very significant formative and integrative role in defining national identity and combining the Arab and Berber communities; it was a basic source for political legitimacy and a catalyst for resistance. These countries are characterized by a dominant Sunni composition and the Maliki school of law, notwithstanding the existence of a small Hanafi minority and Kharijite elements in Tunisia and Sufi brotherhoods in Algeria and Morocco. This common background granted them a sort of legal conformity and a strong sense of cultural affiliation. Up to the sixteenth century, Tunisia, Algeria, and Morocco did not have separate boundaries. The emergence of a reformer-ruler mobilizing the people around a rejuvenated form of Islam and challenging the legitimacy of the incumbent leaders had been a recurring pattern in the middle and even modern history of these societies. Several dynasties, the Almoravids (1042-1147) and the Almohads (1147-1269), for example, rose and fell attempting to revive the Islamic ethos, unite the Muslim community, and defend the Islamic territories against outside threats, particularly the non-Muslims in Spain.

The three countries also share, though with varying degrees, a historical experience of foreign domination. Algeria was subdued to total French colonization in 1830. The French administration in Algeria adopted an integrationist policy that destroyed the pre-colonial Algerian economic, social, and cultural institutions and placed the entire country under French control. To avoid Algeria's fate, Tunisia and Morocco attempted to initiate some reforms.

After a period of modernizing policies followed by financial difficulties, Tunisia fell under the French protectorate in 1881. Elbaki Hermassi characterized the French rule of Tunisia as an "instrumental colonialism," for the French administration assumed control over the economic affairs of the country while reserving the option to interfere in the social structures of the society as circumstances warranted. A major criticism that is often leveled against the French administration is that it introduced a dual educational system, one purely French and the other Franco-Arab. The latter had a major effect on the orientation of Tunisia's future elite, and, eventually, on the status of Islam after independence.

Morocco was acquired by the French in 1912, with the Spanish controlling the northern parts of the country. Hermassi identified the French experience in Morocco as a "segmental colonialism." Despite the economic interest of the French in the country, they avoided dismantling its traditional cultural and political structures. This enabled some traditional institutions to maintain their status and functions in the post-colonial phase.[4]

Finally, the three North African countries have experienced clear manifestations of Islamic reassertion since the beginning of the 1970s. Islam has resurfaced as a dynamic factor in the affairs of these societies and as a vibrant political language expressed by the incumbent elite and protest groups alike.[5]

There are also clear differences between the three countries. The post-independence political structure and institutional orientation of Tunisia, Algeria, and Morocco are different. Officially, Tunisia has adopted a "liberal socialist" system in which power is highly centralized within the state-dominated confines of the Socialist Destourian Party, now the Democratic Destourian Rally,[6] notwithstanding the existence of marginal parties which struggle to function as opposition groups in a highly controlled political pluralism. From its independence in 1962, Algeria was ruled by a single party, the National Liberation Front (FLN), until 1989, when a new constitution was approved, permitting the formation of a multi-party system and abandoning socialism as the state ideology for achieving economic development and comprehensive change. Morocco, on the other hand, is a liberal-clientalist system in which the authority of the state is highly personalized in the institution of the monarchy, which has served as patron of the existing weak political parties.

Despite these differences, however, what is most noteworthy is that, due to the orientation of the incumbent elites, who chose to espouse foreign-inspired models of development to assist them in the process of building a modern state, Islam ceased to play a significant role in the transformation of Tunisian, Algerian, and Moroccan society. As these elites assumed power without an indigenous model of development, they vacillated between different ideologies. This undermined their credibility and in response led to the emergence of rival forces seeking other alternatives.

The Islamic movements in the three countries have not followed the same paths. During the 1970s and 1980s, the Islamists in Tunisia had a mainstream movement that was more discernible, better organized, and more articulate than that of their counterparts in Algeria or Morocco. In Algeria, the Islamic movements did not draw much attention until the end of the 1980s, and particularly in 1990, when the Islamic Salvation Front (FIS) swept the municipal elections and a year later won the first round of the parliamentary elections. In Morocco, the Islamic movements have been highly factionalized and at present pose little threat to the stability of the regime. This, of course, raises the questions of what forces were behind the emergence of these movements and what factors have contributed to their difference in course.

Current Approaches

Having erupted in such a prolific and seemingly sporadic way, the phenomenon of Islamic revivalism has attracted the attention of many analysts since the late 1970s, particularly since the outbreak of the Islamic Revolution in Iran in 1979 and the increasing evidence of religious reassertion in several Islamic countries. This book will not attempt to elaborate on the scattered manifestations of this resurgence—these have been repeatedly dealt with elsewhere—but rather, the intent is to refer to these manifestations only insofar as they are relevant to a comparison of the Islamic movements in Tunisia, Algeria, and Morocco.

A considerable number of studies have also been devoted to the understanding of the nature, causes, and implications of this phenomenon. Most of these studies recognize the complex and multidimensional nature of Islamic revivalism. It has now become a conventional wisdom that "the Islamic movement is not a monolithic one," though sweeping generalizations and simplistic stereotyping still persist. One could possibly attribute this partly to the nature of the ideology that the Islamists propagate. In Muslim societies, religion occupies a central position in their affairs as it is intertwined with many segments of life. For centuries, Islamic precepts have set the foundations of the legal, educational, social, and political systems, permeating the structures of society. This engagement renders it hard to confine the Islamic appeal to a certain realm in society. It has been an element introduced in the conflicts between the modern and the old, the internal and external, the state and the society, the rural and the urban, and the rich and the poor. In some locales, Islamism is militant and radical; in other places, it is revivalist, or reformist, depending on the context. Why does the nature of the Islamic movements change from one country to another, or, why do they take a different course while their ideological reference is presumably the same?

An analyst of the phenomenon who is aware of this complexity suggests that "an appropriate approach for the study of Islamic resurgence has to be interdisciplinary, comparative, and integrative."[7] Most studies combine more than one approach and provide a wide variety of explanations for Islamic revivalism. One can identify four approaches that distinguish the studies on Islamic resurgence. These are the crisis, success, developmental-social, and cultural-historical approaches.[8] This categorization is certainly not extensive, nor is one to assume that each is totally exclusive of the other. Some observers, however, place more emphasis on one or several factors than others and, in doing so, they present only part of the answer.

The Crisis Perspective

Is the rise of Islamic movements mainly a result of a crisis environment? In the past few years, the word crisis (*azma*) has become a very familiar and widely used one to describe, and sometimes to conceal, things in the Middle East.[9] Several studies view the Islamic resurgence through a context of a crisis milieu, notwithstanding the different factors present in this situation. A proponent of this type of analysis is Richard Dekmejian, who describes the contemporary Arab setting as being characterized by "certain specific attributes of protracted and intense crisis, which constitute the catalysts that have triggered Islamic fundamentalist responses."[10] He distinguishes six types of intractable crises that create a "crisis environment." These include a crisis of identity, lack of legitimacy of the ruling elites, misrule and coercion, class-conflict, military defeat and incompetence, and modernization.[11] As such, Islamic "fundamentalism" emerges as a response to these types of crisis, because Islam provides spiritual asylum and psychological relief. In an attempt to find a pattern for revivalism,

Dekmejian proceeds to examine Islamic history in its entirety through a cyclical pattern of crisis and fundamentalist response.[12]

This type of analysis has certain advantages in attempting to find a pattern that explains the dormancy and re-emergence of Islamic revivalist movements. It is also useful in its detailed treatment of the political environment that triggers these movements. However, it assumes that Islam is a constant and unchangeable entity within a changing world. In other words, when things become too bizarre, a Muslim can easily escape this unfamiliar world and fall back on the comfort of recognized values and the refuge of familiar traditions. An analyst of Islamic continuity and change rightfully notes that this type of analysis "runs the risk of ignoring the many developments that have taken place within Islam in modern times."[13]

In addition, it contradicts other studies that overemphasize the diversity and even the "uncertainty" of Islam in general.[14] Furthermore, even after seeking psychological and spiritual relief in Islam, a Muslim fundamentalist, in Dekmejian's analysis, is regarded as fanatic, alienated, dogmatic, inferior, aggressive, authoritarian, intolerant, paranoid, idealistic, rigid, and submissive.[15] This type of perspective is one-dimensional, lacks nuance, and presents an undifferentiated stereotype.

Despite the recognition of an acute crisis situation, Dekmejian still has confidence in the present ruling political elites and volunteers to provide prescriptions by which the Islamic "threat" and fundamentalist "challenge" could be contained and the crisis situation reversed. He advises that in order "to stem the fundamentalist tide and reduce the level of social tension, Arab elites need to pursue three inter-related policies—comprehensive reforms, systematic socialization, and moderation in the use of state power against opponents."[16] With regard to the United States, Dekmejian sees that a "restructuring of American policy is likely to reduce the Islamist fervor and prepare the grounds for possible cooperation with 'moderate' fundamentalist or nationalist elements."[17] He proposes that "any American preemptive effort would have to be applied well in advance of the revolutionary outbreak. In addition to providing intelligence, arms, and organizational know-how to these [pro-American] regimes, there is no substitute for American persuasion to institute political and economic reforms."[18]

Unfortunately, the issue is more complex than these proposed solutions. In fact, Arab political elites have already initiated a series of alleged "reforms," corrective movements, revolutions in all colors (green, red, and white) as well as counter-revolutions. Yet, contrary to the expectations of the proponents of this perspective, the apparent result has been a lack of trust, discontent, or mass apathy between a large segment of society, weary of experimentation, and the ruling political elites. An increasing American involvement on the side of the present Arab political elites is only likely to complicate the matter further. It will at least erode any remaining credibility of these regimes and increase antagonistic sentiments against the United States.

The Success Perspective

Contrary to the crisis analysis common to most studies, the success perspective attempts to present a brighter and more positive explanation of Islamic revivalism. This analysis emphasizes the conviction of Muslims that there is a positive relationship between historical success and proper adherence to the faith. It considers successful events that took place during the 1970s as catalysts for Islamic reassertion. Such events include the 1973 Arab-Israeli war, the Arab oil embargo, the increasing oil revenues, and the triumph of the Islamic Revolution in Iran in 1979. It was during this period that the relation between success and the increasing manifestation of religious reaffirmation was clearly expressed and reiterated by many Muslims. John Esposito notes that, "Events in 1973 provided a new source of pride and served as a positive motivation for Islamic revivalism."[19] The religious symbolism that was given to the war reminded Muslims of their early success and made the war an Islamic victory. This was reinforced by the successful Arab oil embargo against Western countries supportive of Israel, which was led by Saudi Arabia, the birthplace of Islam. The war and the embargo reflected an Arab and Islamic solidarity and increased the Arabs' awareness of their economic and strategic importance: "Their [the Arabs] economic and, hence, geopolitical importance was a source of enormous pride and a sign to many of a return of Allah's blessings."[20]

Some considered the oil wealth, particularly of Arab countries such as Saudi Arabia and Libya, to be the major impetus toward creating and shaping Islamic revivalism in the 1970s. Daniel Pipes, an ardent proponent of such a view, wrote that "the boom in oil exports has, more than anything else, caused the recent Islamic resurgence."[21] His analysis led him to the conclusion that "current waves of Islamic activism will die along with the OPEC boom."[22]

The outbreak of the Iranian Revolution in 1979 and the success of the mullahs' take-over, all observers agree, provided an important boost for the Islamic resurgence throughout the Islamic world. But the success perspective places undue emphasis on factors which postdated the actual emergence of the Islamic movements.[23] In addition, one would expect the 1973 war and the oil embargo to have generated conformity between establishment Islam and the neglected Muslim masses, and not dissent and protest as has been the case in many Arab and Muslim countries. Some observers are also very critical of the simplicity of the oil revenue argument. For example, Esposito considers it "naive to attribute the Islamic revival mainly to oil. ... Oil revenue has assisted a process set in motion by other factors but has not itself been the primary cause or catalyst."[24] James Piscatori, moreover, criticizes the oil argument for being logically fallacious, reducing everything to the material dimension, and for giving the revival more uniformity than it possesses.[25]

It is also hard to argue that the Iranian Revolution has been a cause of Islamic resurgence. It is true that, for a short time, the revolution served as inspiration: Islamic activists looked to the revolution as an exemplar and tried to emulate its language. But they soon realized that revolutions were not transferable. Fouad Ajami contends "the romance of the Iranian revolution that had played havoc with the Middle Eastern system has effectively diminished."[26]

Developmental-Social Perspective

The issue of Islamic resurgence in the 1970s is also examined through the developmental-social perspective. Analysts applying this approach attempt to find explanations for the emergence of revivalist movements in the outcome of the process of development that has taken place in the Islamic countries. This process has increased rapidly the level of urbanization and social mobility that exceeded the absorptive capacity of the system, eventually creating strains and discontent among some disadvantaged groups in society. The most affected of these, as Saad Eddin Ibrahim concluded in his anatomy of the militant Islamic groups of Egypt, are the lower-middle and middle classes, which find themselves on the margin of the system, alienated by "city" values. They resort to Islam and its familiar norms in order to make up for these sentiments of alienation and to regain admission to the system. The development of the means of communication (radio, television, cassettes) has the added effect of assisting Muslim activists in the dissemination of their ideas and in broadening their constituency.[27]

Truly, the developmental-social approach reveals some of the disruptive effects of the process of development on traditional societies. It also succeeds in demonstrating that the base of support of the Islamic revivalists among the social classes continues to grow. However, it runs the risk of overlooking the elements of continuity of an Islamic heritage by not dealing with history as a process of continual evolution. In his study of the ideological evolution of Islamic radicalism, Emmanuel Sivan maintains that the "Islamic revival—while activist and militant— is thus essentially defensive; a sort of holding operation against modernity."[28] He goes further in his sweeping generalization and judges radicals and conservatives: "They are above all united by an intense hatred of the 'evil of evils,' modernity. Modernity is inherently alien to Islam."[29] Such an assertion, one may argue, portrays a Western bias against developing societies as it maintains an ethnocentric definition of modernity and emphasizes the inability of traditional societies to modernize. To cite but one example to disprove this, Rashed al-Ghannoushi, the leader of the Tunisian Islamic movement, al-Nahda, states his position on modernity:

> We want modernity, contrary to the ridiculous allegations made by those adversely inclined against political Islam, but inasmuch it means absolute intellectual freedom; scientific and technological progress; and promotion of democratic ideals. However, we will accept modernity only when we dictate the pace with which it penetrates our society and not when French, British or American interpretations are imposed upon us. It is our right to adopt modernism through methods equitable to our people and their heritage.[30]

It is worth noting that none of the leaders of the Islamic movements in Tunisia, Algeria, or Morocco belongs to, or represents, the traditional religious establishment. The majority of these activists are professionals and lay intellectuals who have generally acquired a modern education and share an exposure to both Muslim and Western cultures.

It must also be pointed out that the appeal to Islam is not confined to a certain social class or a particular group. In fact, the Islamic appeal and the increased adherence to Islamic practices, one may argue, cut across the various social strata, notwithstanding the varying degree of intensity and persistence. In other words, Islamic resurgence is not a class phenomenon and the Islamic movements do not articulate or defend the vested interests of a particular class. In *Islam and Revolution*, Dekmejian declares: "Nor is Islamic revival limited to particular social and economic classes. While much of its grass roots support is based on the lower, lower-middle, and middle classes, there is increasing evidence of widespread emulation of Islamic ways of life among the upper-middle and upper strata."[31]

The Historical-Cultural Perspective

A fourth approach that is often applied to the discussion of Islamic revivalism is historical-cultural. It focuses on the challenges, internal and external, facing Muslim societies and the Muslim response to these challenges.[32] Though aware of the internal ones, Muslim intellectuals consider the external Western encroachment to be the most influential challenge felt by Muslims since the nineteenth century, particularly when they juxtapose the stagnant conditions of the East with the vibrant ones of a more advanced West. This challenge has prompted many Muslim intellectuals to explore and investigate the causes of their decline and reasons behind Western viability in an attempt to reform and invigorate their society. Apparently, these responses have not been symmetrical.

Yvonne Haddad identifies three categories of Muslim intellectuals: the normatives, acculturationists, and neo-normatives. The term normatives refers to Muslims who consider Islam "as a closed cultural system that allows for no change,"[33] and view Western ideals and norms as alien and ungodly. The Muslim acculturationists, on the other hand, look up to the West as a source for emulation and seek to reinterpret Islam according to the model they appropriate. This category includes secularists, nationalists, communists, Islamic modernists, and romantics. The neo-normatives represent the vibrant and militant synthesis emerging out of the conflict between the normatives and the acculturationists. While having no fantasies about Westernization and firmly considering Islam as an eternal message and a living norm, the neo-normatives endeavor to revitalize Islam and give it relevance to the modern world.[34] Contemporary Islamic revivalism is thus viewed in light of this challenge-response syndrome. It is a response to an increasing disillusionment with alien cultural models and the need to revive an indigenous one that can explain and govern Muslim reality.

In examining the Islamic experience in the modern world, John Voll identifies three dimensions: the major actors such as individuals and groups, and their local circumstances; the relationships of Islamic movements to the basic dynamics of modern history; and Islam itself as reflecting a continued process of renewal and revival. He views Islam in the modern world "as the interaction of the special aims and goals of individuals and groups, which are affected by particular local conditions, with the factors of the dynamics of modern development and the continuity of the Islamic tradition."[35]

The historical-cultural approach is capable of explaining contemporary Islamic revivalism more thoroughly and profoundly because it traces the roots of this phenomenon within its historical and cultural context. It succeeds in demonstrating the elements of continuity and change of the revivalist movements in the different environments in which they evolve. However, by focusing on general patterns, the historical approach runs the risk of overlooking some particularities within Islamic revivalism. Moreover, the categorization of Muslim responses, if oversimplified, sometimes appears exclusive and fails to recognize the complexity and diversity of responses even within the same category.

In focusing on the active Islamic movements in Tunisia, Algeria, and Morocco this work draws on the historical-cultural perspective. It seeks to explain the reasons behind their gradual evolution, the nature of their dynamics, and the basic tenets of their ideology. Emphasis will be placed on al-Nahda (Renaissance) Movement, the Progressive Islamic Tendency Movement, and the Islamic Liberation Party in Tunisia; the Islamic Salvation Front (FIS), Hamas, and al-Nahda Parties in Algeria; and the Association of Justice and Benevolence (al-`Adl wa al-Ihsan), the Movement of Reform and Renewal (Harakat al-Islah wa al-Tajdid al-Maghribiyya—HATM), and other Islamic associations in Morocco.

Such a comparative study helps to demonstrate the intricacy of local conditions and highlight their overall effect on the emergence of social movements adopting Islam as a political alternative and as an instrument for social protest. In addition, it allows us to explain the causal relationship between the different orientations and structures of the political regimes and the character, ideology, and extent of the Islamic revival movements. The comparison thus aims at demonstrating how the Islamic movements have evolved, articulated their arguments, and functioned under a single party system—or more specifically, one with marginal parties—as is the case in Tunisia; a system with a dominant party that turned into a highly pluralistic one, as is the example of

Algeria; and a weak multi-party system in which the monarchy plays a pivotal religious and political role, as is the case in Morocco.

In addressing these issues, it is important to begin by providing an analysis of official Islam, as practiced in Tunisia, Algeria, and Morocco, in order to set the groundwork for understanding the emergence of the Islamic movements from outside the official religious institutions. Chapter three explains the rise of the Islamic movements in Tunisia, focusing, in particular, on the evolution of the mainstream organization, the Renaissance Movement. It also deals with less influential organizations such as the Progressive Islamic Tendency Movement and the radical Islamic Liberation Party. Chapters four and five address the emergence and development of the Islamic movements in Algeria and Morocco, respectively. Finally, chapter six analyzes the major themes of the Islamists' ideology and their evolution, as articulated by the main intellectuals of these movements.

Notes

1. Paul Wilkinson argues that for social movements to maintain their original character and have an effective role in society—i.e., not resort to violent means and clandestine activities—they must operate in an environment that allows some degree of pluralism and tolerates dissent, criticism, and differences in opinion. See Paul Wilkinson, *Social Movement* (New York: Praeger Publishers, 1971), p. 109-14.

2. See John Esposito and James Piscatori, "Democratization and Islam," *Middle East Journal*, Vol. 45, No. 3, Summer 1991, p. 440.

3. The only book available in English on the Islamic movements in North Africa is François Burgat and William Dowell's *The Islamic Movement in North Africa* (Texas: Center for Middle Eastern Studies, University of Texas at Austin, 1993), which is a translation of Burgat's excellent volume, *L'Islamisme au Maghreb: La Voix du Sud* (Paris: Karthala, 1988). However, there have been a number of good articles on this topic by, among others, John Entelis, Robert Mortimer, Hugh Roberts, and Lisa Anderson.

4. Elbaki Hermassi, *Leadership and National Development in North Africa: A Comparative Study* (Berkeley: University of California Press, 1972), pp. 56-8.

5. Jean-Claude Vatin, "Revival in the Maghreb: Islam as an Alternative Political Language," in Ali E. Hilal Dessouki (ed.), *Islamic Resurgence in the Arab World* (New York: Praeger Publishers, 1982), pp. 226-8.

6. The Destour Party adopted this new name on February 28, 1988.

7. Ali E. Hilal Dessouki, "The Islamic Resurgence: Sources, Dynamics and Interpretations," in Dessouki (ed.), *Islamic Resurgence in the Arab World*, p. 18.

8. I have benefited from John Voll's categorization of recent approaches on the study of Islamic revivalism in his excellent book *Islam: Continuity and Change in the Modern World* (Boulder: Westview Press, 1985).

9. A whole issue of the periodical *al-Wihda* was dedicated to the discussion of the crisis of the Arab world. See *al-Wihda*, No. 6, March 1985.

10. R. Hrair Dekmejian, *Islam in Revolution: Fundamentalism in the Arab World* (New York: Syracuse University Press, 1985), p. 26.

11. Dekmejian, *Islam in Revolution*, pp. 25-32. Also see Dekmejian's "The Islamic Revival in the Middle East and North Africa," *Current History*, April 1980, p. 169.

12. Dekmejian, *Islam in Revolution*, pp. 9-20.

13. Voll, *Islam: Continuity and Change*, p. 350.

14. James Piscatori, *Islam in a World of Nation-States* (Cambridge: Cambridge University Press, 1986), pp. 13-15. See also Metin Heper, "Islam: Politics and Change in the Middle East," in Metin Heper and Raphael Israeli (eds.), *Islam and Politics in the Middle East* (London: Croom Helm, 1984).

15. Dekmejian, *Islam in Revolution*, pp. 32-5.

16. Dekmejian, *Islam in Revolution*, p. 162.

17. Dekmejian, *Islam in Revolution*, p. 174.

18. Dekmejian, *Islam in Revolution*, p. 175.

19. John Esposito, *Voices of Resurgent Islam* (New York: Oxford University Press, 1983), p. 13. See also his *Islam and Politics* (New York: Syracuse University Press, 1984), p. 211.

20. Esposito, *Voices of Resurgent Islam*, p. 13.

21. Daniel Pipes, "Oil Wealth and the Islamic Resurgence," in Dessouki (ed.), *Islamic Resurgence in the Arab World*, p. 45. See also Daniel Pipes, *In the Path of God: Islam and Political Power* (New York: Basic Books, Inc., 1983), pp. 281-330.

22. Pipes, "Oil Wealth," p. 51 and *In the Path of God*, pp. 331-5.

23. Voll, *Islam: Continuity and Change*, p. 351.

24. John Esposito, "Islamic Revivalism," *The Muslim World Today*, Occasional Paper, No. 3, July 1985, p. 14.

25. Piscatori, *Islam in a World of Nation-States*, pp. 25-6.

26. Fouad Ajami, "The Arab Road," *Foreign Policy*, No. 47, Summer 1982, p. 22.

27. Saad Eddin Ibrahim, "Anatomy of Egypt's Militant Islamic Groups: Methodological Note and Preliminary Findings," *International Journal of Middle East Studies*, Vol. 12, December 1980; Henry Munson, "The Social Base of Islamic Militancy in Morocco," *The Middle East Journal*, Vol. 40, No. 2, Spring 1986; Mohamed Elbaki Hermassi, "La Société Tunisienne au Miroir Islamiste," *Maghreb-Machrek*, No. 103, January-February-March 1984. Mark Tessler, "Social Change and the Islamic Revival in Tunisia," *The Maghreb*

Review, Vol. 5, No. 1, January-February 1980; Piscatori, *Islam in a World of Nation-States*, pp. 26-34.

28. Emmanuel Sivan, *Radical Islam: Medieval Theology and Modern Politics* (New Haven: Yale University Press, 1985), p. 3.

29. Sivan, *Radical Islam*, p. 138.

30. Rashed al-Ghannoushi, "The Battle against Islam," paper presented at the symposium on Islam and Democracy in the Arab Maghreb, London School of Economics, London, February 29, 1992.

31. Dekmejian, *Islam in Revolution*, p. 4.

32. Examples of studies applying this approach are: Esposito, *Islam and Politics*; Yvonne Y. Haddad, *Contemporary Islam and the Challenge of History* (New York: State University of New York, 1982); G.H. Jansen, *Militant Islam* (New York: Harper and Row, Torchbooks Library Binding, 1979); Hamid Enayat, "The Resurgence of Islam," *History Today*, No. 30, February 1980; Bernard Lewis, "The Return of Islam," *Commentary*, Vol. 61, January 1976; and Edward Mortimer, *Faith and Power: The Politics of Islam* (New York: Random House, 1982).

33. Haddad, *Contemporary Islam*, p. 8.

34. Haddad, *Contemporary Islam*, pp. 8-11. See also Haddad, "The Islamic Alternative," *The Link*, Vol. 15, No. 4, September-October 1982, p. 4.

35. Voll, *Islam: Continuity and Change*, p. 4. Esposito, *Islam and Politics*, p. 29. On the cultural dialectics of the ideological orientation of the Maghribi elites see I. William Zartman, "Political Dynamics in the Maghreb: The Cultural Dialectic," in Halim Barakat (ed.), *Contemporary North Africa: Issues of Development and Integration* (Washington, D.C.: Center for Contemporary Arab Studies, Georgetown University, 1985). Salah Eddin al-Jourshi, et al., *Min ajl Tashih al-Wa`i bi al-Dhat* [For Reforming Self-Consciousness] (Tunis: Maktabat al-Jadid, 1985), pp. 11-12.

2

Islam in State Politics

In Tunisia, Algeria, and Morocco, the state controls the institutionalized practice and formal public teaching of Islam. Official Islam is used as a means to silence religious-based opposition and draw mass cohesion to affirm the legitimacy of an elite committed to foreign models of socioeconomic development. To advance the interest of the state, the government has invoked the symbols of Islam without necessarily shaping its policies to fall in line with Islamic doctrines as set down in the *shari`a* (Islamic law).[1] What has been propagated on the part of the regime has been acceptance of Islam in principle but not necessarily its implementation in practice.[2]

It is still possible to argue that in Tunisia, Algeria, and Morocco the political elite has not ignored the paramount role of Islam in the formation and evolution of the political culture of the masses and in their mobilization during the national struggles for independence. In the first years of independence, however, a process of systematic state expropriation of the Islamic institutions took place and inaugurated the current phase of a state-dominated religion known as official Islam. The institutionalization of Islam has set a pattern of relationship between the `ulama' (religious scholars) in charge of these institutions, on the one hand, and the state, on the other. To a large extent, the current official Islamic institutions in Tunisia, Algeria, and Morocco have been shaped by the relationships Muslim scholars maintained with the state and the nationalist movements in the pre-independence period.

The need of the regime to promote actively the traditional forms and values of Islam is two-fold: first, to cultivate a base of support for launching a largely secular-oriented nation-wide modernization drive— that is, to provide a banner of national unity over political issues that may not necessarily draw mass support; and second, to perpetuate the legitimacy and stability of a regime dominated by a Westernized political elite with little in common with the masses. To understand this process, it is useful to examine the historical role of Islam in the Maghribi context, the attitude of the post-independence elites toward the role that Islam should play in the transformation of their societies, and the measures undertaken to undermine the traditional religious institutions.

Pre-Colonial Religious Structures

In highlighting the historical role Islam has played in different contexts in Tunisia, Algeria, and Morocco, it is important to note that, until independence, Islam had a dynamic part in shaping the popular culture of the people and the structures of these societies, and, despite the changes in conditions and circumstances of colonialism, Islam remained a factor of continuity in the political values and responses in the three North African countries. In the eighteenth century, Tunisia, Algeria, and Morocco developed different religious structures that influenced the future course of Islam in those countries.

The *'ulama'* in Tunisia maintained a dominant role in the religious sphere and control over important religious institutions. The most prominent of these were the judicial and educational institutions, such as the *shari'a* courts, the Zaytouna mosque in Tunis, the grand mosque of al-Qayrawan, and local mosques. In addition, the *'ulama'*s knowledge of legal doctrines and their adherence to the Maliki *madhhab* (one of the main Sunni schools of Islamic jurisprudence) granted them privileged status and enabled them to function as representatives of the general population. However, the political elite's patronage of the *'ulama'* and religious institutions ushered in a conservative spirit within the Tunisian religious establishment that made it less susceptible to reformist impulses and prevented it from being the engineer of major social reforms.[3]

During the nineteenth century, however, the major reforms were staged by such modernizing rulers as Ahmed Bay, who ruled from 1837 to 1855, and Khayr Eddin Pasha, Tunisia's Prime Minister from 1873 to 1877. They were motivated by the external European challenge and attempted to combine Western modernism with Islamic tradition. These sweeping reform measures focused on education, finance, and the modernization of the military, and they had the overall effect of expanding the role and authority of the government at the expense of the religious establishment. While the conservative `ulama' accepted the reorganization of the Zaytouna mosque and the religious financial institutions, they were still able to preserve their status in society.[4]

The religious structure in Algeria during the eighteenth century was different from that of Tunisia. Centers of religious learning similar to the Tunisian Zaytouna and al-Qayrawan Mosques or the Moroccan al-Qarawiyyin Mosque did not exist. Instead, the Sufi orders (mystical brotherhoods) were playing an increasingly important political and social role. The eighteenth century witnessed the proliferation of new orders and the restructuring and revitalization of existing ones, such as the Tijaniyya, Rahmaniyya, Tayyibiyya, Qadiriyya, and Darqawiyya, which attracted religious scholars and local leaders to their membership. Through a well-organized structure in rural and urban areas, the Sufi orders were able to influence the life of the population as they became involved in social, economic, and political activities. They acted as intermediaries between the people and the Turkish ruling elites, who, unlike the Hassinid ruling dynasty of Tunisia, remained isolated from the rest of the society. They also mobilized the population against the abuses of the Turkish governors and, at times of weakness of the central power, assumed local authority. The growing influence of the orders continued throughout the beginnings of nineteenth century, particularly as the authority of the central government became confined to the coastal areas.[5] The lack of institutions for religious learning and the predominance of a Sufi-type Islam prevented the emergence of a reformist Islam in Algeria during the eighteenth and nineteenth centuries.

The official religious structure in Morocco at that time, however, was far more complex. It was shared by the ruling sultans, the pervasive Sufi orders (*tariqa* and *zawya*), and the `ulama'. Although the relationship between these three institutions was sometimes characterized by competition and rivalry, no party was able to gain total control over the religious sphere.[6] The ruling Moroccan sultans enjoyed special religious status among the local Muslim community as they were perceived to be endowed with their own spiritual authority. Due to their sharifian lineage (descendants of the Prophet Muhammad), the sultans of the Alawite dynasty, who had succeeded in establishing a relatively strong central authority from the sixteenth century, were important religious figures and were able to mobilize the Muslim population through appeals to Islam.

Local religious leaders, such as *marabouts* (Sufi teachers), and Sufi religious institutions, such as the *zawayas*, enjoyed religious, economic, and political influence in the rural areas and often engineered local dissent and challenged the authority of the central government (the *makhzan*). To counterbalance the influence of the *zawayas*, the sultans (Sultan Muhammad Ben Abdullah, r. 1757-1790; his son Mawlay Ismael, r. 1792-1822) encouraged reformist initiatives and supported religious scholarship. During the nineteenth century, new Sufi orders such as the Tijaniyya emerged with strong following, but they were essentially puritanical and influenced by Wahhabism, attacking the un-Islamic and saint-oriented practices of the old orders and the *marabouts*. At the same time, they maintained close ties with the political establishment.[7]

As scholars and teachers at the major mosques and traditional educational institutions, the formal `ulama' carried some influence in the urban areas. However, this was basically religious, and they did not play a significant political role. Therefore, they tended to associate with either the sultan or the *zawayas*.[8] Following the French and Spanish control, the relationship between the three institutions began to change as the sentiments of nationalism began to mobilize the people against foreign domination.

The Colonial Struggle

Tunisia and Morocco were subjected to similar forms of colonial domination and external challenges. The response to that domination took much the same course and passed through almost the same phases. The various administrative and economic measures taken by the colonial authority resulted in the reshaping of existing structures and posed a threat to the dominant indigenous culture and traditional institutions. Algeria's colonial experience, however, was very different with regards to the intensity of foreign domination and the challenges it posed to the national identity of the population. In the context of the national struggle against colonialism, Islam was to constitute a mobilizing force for people's resistance against foreign penetration and assimilation and for reaffirming their national identity. Examining the various forms that the fight for independence took in each of these countries is instrumental in understanding the subsequent evolution and continuity of each nation's Islamic movements.

Tunisia

Following the establishment of the French Protectorate in 1881, two major reformist trends surfaced within the Tunisian intellectual elites. The first emphasized the Western secularizing aspects of reform and viewed Islam as a personal matter; it was advocated by the secularist wing of a group known as the Young Tunisians. These were graduates of the Sadiki College, which was established by Khayr Eddin Pasha as part of his drive to combine Islamic and Western education. To circumscribe the authority of the monarchy, this group acquiesced to the French Protectorate and attempted to undertake reform within the framework of the French regime. By World War I, however, the Young Tunisians' advocacy of total assimilation had already exhausted their potential as leaders of the community.

The second trend stressed the Islamic dimension of reform, and attempted to assert the Islamic identity of the Tunisian people. This trend was advocated by Shaykh Abdel Aziz al-Tha`alibi (b. 1879), who was educated in the Zaytouna mosque and was influenced by the pan-Islamic politics of the Ottoman Sultan Abdel Hamid and the reformist ideas of Muhammad `Abduh and the *Salafiyya* movement. He was associated with the Young Tunisians before World War I but disagreed with their Western and secular tendencies, and founded the Destour (Constitution) Party in 1920. Until the end of the 1930s, al-Tha`alibi remained the champion of Islamic reform through his identification with the *Salafiyya* program of reform (discussed below). The Destour party, which managed to build an organizational structure and gain influence among the urban Islamic middle and educated classes, mostly from the city of Tunis, stressed the Islamic and Arabic dimensions of Tunisian nationalism and presented itself as the defender of Islam.

Al-Tha`alibi perceived the Western-inspired elements of modernism as a means for reinvigorating Islam, and not as an end unto itself that would sweep Islam aside. In his 1919 book, *La Tunisie Martyre: Ses Revendications*, al-Tha`alibi attacked the French presence in the country. He argued that Tunisia had already been modernizing before the Protectorate, and, in effect, had been undergoing a reform program within the Islamic framework. He criticized the French for introducing alien educational and legal systems to the country, and thus distorting its heritage. He prescribed a program for reform that advocated the restoration of the 1860 constitution; the modernization of the judicial system while maintaining the *shari`a* as the supreme law of Muslims;

the promotion of Arabic as the main language of instruction in schools; the development of health and social services; and the redirection of the economy so that it would serve the native population—not just the foreigners.[9] The original Destour's tactics of focusing on legalistic debates and relying on the educated urban class rather than mobilizing the masses, deprived it of the popular support and mass organization necessary for it to survive the oppressive measures of the French occupation.

The major turning points in the nationalist movement in Tunisia and Morocco were implicitly linked to religious issues. This was clearly manifested in the response to the naturalization issue in Tunisia in 1932 and the Berber *dahir* (discussed below) in Morocco in 1930.[10] Although the old Destour Party presented itself as the defender of Islam in Tunisia, its focus on legalistic issues deprived it of a wide popularity base. The younger members of the party, with modern education and more militant tendencies, realized this predicament and decided to combine violence and dialogue with the French authorities. They intended to mobilize the masses through the use of Islam in affirming the Tunisian national identity. The most prominent of these young leaders was Habib Bourguiba. In 1934, he severed his formal ties with the old Destour to launch the Neo-Destour Party.[11]

It was the naturalization issue which gave these young elements a golden opportunity to associate themselves with traditional popular sentiments of the Tunisian people and to present themselves as defenders of the Tunisian Muslim faith. In 1932, the *mufti* (jurisconsult who gives learned religious opinions) of Bizerte had issued a *fatwa* that naturalized Tunisians (those taking French citizenship) were not to be buried in a Muslim cemetery. Demonstrations had broken out against the burial of naturalized Tunisians in Muslim cemeteries, and the young Destourians had participated in these demonstrations. Bourguiba in the newspaper *L'Action Tunisienne* wrote extensively on this issue, confirming that those Tunisians who had accepted French nationality were assumed to have relinquished Islam.[12]

Despite the modern orientation of the Neo-Destour Party and its realization of the need for social transformation in Tunisian society, it was nonetheless aware of the importance of Islam for the Tunisian people in pursuing their struggle for independence. Bourguiba's first article in *L'Action* in 1929 was a defense of the veil, the traditional dress of the Tunisian women, as a symbol of national identity. The party used religious symbolism as a means to gain appeal among the conservative population. In addition to the reassertion of the Islamic personality of the Tunisian people, party leaders used the mosques throughout the country to disseminate their ideas. New members were admitted to the ranks of the party after swearing allegiance on the Qur'an, and Qur'anic verses dominated the speeches of party leaders. The party's tactics were effective in gaining the support of the Tunisians and in demonstrating its credibility to the French as the *interlocuteur valable* (valid representative) for the Tunisian people.[13] After independence in 1956, however, a severe rupture between Bourguiba's policies for transforming the Tunisian society and Islam emerged.

Algeria

When the French conquered Algeria in 1830, the country lacked a strong central government and was suffering from internal dissent and prolonged disputes over political and religious autonomy from the Ottoman Empire. While the Turkish elite was quickly defeated, it then took the French four decades to bring the entire population under control. The response of the Sufi orders to French colonialism took different forms. Some orders, such as the Tijaniyya, did collaborate with the foreign power against the Turkish authority; most others however, led a fervent resistance against the French presence. Most notable of these was the resistance movement of al-Amir Abdel Qadir Muhyi al-Din (1808-1883). Abdel Qadir was a religious teacher, head of a Sufi order, and an able military and political leader, who organized the urban areas and the local tribes in the countryside under a modern administration of an Islamic state in the interior and at times was even able to extended his authority to the coastal areas. Abdel Qadir's two decade-long resistance was eventually crushed in 1847 thanks to internal divisions and the superior, and often vicious, military powers of the French. Subsequent revolt movements emerged, though they were smaller in scale and effect than Abdel Qadir's. These revolts were led by religious figures of the Sufi orders such as Muhammad al-Muqrani who headed the resistance in 1871 in the east and Bou Amamah who in 1881 began a twenty-three year rebellion in the south.[14]

Following the brutal suppression of these revolts, the French presence in Algeria turned from military occupation to total political, economic, and social domination. The French administration fiercely pursued an assimilationist policy that aimed at making Algeria an integral part of France. This meant the destruction and negation of the traditional cultural, social, and economic structures of the indigenous population. At stake for the Algerians was the issue of their identity in the face of this assimilationist policy. To make Algeria a part of France, the colonial authorities worked on the eradication of the basic components of the Algerian national character. This involved the settlement of a large French community (colons) into the country, the massive confiscation of lands, including those of the religious endowments, the restriction of Arab and Islamic education, the implementation of repressive codes to stifle armed resistance, and the co-optation of the Sufi orders.

Up to independence in 1962, the Algerian nationalist movement combined several currents with different and sometimes contradictory orientations. This is not surprising given the destruction of the traditional native institutions, the prevention of the emergence of new ones, and the absence of unifying symbols such as the institution of the monarchy in Morocco or the Zaytouna in Tunisia.[15] The Algerian nationalist movement had evolved through various phases and was represented by four main trends: the assimilationists, Islamic reformers, anti-colonial nationalists, and, at a later phase, the revolutionaries. Before World War I, the national aspirations of the Algerian population were expressed by the assimilationists and by Islamic reformers. The first were represented by a small number of newly emerging French-educated Algerians who accepted assimilation and pushed for complete equality with the French. They became known as the evolues: gallicized Muslims raised to a high status though their European education and mannerisms. This trend was led by middle class professionals, exiles, and some Algerians who served in the French army. While expressing loyalty to France and its values, the demands of this group focused on limited reforms such as attaining equal political and taxation rights and the cancellation of the *Code de l'Indigenat*.[16] Their activities revolved around establishing social and cultural associations, issuing newspapers and presenting petitions of demands to the French administration. The influence of the assimilationists remained limited due to their alienation from the rest of the population and to the opposition of the French settlers to granting any concessions to the indigenous people.

The advocates of Islamic reform represented the second trend in the nationalist movement. It consisted of a group of Muslim scholars and students who were exposed to the ideas of the *Salafiyya* movement, either directly through its protagonists, such as Muhammad `Abduh and Muhammad Rashid Rida, or while studying at religious institutions in the Arab east. Like Tunisia and Morocco, the influences of the *Salafiyya* were spreading at the turn of the century into Algeria. In 1903, Muhammad 'Abduh briefly visited the country and contacted some of its religious scholars. He was appalled by the deterioration of the Islamic culture in the country. Many Algerian students returned from the east after finishing their education at religious institutions there and began to propagate *Salafi* reformist ideas. Unlike those of the assimilationists, the efforts of this trend focused on asserting the national identity of the Algerians, rejecting the naturalization law, promoting Arabic and Islamic education, and combating the influence of the Sufi orders. They accepted political equality with the French, while emphasizing the independent cultural and social character of the Algerian people.

These trends became more crystallized in the inter-war period as they turned into active parties and associations that survived until independence. In addition, a more populist and radical anti-colonial nationalist stream emerged during the same period. The most prominent figure in the assimilationist trend was Ferhat Abbas (b. 1899). A son of a local governor under the French administration, Abbas was educated in France and joined the nationalist movement at an early age. He was a member of Ben Jalloul's Federation of Elected Muslim Algerians. The Federation, which was established in 1930 by a group of French-educated Algerian elites, called for the gradual integration of Muslim Algeria with France, as well as improving the conditions of the population and expanding their representation in the administration. The demands of the Federation were not met and, more devastating to the aspirations of this group, the Blum-Violette bill which proposed limited reforms was defeated in the French Parliament just prior to World War II. The French intransigence caused Abbas to abandon his integrationist hopes and call for an independent Algeria—though still federated with France. In 1943, Abbas proposed the Manifesto of the Algerian People in which he demanded complete freedom and equality for all Algerians; land reform; recognition of Arabic as an official language; compulsory primary education; direct participation of the Muslims in the administration of the country; and the creation of an Algerian state with associations with France. The demands in the Manifesto were once more rejected by France, which instead proposed limited reforms after the war. Abbas formed a new political party, the Democratic Union of the Algerian Manifesto (UDMA), in 1946. The new party was still unable to extract satisfactory concessions from the French, a situation that led Abbas to join the FLN in 1955. Abbas headed the Algerian Provisional

Government, until he was removed by Youssef Ben Kheddah in 1961. After independence, he became the chairman of the country's first National Assembly, a position which he resigned in 1963 in protest at Ahmed Ben Bella's (president, 1962-1965) chaotic style in securing approval for the country's new constitution.

The founder of the Islamic-inspired resistance to the French in the twentieth century is widely agreed to be a scholar by the name of Shaykh Abdel Hamid Ben Badis. To counter the disorienting effects of the French policies and the advocates of assimilation, a group of Algerian religious scholars led by Ben Badis formed an association that focused on the preservation of the Arab and Islamic identity of Algerians. Ben Badis was born in 1889 in Constantine to a prominent Berber family renowned for its scholarship, wealth, and influence. During his early years, Ben Badis received an Islamic education, and in 1908, attended the Zaytouna Mosque in Tunis. There, he was educated by a number of renowned scholars, particularly Muhammad al-Nakhli and Tahir Ben Ashur, who had been influenced by the teachings of Jamal al-Din al-Afghani and Muhammad `Abduh and introduced Ben Badis to the reformist ideas of the *Salafiyya* movement. After obtaining the degree of `alim (religious scholar), Ben Badis returned in 1913 to Algeria and, until his death in 1940, devoted his entire career to teaching, reforming Islam, and defining the Arab and Islamic basis of Algerian nationalism.

Ben Badis initiated a religious, educational, and social reform movement that aimed at asserting the national identity of Algeria, defending the cultural integrity of its people, and preparing them for eventual independence from France. He began teaching Arabic and the Qur'an throughout the country. In 1925, he published a weekly paper, *al-Muntaqid* (The Critic), in which he disseminated salafi ideas and attacked the practices of the Sufi orders. *Al-Muntaqid* was banned after 18 issues, and he responded by founding yet another newspaper, *al-Shihab* (The Meteor), in which he maintained a more moderate tone.

In 1931, Ben Badis and other religious scholars formed the Association of Algerian Scholars. Electing Ben Badis as president, the Association worked to restore the Arab and Islamic roots of the Algerian nation, reform and revive Islam, and counter the subversive influences of the Sufi orders and the assimilationists. While avoiding direct confrontation with the French administration, it demanded religious freedom, restoration of the *habous* (religious endowments) properties, and recognition of Arabic as the national language. It opened hundreds of free schools and mosques to teach Arabic and Islam, as well as modern subjects; published its own papers to spread religious, cultural, and social reform; campaigned against the marabouts' corrupt practices; and sent delegations to France and opened branches to involve Algerian Muslims there. In 1938, the Association issued a formal *fatwa*, which declared naturalized Algerians as non-Muslims. Its programs disturbed the French administration which tried to restrict the activities of its members.

Ben Badis and the Association of Algerian Scholars shared many viewpoints with the *Salafiyya* movement. They believed in the adaptability of Islam and ascribed the deterioration of the Muslims—their submission to foreign powers—to internal weakness, disunity, despotism, and the spread of non-Islamic practices. The Association offered a modernist interpretation of the Qur'an and emphasized reasoning and free will. Ben Badis's reform movement was anchored in education as the method to purify Islam from popular accretions, restore it to its pure origins, and improve the conditions of the individual as a step toward reviving the entire society. Ben Badis identified Islam, Arabism, and nationalism as the three components of the Algerian national character, which he insisted on being distinct from that of France. The Association's major contribution lies in the linking of reform and education with the promotion of an Algerian nationalism. It instilled in the Algerians a deep sense of pride in their language, culture, and history. Ben Badis and the Algerian Scholars laid the foundations for the national identity of the Algerian people.

The Association of Scholars represented an Islamic nationalist trend within the Algerian nationalist movement. Throughout the Algerian war against France (1954-62), the Association aligned with the National Liberation Front (FLN), and was later represented in the provisional government of the Algerian Republic (GPRA). Commenting on its influence, Muhammad Arkoun writes, "After independence, all expressions of Islam were more or less affected by the spirit and teachings of the `ulama' movement. Constant reference made to Ben Badis and his successor, al-Shaykh al-Ibrahimi, by Algerian officials is evidence of the impact the `ulama' movement's views have had on Algerian Islam."[17]

Ironically, the other main influential current in the Algerian nationalist movement originated in France, of all places, in the mid-1920s. The activist style of its leader, Messali Hajj and the environment in which he operated greatly affected the nature of this trend which was clearly populist and anti-colonial. Messali was born in 1898 to a poor peasant family in Telmencan and suffered from harsh living conditions. He immigrated to France in 1923 and joined the French Communist Party, where he acquired organizational skills that proved useful in his future nationalist career. Messali left the Communist Party to form a group called the North African Star (EAN) in 1926. The EAN was active among North African expatriates (particularly the workers who had immigrated to France in increasing numbers since World War I), students, and North Africans who had served in the French army. Compared to their countrymen in Algeria, the Algerian workers in France enjoyed better standards of living and more freedom. The demands of the EAN included complete independence for Algeria and its neighbors, Morocco and Tunisia, cancellation of the *Code de l'Indigenat*, formation of a national army, expansion of political and press freedoms, confiscation of colons' land, the right to education and freedom, and the establishment of Arabic schools.

Faced with the increasing activism of the EAN and its anti-colonial orientation, the French dissolved the party in 1929. Messali formed a new one, the National Union of North African Muslims (UNMAN), in 1934. The French also banned this party and arrested Messali, who was released in 1935 and went into self-imposed exile in Switzerland for six months. There, he met with Shakib Arslan, the pan-Arab intellectual who emphasized the significance of the Arab and Islamic dimension in the nationalist struggle and convinced Messali to moderate his leftist slant and focus his activities in Algeria. The French allowed Messali to return to Algeria, where he began to build structures for his party and mobilize followers.[18]

When the French once again banned the UNMAN Party in 1937, Messali resurrected the organization under a new name, the Algerian People Party (PPA), a mass-based party combining social and Islamic values aiming to mobilize the semi-proletariat and the traditional segments of society. The PPA contested local elections and demonstrated radical anti-colonial sentiments. The French brutally suppressed the PPA and sent its leaders, including Messali, to prison. On the eve of World War II, all political associations were suspended and eventually the PPA was banned. When the war was over, Messali, who was released in 1946, established a new party, the Movement for the Triumph of Democratic Liberties (MTLD). The MTLD pursued the policy of agitation, insisting on the evacuation of French troops from Algeria and the convening of an Algerian constituent assembly. Some

MTLD members created in 1947 a clandestine group, the Special Organization (OS), to carry out violent attacks against the French. This group included future Algerian leaders Ahmed Ben Bella, Hussein Ait Ahmed and Muhammad Khedir. However, the OS members failed to secure Messali's agreement to a comprehensive armed revolution. After undertaking limited violent actions, the OS was discovered and dismantled by the French, who arrested Messali and deported him to France. Rifts occurred between Messali and members of the party's central committee (the Centralists) who grew impatient with political dialogue and continued French intransigence. More significantly, they were critical of Messali's personalistic style of leadership.

The Centralists were young nationalists who believed in armed struggle as the only effective means to achieve independence. They succeeded in holding a party congress in 1953 in the absence of Messali and laid down new principles emphasizing democratic conduct and setting the stages for an armed revolution. Through his loyal followers in the party, however, Messali was able to expel the Centralists form his organization. These severe divisions within the MTLD led a third group of OS former members, the nine "historic chiefs,"[19] to form in 1954 a new organization, the Revolutionary Committee for Unity and Action (CRUA). The CRUA denounced old political rivalries and declared its firm commitment to the termination of French rule through armed struggle. Its primary task now was to prepare the country for a national insurrection. In late 1955, the CRUA changed its name to the National Liberation Front (FLN) as other political forces began to join the new organization.

The Centralists were the first to merge with the FLN. Ferhat Abbas dissolved his UDMA, and his followers joined the FLN as did the members of the Association of Algerian Scholars. The party in time evolved to encompass diverse groups with contending tendencies and contrasting political socialization: liberal politicians, Ferhat Abbas; radical politicians, Youssef Ben Kheddah; revolutionaries, Ahmed Ben Bella; Islamic reformers, Ben Badis's associates; and military leaders, Boumedienne. In fact, there was little agreement between the different elements that made up the FLN, except for one objective, the violent overthrow of the French. Despite the FLN success in mobilizing the Algerian population and recruiting various segments of society such as the peasants, workers, students, and townspeople, the diverse background of the party leaders prevented the FLN from drawing a unifying ideology concerning the post-independence political program.

The only political force that did not join the FLN were Messali Hajj and his loyalists who formed a rival party, the Algerian National Front (FNA), with the double objective of fighting the French and the FLN. However, the FNA was no match to the FLN which indeed at this stage had embodied the national aspirations of the Algerian people. Eventually, many of the members of the FNA joined the FLN, and Messali ended his long-time nationalist career by accepting to cooperate with the French government, hoping, after undermining the FLN, to later settle the issue of independence with France. These hopes were proven wrong when the French agreed in 1962 to negotiate the independence of Algeria with the FLN.

Thus, unlike Tunisia and Morocco, French colonialism in Algeria posed an existential threat to the Arab and Muslim identity of the Algerian people. The evolution of the Algerian nationalist movement was in large part a struggle to preserve the traditional components of the Algerian national character. As this movement advanced, it grew frustrated with the unsatisfactory concessions of the French rule and the gloomy reality of political inaction. By the mid 1940s, all political forces aspired for total independence, including the moderates who had abandoned their integrationist fantasies and rediscovered their national identity. However, the means to achieve this objective was unclear, until the FLN espoused armed resistance as a way to break the existing deadlock and regain independence. The fact that the FLN was an umbrella organization for different political forces had bearings on its role in the post-independence era. The pre-independence contradictions within the nationalist movement were infused into the FLN from 1954 and carried over in the post-independence period.

Morocco

In Morocco, one major effect of foreign control was the weakening of the economic base and authority of the central government, and, eventually, the sultan. His inability to defend the country against the non-Muslims stimulated popular dissent and raised religiously-inspired opposition to his rule. Indeed, the decline of the authority of the central government led to an increase in the influence of the `ulama' and the zawayas.

By the end of the nineteenth century, the `ulama', especially, began to acquire and play an important political role as they adopted an anti-colonial position. This position increased their popularity among the

Muslim population and reinforced their importance to the monarchy, which felt the need for their support in justifying its policies and consolidating its rapidly diminishing legitimacy. The `ulama's support, however, was not unconditional. It depended on the stand that the monarchy took vis-à-vis the foreign powers. Although the `ulama' did at times issue *fatwas* (religious opinions) to support the status of some sultans, in 1912 and immediately before the protectorate in 1908, they participated in the deposition of Sultan Mawlay Abdel Aziz for his failure to launch the obligatory *jihad* against the colonial powers.

The French protectorate also provided the Sufi orders with the opportunity to increase their influence and challenge the authority of the central government. The leaders of the Sufi orders began to spread their influence in the areas over which the central authority had lost control. In fact, many of the Sufi orders, such as the Kataniyya, the Tayibiyya, and the Darqawiyya, collaborated with the foreign powers in an attempt to undermine the authority of the sultan. At a later stage, however, the collaboration of many of the Sufi orders with the French administration made them vulnerable to the attacks of the growing nationalist movement.[20]

A major development that occurred in Morocco (and for that matter Tunisia and Algeria) by the end of the nineteenth century was the emergence of an Islamic reform movement, the *Salafiyya*, influenced by the ideas of Islamic modernism propagated by Afghani, `Abduh and the *Manar* group in Egypt.[21] The founders of the *Salafiyya* in the Maghrib were not members of the `ulama' establishment, but rather were people who had received their education in such traditional educational centers as the Zaytouna mosque in Tunis or the Qarawiyyin in Fez, or had studied at eastern centers of learning such as Mecca or Cairo. The most prominent of these scholars were Abdullah Idris al-Sanusi (d. 1931), who introduced the movement to Morocco, Abu Shu`ayb al-Dukkali (d. 1937), and al-Arabi al-Alawi, who educated emerging Moroccan nationalists such as Allal al-Fasi.

The reformist program of the *Salafiyya* expounded a return to the basic sources of Islam, the Qur'an and the Sunna, the exercise of *ijtihad* (independent reasoning), and relentless opposition to the mis-practices of the Sufi orders, which the *Salafiyya* leaders held responsible for the deterioration of the Muslim community. The *Salafiyya* movement had a significant impact in Morocco as it laid the foundations for a modernist ideology, succeeded in undermining the influence of the Sufi orders, and paved the way for its post World War I emergence as a political force against foreign domination.[22]

After the war, resistance to foreign domination intertwined with Islam to produce a religio-nationalist movement. Two major movements emerged: the Rif uprising and the political *Salafiyya*. The first movement was led by Muhammad b. Abdel Karim al-Khattabi, a tribal leader, a religious scholar, and judge of Ajdir, who succeeded in mobilizing the tribes of the Rif mountains through a modern religio-political ideology and launched armed resistance against Spanish rule. After mounting a number of successful attacks on the Spanish army, al-Khattabi went on to proclaim an Islamic republic in the northern part of Morocco in 1923. As a Muslim modernist, he attempted to combine the teachings of Islam with modern Western achievements in the administration of his republic which contained certain aspects of a modern organizational structure. The new republic, however, came to an abrupt end after al-Khattabi was routed by the French legionaries in 1926.[23]

Until the mid 1920s, the activities of the *Salafiyya* movement were mainly reformist and concerned with the purification of religion from Sufi mysticism and with the implementation of orthodox Islam. These activities took shape in the formation of modern Islamic schools (known as the Free Schools) in which the *Salafi* teachers spread their reformist ideas. The formation of the Free Schools rose as a challenge to and a substitute for the parallel French schools, established by the colonial regime. The *Salafi* leaders' attacks against the un-Islamic practices of the Sufi orders and against their collaboration with the French regime led the movement to acquire a political, anti-colonial dimension. The actual transformation of the *Salafiyya* movement into a political and a nationalist force was achieved by Allal al-Fasi, a student of al-Arabi al-Alawi and the Qarawiyyin university. Al-Fasi linked Islamic and political reform to independence from foreign domination, and managed through his political career as the leader of the Istiqlal Party to articulate the reformist message of the *Salafiyya* movement and the national aspirations for independence.

In the case of Morocco, like the naturalization issue in Tunisia, the Berber *dahir* (law) in 1930 was a turning point for the Moroccan nationalist movement. In an attempt to divide the Arabs and Berbers, the French administration tried to impose a law on Sultan Muhammad Ben Youssef to place the Berbers under French and tribal customary laws. This law, if implemented, would have had the effect of excluding the

Berbers from the Islamic jurisdictions. It was considered a clear threat to Islam and the unity of the Moroccans, which were perceived as one and the same.[24] This incident enabled the *Salafiyya* to develop into a politically active movement and gain mass support. The *Salafiyya* leaders organized demonstrations in which religious and political protests were expressed. This was later followed by the establishment of the National Action Bloc in 1932, which brought together nationalists of differing orientations—conservative, reformist, and modern. The activities of the leaders of the Bloc led to its dissolution by the French administration in 1937. It was reorganized in 1943 as the Istiqlal Party and Al-Fasi assumed its supreme leadership after his return from a nine-year exile in Cairo in 1946.[25] The Istiqlal under this new leadership rallied the Moroccan people around the traditional values and religious symbols of Islam.

During the national struggle for independence, the monarchy, which had been undermined by the French Protectorate, began to regain much of its traditional influence. Aware of this influence among the masses, the nationalist movement perceived the monarchy as a symbol of the Moroccan nation and organized a number of demonstrations expressing loyalty to Sultan Muhammad V. He, in turn, quietly supported the nationalist movement, finding in it a means to protect the integrity of the throne. This forged a close relationship between the two that was to last until independence. After World War II, the Sultan became closely associated with the cause of the Istiqlal Party. He made a number of protests against French rule, and, upon the encouragement of the Istiqlal, refused to sign decrees that jeopardized Morocco's sovereignty. As a result, Muhammad V was deposed and exiled by the French in 1953, only to return, however, two years later as a national hero.[26]

In brief, despite the different structures and phases of the nationalist movements in Tunisia, Algeria, and Morocco during the pre-independence period, Islam remained a major factor of continuity within the changing circumstances. It was used by the modernist-oriented elites of Tunisia and Algeria, as well as by the religio-nationalists of Morocco, as the means to maintain national integration, preserve the legitimacy of the traditional heritage, mobilize the masses for resistance, and assert national identity against Western encroachments.

Following the departure of the colonial power, however, the religious sentiments, heightened during the national struggle, began to relax. These countries began to face the difficult and pressing tasks of state-building and social transformation. It was the French-educated elements that were better equipped with the necessary technical skills to perform these tasks. This eventually undermined the power and influence of the traditional elites, especially the religious scholars (*'ulama'* and *shaykhs*), and minimized their future participation in the building of the post-colonial national state.

Islam and the Post-Colonial State

Tunisia: Secularism Manipulating Islam

Educated in law and political science at the Sorbonne in the 1920s, and influenced by the French ideals of enlightenment, positivism, and progress, Habib Bourguiba set out, following independence, to launch a process of change with the purpose of bringing about the modern transformation of the Tunisian society. Throughout this process, he equated social reform with the reform of the traditional religious institutions by bringing them under the direct auspices of the state. In one of his early speeches in 1957 at al-Qayrawan mosque, Bourguiba pledged to carry on the plan of religious reform on the basis of a more general program of reforming the structure of the state.[27] The provisions of the Constitution of 1958 proclaimed Islam as the official religion of the state. As noted by the Qur'anic citation in the Preamble of the Constitution, "In the name of Allah the Merciful, the Compassionate. ... We, the Representatives of the Tunisian people proclaim that the people are determined on...remaining true to the teachings of Islam."[28] Nevertheless, the state would shortly embark on a process of expropriating the formal practice of religion, which was traditionally the exclusive domain of the *'ulama'*.

Bourguiba's attitude towards Islam was very much shaped by his declared desire to free it from the shackles of outdated traditions by seeking an innovative interpretation of Islamic practices. Presenting himself to the Tunisian people as a religious reformer inspired by the precedents of the Prophet, Bourguiba explained in one of his speeches:

I have realized that the real secret behind the glory, strength, and civilization which Islam achieved during its first phase was its (ability) to open the minds, break the chains, and liberate the human intellect. The secret behind the decline of Muslims in their dark ages lay in their rejection of reason, their conservative imitation, and submission to dubious leaders, fake religious characters, conservative scholars, and Sufi orders that restricted reasoning and stagnated religion.[29]

Bourguiba would thus emphasize reason over commitment to religious principles whenever he perceived them as an obstacle to his program of change. As he put it, "The gates of *ijtihad* (individual reasoning) should be re-opened."[30] The rationale of Bourguiba was that Islamic teachings should be reinterpreted in the context of the modern-day way of living and the outdated conventions of tradition should not dictate the customs and behavior of modern-day man.[31]

Unlike Kamal Ataturk, whom Bourguiba greatly admired, however, Bourguiba was careful not to endorse a strictly secularist program. This was partly out of pragmatism to avoid the resentment of the Tunisian Muslim population and to generate legitimacy for his programs. In different ceremonies held in the historical Tunisian mosques and through the political declarations of his public speeches, Bourguiba elaborated on the various Islamic bases of the sweeping reforms he introduced in the religious and social structures of the Tunisian society.[32] These included reference to the Qur'an and the precedents of the Prophet and covered such measures as the abolition of polygamy, the non-observance of the fasting during the month of Ramadan, and the equality of men and women.

On the subject of Ramadan, for instance, Bourguiba equated the need for socioeconomic development and the struggle against underdevelopment with holy wars of the Prophet Muhammad and even referred to it as *al-jihad al-akbar* (the greater struggle). He condemned the drop of productivity during Ramadan as a result of the fast and said: "If we want to show our earnestness and sincerity as Muslims, we should work harder in this month of Ramadan than any other month."[33] Bourguiba also criticized excessiveness in performing *hajj* (pilgrimage) on the ground that the foreign exchange spent could be invested in the programs of economic development, which was also a duty. When the Neo-Destour Party moved to a socialist format in 1962, the support of religion and the precedents of the Prophet Muhammad were once more invoked:

Socialism, once adopted as an ideological label, was perfectly neutral; even the companions of the Prophet...were socialists before the invention of the word. ... By turning back to the sources of Islam, we are to imitate them in their self-sacrifice, their love of their neighbors, and their sense of solidarity.[34]

These are classic examples of how Bourguiba attempted to manipulate Islam to advance change and extend the control of the state over society. One may argue that even though Bourguiba appeared to violate the basic understanding of the Islamic texts, this emphasis on the Islamic aspects of his policies was a way of defending his position as a Muslim leader in the eyes of the Tunisian masses. In one of his speeches, he declared that "I issue a *fatwa* to you in my capacity as the *imam* (leader) of the Muslims in this country."[35] The monopoly over the interpretation of Islam became evident when in 1962, for example, the state's attorney general demanded the execution of shaykh Rahmouni on the ground that, "The defendant has permitted himself to have an understanding of the Qur'an contrary to the understanding of his excellency the president."[36]

But the Tunisian regime did not rely solely on the religio-political discourse of President Bourguiba in order to carry out the transformation of the Tunisian society. On the contrary, it went on to assert its control over the religious establishment, even if this meant the disintegration of some of its institutions and the discrediting of the *'ulama'*. Indeed, a massive campaign was launched against the religious scholars, who were portrayed by Bourguiba as an obstacle for bringing about the modernization of the country. This included criticizing their past record as misguided and denouncing them as anachronistic and incapable of being involved in running the affairs of post-independence Tunisia.

Bourguiba's attitude toward the religious establishment can be traced to just a year before independence when the *'ulama'* took the wrong side in a personal conflict between Bourguiba and his popular rival Saleh Ben Youssef. In 1955, two opposite trends emerged within the Neo-Destour Party. The first was headed by Bourguiba, who drew his support from the Sahel (the middle coastal area) and advocated moderation and conciliation with the French protectorate; the second was represented by Saleh Ben Youssef, the Secretary General of the Neo-Destour Party, who promoted adherence to Arab-Islamic values and to armed struggle against the French until the total liberation of North Africa was achieved. Ben Youssef's followers were drawn from the south and from the more conservative nationalist elements among the intellectuals, *'ulama'*, and Zaytouni students (Ben Youssef succeeded in getting the support of an old Zaytouni association, *Sawt al-Talib* (The Student's Voice), which was established in 1907). With the help of the party and of the *Union Generale des Travailleurs Tunisiens* (UGTT) headed by

Ahmed Ben Saleh, Bourguiba succeeded decisively in overcoming Ben Youssef and consolidating his position as the sole leader of the party and the country. In the process of repressing Ben Youssef and his followers, the Destour Party of Bourguiba endeavored to dismantle the ideological and institutional base of Ben Youssef's Zaytouni supporters.[37] One dimension of Bourguiba's "reformist policy," therefore, was effectively to dilute the strength of the religious establishment and to contain the `ulama'`.

In the first five years of independence, in fact, the state undertook a number of reform measures that had a drastic impact on the religious structure. In 1956, the public and religious *habous (*endowments) were dismantled and integrated into the state domain. Historically, the *habous* were controlled by the `ulama'` and provided them with a measure of financial independence. The public *habous* that were confiscated amounted to one hundred and fifty thousand acres of land.[38] In 1957, the state abolished the private *habous* land as well, thereby reducing the power of the `ulama'` even further.

In the field of jurisprudence, a unified judicial system was established in 1956 to replace the Islamic *shari`a* courts and the French tribunals established during the protectorate. In doing this, certain fundamental changes were introduced in the field of Islamic jurisprudence. For example, a new Personal Status Code, regulating marriage, divorce, and inheritance, was introduced and became applicable to all Tunisians— Muslims and Jews. Purporting to improve the status of women in society, the Code stipulated the equality of men and women, set minimum ages for marriage, and required the consent of women to marriage.

Several of the articles of the Code, however, were clearly in opposition to the explicit provisions of the Qur'anic text. The law prohibited polygamy and denied men the right of repudiation of marriage by oral declaration; it also restricted divorce by placing it under the jurisdiction of civil courts. Moreover, it permitted the marriage of Muslim women to non-Muslims, and made women equal to men in inheritance. The passage of the civil and commercial legislations in 1959 and the criminal law in 1968, which were influenced by Western legislative concepts, undermined further the *shari`a* law. The process of establishing a modern legal system was a gradual one by which the government made steadfast gains in attempting to establish a Western-inspired *qanun* (law) that would overshadow the traditional model of Islamic jurisprudence.

Another important step which had decisive consequences in curbing the influence of the `ulama' was the nationalization and unification of the school system on the secular French model. Upon independence, Tunisia suffered from the lack of trained and educated native cadres that could shoulder the task of developing the country. The government, therefore, placed great emphasis on reforming and expanding the educational system for the purpose of creating the required qualified elite. During the 1960s, more than one-third of the national budget was allocated to improving education, building new schools throughout the country—primary and secondary as well as universities—sending students abroad, and initiating new teaching programs. Despite independence, however, French remained the primary language of instruction in Tunisian schools and Western culture dominated the educational curriculum. With the spread of schools in rural areas, the French language was finally introduced into the remote parts of the country; ironically, it was introduced by a "national" elite, an "achievement" which even the foreign colonizer had failed to accomplish due to the violent resistance of the indigenous population.

The traditional education system of the country—the Qur'anic schools, the *madrasas*, and the Zaytouna college—were gradually taken over by the Ministry of National Education. This meant the nationalization of 208 Qur'anic schools previously administered by the scholars of the Zaytouna.[39] The Zaytouna college which traditionally had emphasized formal Arabic and Islamic education, was closed down in 1957, and in 1961 was transformed into a part of the University of Tunis as the Faculty of Theology and Religious Science. In addition to religious studies, modern subjects were introduced into the curriculum of the new faculty.

The mosque, its scholars, and graduates rapidly began to lose their prestige as they entered into a process of marginalization. The graduates of the Zaytouna religious schools, educated in the Arabic language, had little chance of joining the state university, which used French as the main language of instruction. At the same time, many Zaytouna graduates (an estimated figure of 800) who had been serving as teachers were gradually eliminated from the national system of education on the pretext that they lacked the appropriate educational standard. To address this problem, the government enlisted some of the unemployed Zaytouna graduates into retraining programs emphasizing manual skills, but for the Zaytounis this was regarded as adding insult to injury.[40]

The religious personnel throughout Tunisia were gradually bureaucratized under the control of the Administration of Religious Affairs, which was established in the early years of the 1960s and placed under the jurisdiction of the Prime Minister. (In 1986, this office was returned to the control of the Ministry of Interior in order to ensure security and state control over the mosques). Kamal al-Tarzi, the former Director of the Administration, summarized the functions of the Administration as: building and supervising mosques, training preachers and renewing the methods of preaching. On the limited and subservient role of the *imams*, al-Tarzi asserted that the scholars had no political role in the implementation of the *shari`a*. He explained that "the function of the *imam* is to teach people religion, before he enjoins the good or forbids the evil. He should say that alcohol and gambling are *haram* (forbidden), but it is not his responsibility to stand in front of a bar and demand it to be closed."[41] The administration publishes a monthly religious magazine *al-Hidaya* (Guidance), which promotes the official doctrine of Islam. The articles of the periodical elaborate on historical and theological issues, but to a large extent these are divorced from the current problems of society.

It is difficult to argue that Bourguiba's measures regarding Islam received popular support or went without opposition. The Personal Status Code, for example, was opposed by several scholars as a clear contradiction of the Qur'anic provisions. It was not surprising that fourteen of the `ulama' took the bold step of overriding the legislation by issuing a *fatwa* to denounce it.[42] It was the sanctioning of the breaking of the fast of Ramadan, however, which actually aroused most popular opposition. As one observer noted, "...Bourguiba miscalculated the depth of popular attachment to tradition. Almost all Tunisians observed the fast. ...Even in the upper echelons of the Neo-Destour, Bourguiba's public breaking of the fast and his urging others to do likewise had limited support."[43] The majority of the `ulama' rejected Bourguiba's reasoning, and the grand *imam* of the Zaytouna mosque issued a *fatwa* in which he insisted that the fast of Ramadan remained a religious duty that must be carried out, except in time of illness or war. Public demonstrations broke out a few days before Ramadan in 1961 in Qayrawan after the regime tried to transfer the *imam* of the mosque for criticizing its religious policies in an open sermon. Although the protesters were crushed by the police and the army, these incidents indicated that, despite Bourguiba's secularizing measures, Tunisians remained faithful to the basic values of their religion and the religious scholars still enjoyed some influence among the masses.[44]

Later developments in the Tunisian political process reveal that while Islam was more commonly invoked, it remained a tool for the regime to generate legitimacy for its policies. When Tunisia was undergoing grave economic difficulties in the mid-sixties, for example, President Bourguiba began to urge the need to return to stringent conformity with Islamic teachings. This was the same person who had strongly pushed for the gradual replacement of the *shari`a* by European legal codes. Then, when he lashed out at the moral decadence of Tunisian youth and their slavish imitation of Western cultural trends, he sounded more like a conservative religious scholar than a Westernized social reformer.[45] In the beginning of the 1970s, moreover, the government-controlled press began to make a show of the official observance of Ramadan.[46] To demonstrate increasing piety, the government established the National Association for the Preservation of the Qur'an to promote the teachings of Islam and encourage the presence of mosques in schools and factories.

To sum up, as the government moved to assert its control over the religious domain to facilitate the wheels of modernization, religious officials were discredited and stripped of their authority and their right to interfere with the administration of the government. The undermining of institutional Islam was undertaken to dismantle the traditional establishment and eliminate a rival power center in society, yet this was to set the stage for the unleashing of those forces of opposition that felt the need to defend the Islamic values of the Tunisian people.

Algeria: Religious Monopoly

Algeria's independence in 1962 posed tremendous challenges to the new ruling elite. Faced with a long colonial experience that had suppressed the formation of a national identity of the native population and negated the existence of an Algerian state, the national elite had to foster a new legacy to reverse the colonial era. This new legacy, which dominated the politics of independent Algeria, was based on three components: instilling a strong feeling of nationalism, building a strong state, and achieving comprehensive development. These elements determined the future course of the Algerian state regarding its relation with the role of religion in society, the ideology it espoused, and the institutions it created. More importantly, since they constituted the main source for its legitimacy, they set clear parameters for regime's successes or failures.

The post-independence elites inherited a strong state and a highly centralized administration from the colonial experience. Paradoxically, the regime maintained this negative aspect of colonialism as a means to consolidate its power over society and prevent the emergence of any opposition to its policies. Much the way the policies of the colonial state controlled the religious activities of the local community, the national state placed the Islamic institutions under its auspices. The nationalization of religion took place on three different levels: ideological, institutional, and political.

On the ideological level, Algeria's ruling elites were aware of the historical role that Islam had played throughout the nationalist movement and war of liberation. In building a modern ideological base for its rule, the national state appropriated Islam not as an ideology to lead the post-independence phase, but to claim historical legitimacy and gain support for its socialist model of development. This was achieved by linking modern Algerian nationalism with its Islamic components, adopting a reformist Islamic orientation—as originally advocated by Ben Badis and the Association of the Algerian Scholars—and then intertwining it with socialism.[47]

The official discourse since independence has highlighted the Islamic dimension of the Algerian nation. The 1976 National Charter states:

> Islam, as an integral part of our historical identity, has proved to be one of its most powerful defenses against any attempt to remove that identity. It was to Islam, militant, austere, and inspired by a sense of justice and equality, that the people of Algeria turned at the worst moments of colonial rule, and from Islam it drew that moral energy and spiritual fervour which saved it from despair and enabled it to win victory.[48]

Despite recognition of the essential role of Islam, it is noteworthy that the section of Islam was mentioned in association with the socialist revolution. The Charter emphasized the revolutionary and socialist aspects of Islam by characterizing it as a religion of struggle, justice, and equality. Commenting on how the Algerian elites utilized Islam, John Entelis writes, "From the perspective of the revolutionary leadership Islam was to serve as an identity-forming instrument, not as a legal code by which to reorder state and society. Ideologically, it was one of the dominant themes in the Algerian nationalist consciousness but had no influence on political structures."[49]

The other component of the Algerian character, the Charter stated, is the Arabic dimension. In this respect, the post-independence elites considered the achievement of Arabization as one of its objectives in reasserting the Arabo-Islamic identity of Algeria. Therefore, it was natural that the Charter confirmed that "Arabic is an essential element in the cultural identity of the Algerian people. Our personality cannot be separated from the national language that expresses it. Consequently, the generalized use of Arabic and a command of it as a creative functional instrument must be one of the major priorities in the Algerian society."[50] The expansion of education and Arabization were included as national objectives and remain an official policy in the various charters and constitutions that have been produced since independence.[51] Houari Boumedienne (president 1965-1978) stated in 1970 that "the issue of Arabization is a national demand and a revolutionary objective. We do not make a distinction between [achieving] Arabization and achieving the objectives of the revolution in other fields."[52] Thus, Arabization became part of the revolutionary legitimacy of the national state. In fact, the state, particularly under Boumedienne, took the practical steps of launching a phased process of Arabization that targeted the educational system and the official institutions.

The issue of Arabization is an extremely sensitive one that reflects competing currents, the Arabophones and the Francophones, within the Algerian elites and the state apparatus. The Arabophones, the Arabic-Islamic educated elites, used the party to advance the process of Arabization, while the Francophones, the French-educated elites, used the state administration to stall it. This competition has affected the consistency and quality of the Arabization process, revealed the influence of the Francophone elites within the administration, and created a severe conflict among the newly educated generations.

After independence, the state appropriated the reformist ideology of Ben Badis and the Association of Algerian Scholars. As we have noted, the Ben Badis's triad—Islam, Arabism, and Algerian nationalism—have been integrated in the national charters, constitutions, and the official discourse of the state. These elements of Algerian nationalism were also embodied earlier in the FLN's declaration of November 1954 that announced the war of liberation and called for the establishment of a democratic state within the Islamic principles. In its official discourse, the new regime presented itself as the only legitimate heir of Ben Badis and the reformist scholars.[53] The reformist legacy was in fact needed after independence to assert the continuity of the historical legitimacy of the FLN, introduce the new state as the embodiment of religious reformism, and contain or eliminate political rivals.[54]

The new elites undertook symbolic and practical measures to reinforce this image. After Ben Bella took over power in 1962, he banned the use of alcohol, re-converted Christian churches into mosques, and replaced Christian symbols with Islamic ones. When Boumedienne, a graduate of Al-Azhar university, ousted Ben Bella, he in turn criticized the personalistic leadership style of the deposed president and his deviation from the true Islamic principles embodied in the November 1, 1954 Declaration.

The official Islamic ideology inherited from the 'ulama' a hostile attitude towards the Sufi orders and their heterodox beliefs and practices, thus confining Sufi influence to local communities and rural society. The state also adopted the reformist scholars' modernist interpretation of Islam, which emphasized its compatibility with modernity and the need to devise a rationalist outlook that draws on the original sources of religion. While maintaining a similar perspective, the post-independence regime, however, propagated a progressive, socialist Islam that would legitimize its revolutionary alternatives and the adoption of "scientific socialism."

The post-independence regime in Algeria adopted socialism as a model for achieving extensive development and economic independence. To justify its choice and gain popular acceptance of it, Islam was interwoven with socialism and the two were always portrayed as fully compatible. According to the official ideology, there would be no real independence without socialism and no socialism without Islam. The 1986 National Charter further emphasized this attitude by stating that "adhering to Islam is not only confined to the performance of rituals. Islam has many precepts that call for social justice and condemn the hegemony of wealth and the tyranny of material fortune. This has made Algeria adopt socialism while being confident of its continued commitment to Islam."[55] Hence, socialism does not become an alien ideology to the teachings of Islam, but a fulfillment of its admonitions. In this respect, the Charter explains, "a precise reading of the phases through which the revolution has passed clearly demonstrates that the choice of socialism as a model to achieve development and guarantee the equal distribution of the country's resources has not been an arbitrary decision or an imported idea superimposed on the people. It [socialism] is closely linked with the process of national liberation and fully compatible with the call of Islam for achieving social justice."[56]

The marriage between socialism and Islam was also useful in countering any opposition to the regime's socialist orientation and the nationalization measures that were implemented in the two decades that followed independence. Such measures included the nationalization of agricultural land, industrial firms, and commercial companies, and the establishment of a large public sector that would constitute the basis for the transformation into socialism. The state's socialist policy, particularly the confiscation of privately owned lands, raised opposition and discontent among some rural segments as well as Islamic activists, who were opposed to socialism. Some `ulama' issued a *fatwa* prohibiting prayers on confiscated land. To discredit this opposition, the regime criticized opponents to its policy as regressive and anti-social elements that were incapable of understanding the revolutionary and progressive message of Islam.

A personal status code, which had been subject to long revisions and debates reflecting the contending orientations within the government, was finally approved in 1984. For twenty years, the regime had been trying to introduce a liberal code that was always resisted by the Islamic elements in the government and in society. In contrast to the Tunisian personal status code, the Algerian code appears more conservative and closer to the rules of the Islamic *shari`a*. It permits polygamy, does not sanction the marriage of a Muslim woman to a non-Muslim, and maintains the Islamic rules regarding inheritance and adoption. As previous drafts of the code had raised the objections of the Islamic forces in society, so the new code has been a source of protest by Algerian feminists.

The nationalization of the Islamic ideology was one component of the regime's policy of controlling the religious domain. Another measure was to bring Islam under direct state control through the institutionalization and organization of religious activities. Religious affairs were placed under the government's civil service bureaucracy. In this respect, Algeria has not been different from Tunisia or Morocco. In 1964, Ben Bella's regime nationalized the public and private *habous* and placed them under state supervision. Two years later, the Supreme Islamic Council was formed. The members of the Council, who were given the right to select their head, were all appointed by the state.

According to the 1989 Constitution, the Council is affiliated to the Presidency that selects the members of the Council. The main function of the Supreme Islamic Council is to issue *fatwas* (religious opinions) and give advice to the government on religious issues, though it does not have any political bearing on the government's decisions. Commenting on the marginal political role of the religious establishment, Richard Parker remarks, "The religious establishment was given no role to speak of in running the government, which was left to technocrats, few of whom even went near a mosque. Indeed in Boumedienne's time, mosque attendance in Algeria was like church attendance in Moscow—the old, the infirm and the idle made up the congregation."[57]

A Ministry of Religious Affairs was established following independence. It was entrusted with the tasks of propagating the official religious discourse of the state; administering mosques, religious schools, and *habous* properties; and appointing and training religious leaders. Commenting on the functions of the ministry, John Entelis explains, "The principal objective in these multiple efforts has not been only to raise the level of national religious consciousness as a moral prerequisite for revolutionary advancement, though this remains important. The objective has always been to ensure that Islamic symbols and appeals are not confiscated by autonomous forces hostile to the current regime and its secular policies."[58]

Since independence, the Ministry of Religious Affairs has always been headed by subservient bureaucrats implementing the state's official religious policy. The first to assume the post of minister of religious affairs after independence was Tawfiq Madani, a former member of Ben Badis's association and a member of the Algerian Provisional Government (GPRA). The two most active ministers, however, were Mouloud Kassim and Abdel Rahman Chibane. Assuming the post in the 1970s, Kassim dedicated his ministry's activities to enhancing religious education and demonstrating the compatibility of Islam and socialism. In 1976, all Qur'anic schools, traditional schools, and institutes were nationalized and placed under the directorship of the Ministry of Religious Affairs. Under Kassim's tenure, the ministry produced two publications, *Al-Asala* and *Al-Risala*. Both expressed official Islam, defended the socialist policies of the state, and affirmed their Islamic character. Chibane, who was a minister from 1980 till 1991, assumed his post amidst increasing manifestations of religious protest.[59] The 1980 law organizing mosques aimed at assuring his ministry's tighter control over the country's mosques and their activities. Under President Chadli Benjedid's (1978-1992) directives, Chibane launched morality campaigns to counter the demands of the Islamic activists and give the impression of official concern for the moral and Islamic standards of the country's youth. Recently, the ministry has been headed by successive religious figures who lack the caliber of Kassim and Chibane and follow the line of defending the government's religious policies and ensure official control over the mosques.[60]

Politically, the Algerian regime took measures to undermine any opposition to its policy on religious grounds and prevent the rise of autonomous religious figures. Jean-Claude Vatin notes, "Following the example of the colonial state, the national state tried not to allow any kind of autonomy either to local culture or to associations and organizations based on Islamic principles."[61] In line with this policy, Ben Bella's regime dissolved the Association of Algerian Scholars in 1964, claiming that the Association was no longer needed particularly since its message had been incorporated as the official religious ideology of the state. In fact, the banning of the Association was an important initial indicator of the new state's tendency towards exercising political monopoly through a single party system. In particular, it also disclosed Ben Bella's dislike of Ben Badis's associates. In 1966, Boumedienne's regime banned the activities of al-Qiyam (Values) Association, which adopted the reformist line of the Association of Algerian Scholars and attempted to play a political role. Its periodical, *Humanisme Musulman*, was suspended and finally outlawed in 1970. Following that date, all religious publications, except those issued by the Ministry of Religious Affairs, have been banned. The religious scholars who opposed the state's secular policies were either sent to exile, such as shaykh Misbah al-Huwaiziq (d. 1973), or confined to house arrest as in the case of Shaykh al-Bashir al-Ibrahimi (d. 1965), the head of the Association of Scholars, and Abdel Latif Sultani (d. 1983), who vehemently opposed the socialist orientation of the regime.

Official Islam was used by the post-independence regime only to advance its secular choices: a strong state, socialism, and comprehensive development. This can best be grasped in the following statement which Boumedienne delivered to the members of the Organization of the Islamic Conference in Lahore, Pakistan, in 1974:

Human experience in many regions of the world has confirmed that spiritual links, whether Islamic or Christian, have not been able to withstand the painful strokes of poverty and ignorance. This is due to a simple reason: people do not desire to go to paradise on an empty stomach. Here is the essence of the problem. A hungry people does not need Qur'anic verses, with all respect to the Qur'an which I memorized since the age of ten. Hungry people need food, the ignorant need knowledge, and the sick need medicine.[62]

Official Islam was used to extend the state's monopoly over the political and religious domains. The state control over all aspects of the religion—its ideology, institutions, and figures—did not prevent the emergence of discontented groups who then challenged the legitimacy of the regime on religious grounds.

Morocco: Religious Symbolism

Unlike the leadership of Tunisia and Algeria, where transformation of society was pursued by steering the country away from its traditional roots, King Hassan II of Morocco has seemed satisfied with combining the best of both worlds: the old, from which he draws the basis for traditional legitimacy; and the modern, which provides him with the necessary means for the transformation and institutionalization of the regime.

The religious structure that survived in Morocco upon independence was different from those that existed in Tunisia and Algeria. As mentioned earlier, it was dominated by three major actors—the monarch, the `ulama', and, less significantly, the Sufi orders. The protectorate affected the influence and the relationships among these three institutions principally by weakening the monarchy, or the *makhzan*, in relation to the power of the scholars and the Sufi orders. However, following independence, this situation was immediately reversed as the monarchy emerged as the dominant of the three institutions. The scholars were placed under the control of the state's administration, and the majority of the Sufi orders were discredited for their collaboration with the French.[63]

The transition of King Hassan to the throne was paved by the popular nationalist and heroic role of his father, Muhammad V, in safeguarding the values of Islam and defending the Muslim community against foreign penetration. Unfortunately, the young king lacked the experience and charisma that his father enjoyed, and, therefore, had to consolidate his own legitimacy. In the religious realm, this was successfully achieved through his manipulation of the sources of the historical and religious legitimacy of his dynasty, his monopoly over the production of religious symbolism, and his control over the religious institutions.

King Hassan cultivates his status as the political and religious head of the country by asserting his legitimacy through the historical lineage of religious descent. He plays up the fact that he is a descendant of the

Prophet Muhammad, which implies that, in terms of religious authority, he ranks third after God and the Prophet. Each year, he receives the *bay`a* (oath of allegiance) from the political elites of the country, and this is usually articulated in a purely classical Arabic and loaded with heavy religious symbolism—hearkening back to the days of the Islamic Caliphate. A good example is the *bay`a* presented by the Moroccans in the different regions of the Sahara to King Hassan in 1979. They praised God for regulating the system of the Caliphate, explained the necessity of the *bay`a*, recognized the significance of the sultans, kings, and caliphs for maintaining security, peace, and justice in the land, renewed the allegiance of their forefathers to the king's dynasty, and self-consciously reaffirmed an oath similar to the one that had been given to the Prophet fourteen centuries earlier.[64] As such, the possession of religious descent and the annual submission of the *bay`a* allies the king with the religious institutions of the country and enables him to place himself at the top of the religious hierarchy and impose his authority on it.

Islamic values were carefully inserted in the Moroccan constitution, which was completed in 1962, a year after the proclamation of the "Fundamental Law." The articles of this law are inscribed in the preamble and General Principles. The preamble states *inter alia*: "The Kingdom of Morocco, a sovereign Muslim State [*dawla islamiyya*], whose official language is Arabic, shall be a part of the Greater Maghreb."[65] Article 6 states that, "Islam shall be the religion of the State, and the State shall guarantee to all the freedom of worship"; and Article 7 states that "the motto of the kingdom shall be: God, country and king."[66] The same references to Islam were confirmed in the subsequent four constitutions of 1962, 1970, 1972 and 1994. Erwin Rosenthal, nonetheless, has noted that the "Islamic" provisions of the constitution "are no stronger than those contained in the Tunisian Constitution, apart from the duty of the king, who is styled *amir al-mu'minin* (Commander of the Faithful) like the caliph, to defend religion."[67]

King Hassan is in charge of maintaining the religious symbols of Islam. This includes his reception of the *bay`a* from the political elites of the country on the third of March every year, the extensive use of classical Arabic and Qur'anic references in his political discourse to the Moroccan people, and his emphasis on his *baraka* (God-given good fortune), particularly after the two failed attempts on his life in 1971 and 1972. He also frequently participates in Friday prayers in the mosque near his palace, appears in the public garb of an `alim (religious scholar), sacrifices the first ram on `Id al-Adha, and donates generous personal gifts of alms to the poor during the various religious anniversaries. As an `alim, the king presides over *al-Durus al-Hassaniyya* (the Hassanite lectures), which are held annually during the month of Ramadan. In these lectures to the `ulama', the king presents his personal interpretations of the Qur'an and the Sunna.

In addition, Islamic rhetoric is noticeably heard with reference to issues of national and territorial consolidation, as in the case of the Green March to the Western Sahara in 1975. The marchers were ordered by the king to hold the Qur'an, the flag, and his portrait. The removal of Spain was likened to the famous Islamic battle, the Battle of Siffin.[68] To underscore the significance of the Green March in reformulating the religious and patriotic sentiments of the Moroccan people, King Hassan stated to his countrymen that "The March did not create a new people or a new Morocco out of you, but indeed it renewed your religion and patriotism, and as such, it makes you prisoners to what it has renewed and created."[69]

The smooth continuation of this role of Commander of the Faithful, however, requires the king to seek the general approval of the `ulama', who command a significant share of influence over public opinion in Morocco. In theory, the `ulama', as the guardians of the Muslim community, have the right to depose its head if he acts in clear contradiction to the principles of Islamic *shari`a* or against the interests of the community. As we have seen, one sultan was indeed deposed by the `ulama' in the beginning of this century.

Historically, the `ulama' have their own version of religious legitimacy and influence, which is different from that of the king. Whereas the king relies on his Prophetic descent, the `ulama'-related religious legitimacy is based on their status in society as learned men who acquire proficiency in the comprehension and interpretation of the various sources of Islamic teachings. As highly educated men in the matters of religion, they are venerated for the role they are expected to perform in defending the moral values of the community. In addition, the majority of the Moroccan `ulama' refused to collaborate with the French protectorate and allied themselves with the sultan and the Istiqlal Party in their struggle for independence. Therefore, they were able to maintain their status as a respected elite once independence was achieved.

Generally, the king refrains from questioning the authority of the *'ulama'*, and the *'ulama'*, in turn, recognize Hassan as their head and rarely dispute the legitimacy of him personally or his dynasty. Yet, by undermining political rivals to the monarchy, notably the Istiqlal Party with which the *'ulama'* had allied during the pre-independence period, the king succeeded during the 1960s in minimizing the strong position which the *'ulama'* had enjoyed. As in Tunisia and Algeria, this was achieved through the restructuring of the *'ulama'* within the state's institutions, and eroding their control over financial resources and national education. This strategy aimed at reducing any potential oppositional role that the scholars might play in the political arena—especially with regard to any possible conservative criticism of the secular-oriented national development programs.[70] In brief, such a policy was designed to bring about a nationwide modernization program that was not subject to the scrutiny of the *'ulama'*.

The Ministry of Endowments and Islamic Affairs was established in 1961 to administer matters that for long had been considered the exclusive domain of the *'ulama'*. The Ministry is divided into twelve central offices and thirty-two regional offices. They are in charge of administering and investing the majority of the *habous* lands, which were nationalized from the landowning families, Sufi brotherhoods, and the *'ulama'* in 1961. The government directly imposes its jurisdiction by levying rent payments based on the use of the agricultural land, collecting the revenue generated directly from the land, and maintaining other *habous* properties and agricultural facilities. The nationalization of the *habous* enabled the government to consolidate its control over the financial resources of the scholars, who now rely on the government for their income.

As is the case also in Tunisia, the ministry directs the annual pilgrimage of the Moroccans to Mecca and administers the function and operation of the state's mosques as well as supervises the building and maintenance of new ones. It also appoints their personnel and provides their salary. Only a handful of scholars, however, preach regularly in the mosques. According to the *habous* statistics of the government, only 241 scholars out of a few thousand holders of the *shari'a* diploma perform this duty. Most of these *'ulama'* serve as public functionaries.[71] The government, however, does not prohibit the private construction of mosques. Mosques that are built under private supervision are permitted to function independently; nevertheless, all speeches and sermons are carefully watched by the civil servants of the Ministry of Interior. The ministry also publishes two journals of Islamic thought that circulate freely. One is *Da`wat al-Haqq* (The Call for Truth) and the other is *al-Irshad* (Guidance). Both are filled with the views of the prominent *`ulama'* and the administrative personnel on various Islamic thoughts and teachings.

As for the composition of the Ministry of Habous and Islamic Affairs, it is staffed by graduates of the Islamic teaching institutions of Morocco. The department is open to and encourages the appointment of secular-trained personnel. The upper echelon of ministry officials are well-trained in the various Islamic sciences. The ministry controls the hiring and training of the staff assigned to supervise its functions. It is noteworthy that the traditionally-trained *`ulama'* constitute a disproportionately vocal minority, but are by no means a dominant force in the overall decision-making and policy formulation of the ministry. This was clearly illustrated in 1984 when the ministry was reorganized and placed under the control of the Ministry of the Interior. This shift officially made the *`ulama'* a body totally dependent on the regime,[72] and placed the religious activities of the mosques under the security surveillance of the ministry.

As in Tunisia and Algeria, the containment and reduction of the power and influence of the *`ulama'* is clearly tied to the increasing secularization of the education system of the country. Following independence, all education was nationalized and administered by the Ministry of Education. Two divisions were established: modern and traditional. The former is secular oriented and fashioned on the French model of education—and thus more attractive for those who desire to join the government. The latter, less prestigious because it appears to provide fewer career opportunities, is based on the Islamic curriculum and religious education, with the *`ulama'* functioning as instructors and school administrators. Nevertheless, both systems of education are administered by the Western-trained bureaucrats of the ministry. The *`ulama'* have little influence, if any, over the administration of the traditional system, even though it provides instruction in religious subjects in which they specialize.[73]

As the *`ulama'* were gradually brought under the authority of the regime, they lost their strength at the local level as important institutions in shaping the political culture of the community. As was the case in Tunisia, the *`ulama'* became no more than state-dominated theologians for purposes of supporting the state. The change in the situation of the *'ulama'* was described by the president of the Council of Scholars of Rabat, Si al-Makki al-Nasiri, thusly:

> Before 1912, the *'ulama'* were very free because of the fact that they were not integrated in a hierarchical system and were not receiving a salary. The notables of a town would endow goods to sustain the *'ulama'*s needs, just as a sultan visiting the town would offer them *kessoua* [clothes] and *mouna* [wheat]. In the 1920s, the sultan began to call upon the greatest *'ulama'* and integrated them into the *makhzan*, which caused the *'ulama'* to lose the privileges they had before because of the increasing domination of European positive law over the *shari'a* and especially because of the new process of their bureaucratization after the Qarawiyyin reform.[74]

King Hassan realizes, however, the potential threat in totally reducing the status of the religious scholars. He recognizes the importance of the historical and religious bases of his legitimacy and the need to sustain popular endorsement of his religious legitimacy. In this process, the support and approval of the scholars are very significant. In fact, by alienating and minimizing the stature of the scholars, he would indirectly be eroding his own religious legitimacy. In 1980, he expressed concern about the demise of the *'ulama'* and addressed them as follows:

> I do not know and do not want to know, venerable *'ulama'*, to whom or what—to you, to the administration, to politics or programs—your absence from daily Moroccan practice can be ascribed to. Gentlemen, I can affirm that you became strangers. ... We are all paying, children and young, adults and old, the price of this phenomenon, because in the universities and secondary schools the method of teaching of Islam only invokes the causes of the rupture of the *wudu'* (ablution before prayers) and the prayers. ... Where is the analysis of the economic, social, truly socialist, system of Islam? The students do not learn anymore that religion is first of all relationships among individuals.[75]

To resurrect the scholars, the king issued a *dahir* on April 18, 1981, ordering the establishment of Scientific Councils in which the religious scholars would be restructured under the presidency of the monarch. As the king explained, these councils were to act as intermediaries between him and the scholars and to stand against any subversive religious ideology,[76] whether propagated by the Iranian Revolution or the Islamic militants in Morocco. The councils are divided into two levels, *al-Majlis al-'Ilmi al-A'la* (the Supreme Scientific Council) and *al-Majalis al-*

`Ilmiyya al-Iqlimiyya* (the Regional Scientific Councils). The former consists of the heads of the Regional Councils and is chaired by the king. As specified in the *dahir*, this Council is assigned with the following functions: discussing issues presented (by the head scholars) to the king; coordinating the functions of the Regional Councils; and maintaining links with the international Islamic organizations, such as the League of the Muslim World and the Organization of the Islamic Conference. The Council convenes twice a year, but reserves the right to hold emergency sessions whenever the king warrants it necessary.

With regard to the second institutional level, fourteen Regional Councils have been established and headed by a Secretary-General, Muhammad Ben Ahmed al-Hajawi al-Tha`alibi, the director of traditional education in the Ministry of Education. Each council is composed of seven members and a chairman, who are all appointed by a royal decree. The Councils are assigned with the functions of reviving the chairs of preaching, guidance, and religious education in the mosques; educating the masses as to the spiritual, moral, and historical characteristics of the nation through the organization of lectures and seminars; contributing to the preservation of the doctrinal unity of the country by upholding the principles of the Qur'an and the Sunna; and executing the directions of the Supreme Scientific Council. The Regional Councils convene twice a month, and are allowed to hold emergency sessions, after consulting with and obtaining the consent of the king.[77]

In practice, the mechanism and policies dictated by the king for the operation and conduct of the Councils have rendered them void of content. The Councils work under the complete supervision of the state and in collaboration with the king's local governors. In addition, the governors are assisted by civil servants with religious background who are recruited from the Ministry of Interior. The functions of these civil servants, who coordinate their activities with the security forces of the Ministry of Interior, are to supervise the mosques, monitor the radical Islamic groups inside them, and make sure that the religious sermons (*khutba*) that are delivered by the scholars are in accordance with the state's official religious ideology.[78]

The king also drew the limits of the `ulama's activities in the Councils and the mosques. In his speech to the scholars in the concluding session of the Supreme Council, King Hassan warned them against interfering in politics. He stated firmly that the sermons which the scholars deliver must not be political, and that it should not be their concern if the price of any commodity went up. Otherwise, the king warned, "my duty is to defend religion against anything...even against some of the scholars if necessary."[79] He also expressed his confidence that the Councils would monitor the daily activity of each scholar. Hence, the restructuring of the `ulama' was designed to place them under the regime's scrutiny and to defend the regime against rival ideologies.

Another religious institution that has been noticeably undermined in the post-independence period is the Sufi orders. Unlike in Tunisia, the Sufi orders had historically played an influential role in the popular culture of the masses and in the politics of Morocco. The collaboration of some orders—the Kattaniyya, the Darqawiyya, and the Tayibiyya—with the French protectorate and the onslaught of the *Salafiyya* orthodox movement have tremendously eroded their credibility and reduced their influence. Furthermore, the nationalization of the *habous* lands under Sufi control deprived them of an important source of income and financial independence. Consequently, they long ceased to pose a threat, religious or political, to the institution of the monarchy.

However, a relatively recent order, the Boutchichiyya, has begun to gain some importance and popularity. According to Mohamed Tozy who studied this order, the Boutchichiyya has its origin in the 1920s in the Qadiriyya order in the city of Oran (Algeria), and was led by the descendants of its founder, Sidi Ali Boutchich. This brotherhood has five local *zawayas* in Casablanca in addition to basic groups known as *jama`a*. In the 1960s, this group went from a passive stage that just involved prayers and meditation to a more active phase—basically educational—in order to protect the practice of the faith. A member of the brotherhood explained its orientation by stating that, "We do not have the pretension to change the world; all we want is to be left in peace to be able to educate and purify Moroccan society from within; we are against any political manipulation of religion; we are *turuqis* [brotherhood followers], not Khomeinists."[80]

The primary objective of this group, as Tozy explained, is one of deepening faith through mystical rituals, which puts them in conflict with both the Islamist groups and the scholars. The members of the brotherhood consider the Islamist groups in Morocco as misguided and opportunistic. They believe that the "Islamists are wrong, because they want to change power, that is to say, they want to replace a bad leader with a worse one. The important thing is to change all of society from within."[81] Finally, what serves as an irrevocable gap between the Boutchichiyya and the scholars is that the former finds its paramount source of divine guidance in mystical and abstract concepts such as the *haqiqa* (truth) as opposed to the *shari`a*. They consider the *haqiqa* as the supreme law, which, in essence, is comprised of esoteric truth. As such, they declare: "The *`ulama'* are people of the *shari`a* and do not understand anything about Sufism."[82]

The relationship between the Moroccan regime and religion can be characterized as the state's use of religious symbols to formulate its own objectives. It considers the religious opposition groups within the country as marginal. The government portrays them as reactionary, and, to support its case, it relies on the *`ulama'* and the Scientific Councils to defend its actions against these groups. It is interesting to note that although Morocco is a Muslim state with a dominantly Muslim population, Islamic laws are not put into official practice. The national legal code refers to the *shari`a*, but it has been adapted and modernized in favor of Western codes of law. Rituals and ceremonies are broadly practiced, but these are not directly linked to a national ideology of social and political transformation. Morocco is a Muslim country, but like Tunisia and Algeria it does not reflect the political, legal, and social values of an Islamic state.

Conclusion

In brief, while Islam had been mobilized in the fight for independence throughout the colonial phase it has been marginalized during the struggle for development in the post-colonial period. In post-independent Tunisia, Algeria, and Morocco, the state, due to the foreign-inspired development policies of its leadership, has adopted various measures to enhance its authority over society and appropriated the religious institutions of the country. These measures have constituted systematic attempts to preempt religious opposition to government policies. Islam was in the process distorted and ceased to be a force of change in directing national development programs. This marginalization of traditional Islam and emasculation of the *`ulama'* as a political force created a vacuum in society. It was this vacuum that caused Islamic movements to rise beyond the domain of state-controlled religious institutions and attempt to create a new force to fill the old role of the scholars as arbitrators between the state and society. The members of these movements hold the state fully responsible for seeking to dislodge the traditional practice of Islam in favor of a secular-oriented modernization program. The conservative religious establishment has lost nearly all of its credibility for allowing itself to become, in the hands of the government, a tool with which the masses can be manipulated and the state agenda sanctioned.

Notes

1. Technically, the word *shari`a* refers to the Islamic law. However, "Shari`a is more than law; it is also the right teaching, the right way to go in life, and the power that stands behind what is right." Frederick Mathewson Denny, *An Introduction to Islam* (New York: Macmillan Publishing Company, 1994), p. 195.

2. See Alya Chaouachi, "L'Islam et les Tunisiens," *Dialogue*, No. 108, September 27, 1976, p. 22.

3. Voll, *Islam: Continuity and Change*, pp. 74-5.

4. Arnold Green, "A Comparative Historical Analysis of the `Ulama' and the State in Egypt and Tunisia," *Revue de L'Occident Musulman et de la Méditerranée*, No. 29, 1980, pp. 40-4.

5. John Ruedy, *Modern Algeria: The Origins and Development of a Nation* (Indianapolis: Indiana University Press, 1992), pp. 27-9, and Voll, *Islam: Continuity and Change*, pp. 75-6.

6. Mohamed Tozy, "Champ Politique et Champ Religieux au Maroc: Croisement ou Hiérarchisation." (Mémoire pour l'Obtention du Diplôme d'Etudes Supérieures de Sciences Politiques, Faculté des Sciences Juridiques, Economiques, et Sociales, Université Hassan II, Casablanca, 1980), pp. 49-59. See also Jamal Benomar, "The Monarchy, the Islamist Movement and Religious Discourse in Morocco," *Third World Quarterly*, Vol. 10, No. 2, April 1988, p. 544.

7. Voll, *Islam: Continuity and Change*, pp. 76-9.

8. Mohamed Tozy, "Monopolisation de la Production Symbolique et Hiérarchisation du Champ Politico-Religieux au Maroc," in Christiane Souriau et al., *Le Maghreb Musulman en 1979* (Paris: CNRS, 1981), pp. 219-35.

9. Jamil Abun-Nasr, *A History of the Maghrib in the Islamic Period* (London: Cambridge University Press, 1975), p. 342. See also, Nicola A. Ziadeh, *Origins of Nationalism in Tunisia* (Beirut: The American University in Beirut, 1962), pp. 103-8.

10. Brown, "The Role of Islam," p. 104.

11. On the difference between the Old and Neo-Destour Parties see Nora Salem, *Habib Bourguiba, Islam, and the Creation of Tunisia* (London: Croom Helm, 1984), pp. 96-7. Salem maintains that the difference between the two parties was neither ideological nor social since the leaders of both parties came

from the same background. The main difference was tactical as demonstrated in the Neo-Destour's tendency to mobilize the masses and to use violence.

12. Salem, *Habib Bourguiba*, p. 82. See also Kenneth Perkins, *Tunisia: Crossroads of the Islamic and European Worlds* (Boulder: Westview Press, 1986), p. 103.

13. Salem, *Habib Bourguiba*, pp. 98-131. To demonstrate the support which Bourguiba had enjoyed as a result of the identification of the Neo-Destour with Islam, Voll quoted a comment attributed to an old Zaytouni shaykh in 1958, who said, "Whoever does not believe in the word of Bourguiba does not believe in the word of God and his Prophet." Voll, *Islam: Continuity and Change*, p. 209.

14. For an excellent study by an Algerian historian of the early resistance movements to the French occupation, see Abu al-Qasim Sa`dallah, *al-Haraka al-Wataniyya al-Jaza'iriyya: 1900-1930* [The Algerian National Movement] (Beirut: Dar al-Adab, 1969), pp. 49-69.

15. Abdullah Shrit and Muhammad al-Mili, *al-Jaza'ir fi Mir'at al-Tarikh* [Algeria in the Mirror of History] (Algeria: Maktabat al-Ba`th, 1965), p. 221.

16. This law was promulgated by the French in 1881 to control and contain the Muslim population and remained in effect until after World War II. See John Entelis, *Algeria: The Revolution Institutionalized* (Boulder: Westview Press, 1986), p. 32.

17. Mohammad Arkoun, "Algeria," in Shireen Hunter (ed.), *The Politics of Islamic Revivalism: Diversity and Unity* (Bloomington and Indianapolis: Indiana University Press, 1989), p. 172.

18. It was reported that Messali's party had 11,000 followers, 7 branches in France and 61 in Algeria. See Moustapha al-Aqqad, *al-Maghrib al-Arabi* [The Arab Maghrib] (Cairo: Maktabat al-Anglo al-Masriyya, 1993), p. 302.

19. These were Ahmed Ben Bella, Muhammad Khedir, Rabeh Bitat, Hussein Ait Ahmed, Karim Belkacem, Muhammad al-Arabi Ben Mehidi, Muhammad Boudiaf, Murad Didoush, and Moustapha Boualid. For the evolution of the war of liberation, see Muhammad Harbi, *al-Thawra al-Jaza'iriyya: Sanawat al-Makhad* [The Algerian Revolution: Years of Deliverance] (Muhammadiyya: Matba`at Fadala, 1988).

20. Benomar, "The Monarchy, the Islamist Movement," pp. 246-8.

21. *Al-Manar* was a monthly periodical published by Muhammad Rashid Rida, a disciple of `Abduh, in Egypt in the period from 1898 to 1935. See Emad Eldin Shahin, "Muhammad Rashid Rida," *The Oxford Encyclopedia of the Modern Islamic World*, Vol. 3 (New York: Oxford University Press, 1995), pp. 410-12.

22. Voll, *Islam: Continuity and Change*, p. 105. On the *Salafiyya* movement see Abdel Hadi Abu Talib, "Dhikrayat wa Shahadat wa Wujouh" [Memories, Testimonies, and Personalities], *Asharq al-Awsat*, June 1, 8, 15, and 22, 1988.

Leon Carl Brown, "The Role of Islam in Modern North Africa," in Leon Carl Brown (ed.), *State and Society in Independent North Africa* (Washington, D.C.: The Middle East Institute, 1966), pp. 101-6. Leon Carl Brown, "The Islamic Reformist Movement in North Africa," *Journal of Modern African Studies*, Vol. 2, No. 1, March 1964. Jamil Abun-Nasr, "The Salafiyya Movement in Morocco: The Religious Base of the Moroccan Nationalist Movement," *St. Anthony's Papers*, No. 16, Middle East Affairs, No. 3 (London: Chatto and Wind, 1963). Emad Eldin Shahin, "*Salafiyah*," *The Oxford Encyclopedia of the Modern Islamic World*, Vol. 4 (New York: Oxford University Press, 1995), pp. 463-9.

23. Abun-Nasr, *A History of the Maghrib*, pp. 378-82.

24. Brown, "The Role of Islam," p. 104.

25. Abun-Nasr, *A History of the Maghrib*, pp. 384-92.

26. John Waterbury, *The Commander of the Faithful: The Moroccan Political Elite* (New York: Columbia University Press, 1970), pp. 47-58.

27. Habib Bourguiba, "Itarat Tunisiyya li-Tahamul al-Masu'liyya" [Tunisian Cadres for Bearing Responsibility], a speech delivered in the Mosque of Qayrawan in October 5, 1957, in Habib Bourguiba, *Khutab Mawlidiyya* [Speeches on the Occasion of the Prophet's Birthday] (Tunis: The Ministry of Information, 1979), p. 8.

28. Erwin Rosenthal, *Islam in the Modern National State* (London: Cambridge University Press, 1965), p. 319.

29. Habib Bourguiba, "al-Islam Din al-Haya" [Islam: Religion of Life], A speech delivered in the Mosque of Qayrawan, September 3, 1960 in Habib Bourguiba, *Khutab Mawlidiyya*, pp. 26-7.

30. Sadok Belaid, "Role of Religious Institutions in Support of the State," in I. William Zartman and Adeed Dawisha (eds.), *Beyond Coercion* (London: Croom Helm, 1988), p. 156.

31. Rafik Abdallah, "Bourguiba et l'Islam," (Mémoire pour le Diplôme d'Etudes Supérieures de Sciences Politiques, Université de Paris, 1973). Abdallah stated that Bourguiba had an eclectic and hostile attitude towards rigid doctrines. He used different interpretations and adopted reform according to Tunisian reality, see p. 98.

32. See Habib Bourguiba, *Khutab Mawlidiyya*; "Bourguiba: Les Valeurs Islamiques," *L'Action,* July 29, 1981; and "Les Valeurs Islamiques Ont Toujours Guidé l'Action de Notre Parti," *L'Action*, December 5, 1984.

33. Susan E. Marshall, "Islamic Revival in the Maghreb: The Utility of Tradition for Modernizing Elites," *Studies in Comparative International Development*, No. 14, Summer 1979, p. 97.

34. Marshall, "Islamic Revival," p. 103.

35. A speech delivered in Sfax on April 19, 1964.

36. Quoted in Ghannoushi, "The Battle against Islam."

37. Gilbert Naccache, "Idéologie et Projet de Société: L'Inéquation Tunisienne," *Le Mensuel*, No. 3, October 1984, pp. 33-5.

38. Marion Boulby, "The Islamic Challenge: Tunisia since Independence," *Third World Quarterly*, Vol. 10, No. 2, April 1988, p. 592.

39. Hafedh Ben Salah, "Système Politique et Système Religieux en Tunisie," (Memoire pour le Diplôme d'Etudes Supérieures de Sciences Politiques, Université de Tunis, Faculté des Droit et des Sciences Politiques et Economiques, Tunis, 1973-4), pp. 27-8. See also Yadh Ben Achour, "Islam Perdu, Islam Retrouvé," in Christiane Souriau et al., *Le Maghreb Musulman En 1979*, pp. 66-7.

40. Brown, "The Role of Islam," p. 109. See also Al-Monji al-Ka`bi, "al-Zaytouna fi Mir'at al-Damir al-Tunsi" [al-Zaytouna in the Tunisian Conscience], *al-Marji`* , Vol. 1, No. 2, October 1982, pp. 43-50.

41. "Idarat al-Sha`ai'r al-Diniyya: Limadha Taba`t Wazart al-Dakhiliyya" [Why Was the Directorate of Religious Affairs Placed under the Supervision of the Ministry of Interior], *al-Anwar*, May 11, 1986. "Innana Nad`u ila Islam al-I`tidal" [We Call for a Moderate Islam], interview with Shaykh Kamal al-Tarzi, the Director of the Administration of Religious Affairs in *Haqa'iq*, No. 31, June 1, 1984.

42. Brown, "The Role of Islam," p. 111.

43. Perkins, *Tunisia*, p. 119.

44. Clement Henry Moore, *Tunisia Since Independence* (Berkeley: University of California Press, 1965), p. 59.

45. Marshall, "Islamic Revival," p. 105.

46. "Quelle Politique de Ramadan pour les Tunisiens?," *Democratie*, August 28, 1979.

47. Muhammad Darif, *al-Islam al-Siyasi fi al-Jaza'ir* [Political Islam in Algeria] (Casablanca: Manshurat al-Majalla al-Maghrebiyya li-`Ilm al-Ijtima` al-Siyasi, 1994), p. 86-97.

48. *The 1976 National Charter* (Algeria: Ministry of Culture and Information, 1981), pp. 18-19.

49. John Entelis, *Algeria: The Revolution Institutionalized*, p. 81.

50. *The 1976 National Charter*, pp. 58-9.

51. The 1962 Charter of Tripoli that was approved one month before independence states that "The Algerian culture will be nationalist, revolutionary and scientific. Its role as a national culture, as a first phase, is to give the Arabic language, which genuinely expresses the cultural values of our country, its dignity and efficacy as a language of civilization. The Algerian culture will reconstruct the nation's heritage, both its ancient and modern humanistic aspects, assess it, disseminate it and introduce it in the intellectual life and the structure of the national sentiments. Consequently, it [the Algerian culture] will be able to withstand the cultural domination and Western influence which have

instilled in many Algerians disdain for their national language and values." See Muhammad Abid al-Jabri, *al-Ta'lim fi al-Maghrib al-'Arabi* [Education in the Arab Maghrib] (Casablanca: Dar al-Nashr al-Maghribiyya, 1989), p.118.

52. Quoted in al-Jabri, *al-Ta'lim fi al-Maghrib al-'Arabi*, p. 131.

53. Jean-Claude Vatin, "Revival in the Maghreb: Islam as an Alternative Political Language," in Dessouki (ed.), p. 235.

54. Darif, *al-Islam al-Siyasi*, p. 120.

55. Quoted in Darif, *al-Islam al-Siyasi*, p. 92.

56. Darif, *al-Islam al-Siyasi*, pp. 93-4.

57. Richard Parker, *North Africa: Regional Tensions and Strategic Concerns* (New York: Praeger Publishers, 1984), p. 97.

58. Entelis, *Algeria: The Revolution Institutionalized*, p. 82.

59. Jean-Claude Vatin, "Popular Puritanism versus State Reformism," in James Piscatori, ed., *Islam in the Political Process* (London: Cambridge University Press, 1983), p. 111.

60. See interview with Muhammad Ben Radwan, the Minister of Religious Affairs, in *al-'Alam*, No. 397, September 21, 1991, pp. 30-2.

61. Vatin, "Revival in the Maghreb," p. 233.

62. Quoted in Darif, *al-Islam al-Siyasi*, p. 62 from Jean Leca and Jean-Claude Vatin, *L'Algérie Politique* (Paris: Presses de la Fondation Nationale des Sciences Politiques, 1975).

63. Jamal Benomar, "The Monarchy, the Islamist Movement and Religious Discourse in Morocco," *Third World Quarterly*, Vol. 10, No. 2, April 1988, pp. 546-50.

64. *Al-Iman*, Vol. 13, Nos. 128-130, July-October 1983, pp. 81-3.

65. Rosenthal, *Islam in the Modern Nation State*, p. 329.

66. Rosenthal, *Islam in the Modern Nation State*, p. 329.

67. Rosenthal, *Islam in the Modern Nation State*, p. 331.

68. Donna Lee Bowen, "The Paradoxical Linkage of the *'Ulama'* and Monarch in Morocco," *The Maghreb Review*, Vol. 10, No. 1, 1985, p. 7. The Battle of Siffin, a decisive one, that took place in 657 between the Islamic armies of Ali Ben Abi Taleb and Mu'awiya Ben Abi Sufian. The army of Mu'awiya on the verge of defeat, raised copies of the Qur'an and called for arbitration.

69. The king's speech in the Third Anniversary of the Green March, *Da'wat al-Haqq*, Vol. 20, Nos. 2-3, March 1979, p. 9.

70. Bowen, "The Paradoxical Linkage," p. 3.

71. Mohamed Chaoui, "Islam et Politique au Maroc," *Lamalif*, No. 121, December 1980, p. 12.

72. Bowen, "The Paradoxical Linkage," pp. 4-5.

73. Bowen, "The Paradoxical Linkage," p. 5.

74. Tozy, "Champ Politique et Champ Religieux au Maroc," p. 105.

75. King Hassan's speech to the scholars, *Da'wat al-Haqq*, Vol. 21, No. 1, March 1980, p. 16.

76. King Hassan's Speech, Ibid., p. 15.

77. The Royal Decree of April 18, 1981, regarding the establishment of the Scientific Councils, see *Da'wat al-Haqq*, Vol. 22, No. 4, June-July 1981, pp. 6-8. See also Muhammad al-Hajawi al-Tha'alibi, "al-Majalis al-'Ilmiyya al-Iqlimiyya" [The Regional Scientific Councils], *Da'wat al-Haqq*, Vol. 22, No. 6, October 1981. Al-Tha'alibi, the Regional Councils secretary general, stated that "the first task to be expected from the Councils is to defend the country against moral, doctrinal, and intellectual disintegration so they would become a royal army, defending our spiritual entity in the same way the Royal Army is defending our territorial unity" (p. 34).

78. The king's speech to the scholars in the Supreme Scientific Council, *Da'wat al-Haqq*, No. 235, April 1984, p. 9, and his directions to the civil servants in *Da'wat al-Haqq*, No. 238, July 1984, pp. 4-5.

79. King Hassan's speech to the scholars in the concluding session of the Supreme Council in *Da'wat al-Haqq*, No. 224, August 1982, p. 9.

80. Tozy, "Champ Politique et Champ Religieux au Maroc," p. 127.bis.

81. Tozy, "Champ Politique et Champ Religieux au Maroc," p. 128.

82. Tozy, "Champ Politique et Champ Religieux au Maroc," p. 129.

3

The Rise and Repression of an Islamic Movement: Harakat al-Nahda in Tunisia

Throughout the 1970s and 1980s the Tunisian Islamist current set the standard for the rest of the Maghrib. The Islamic movement in Tunisia was by far the best organized and most articulate in the area. Its intellectual discourse, as advanced by thinkers such as Rashed al-Ghannoushi and groups like the Progressive Islamic Tendency Movement (MTPI), gave the most coherent and trenchant analyses to some of the major questions pertaining to political Islam—questions that the movements in the other Maghribi countries had addressed only in the vaguest terms. Historically, the Tunisian Islamic trend played a key role in protecting civil society from the regime and preventing a dangerous polarization between state and society—a role that since the movement's repression has remained unfilled.

Examination of the Islamic movements in Tunisia, particularly the mainstream organization, Harakat al-Nahda (The Renaissance Movement),[1] reveals a pattern of increasing growth and importance during the Bourguiba era, followed by repression under Ben Ali's regime. In this chapter, the characteristics and dynamics of al-Nahda will be assessed with regard to its origins, expansion, and politicization through four distinct phases: the formative phase (1960s-1973); the expansion phase (1973-1979); the politicization phase (1979-1987); and the post-Bourguiba phase (1987-present). The particular characteristics and dynamics of each of these phases will be addressed in the context of political, cultural, and socioeconomic factors.

The historical formation and political evolution of al-Nahda in the late 1960s can be traced to the socialist program launched by Ahmed Ben Saleh under the Bourguiba model of national development; the bureaucratization of Islam through the nationalization of the religious institutions and the undermining of the traditional role of the religious scholars; and the ability of a new generation of Muslim intellectuals to utilize effectively the key resources of the mosque and the secondary schools to promote an alternative ideology. The expansion and politicization of al-Nahda, as such, reflected the dislocating effects of the economic policies of the state, the marginalization of traditional Islam, as well as the outbreak of the Islamic revolution in Iran.

By the late 1970s and 1980s al-Nahda was a dynamic actor and a viable force in Tunisian politics. This was achieved in part by an expansion of the social base of the movement to include—in addition to students and teachers—professionals, workers, and civil servants. More important, the movement successfully managed to institute a cohesive organizational structure capable of sustaining government repression, promoting the political consciousness of its constituency, and resocializing its membership along Islamic lines. In addition, al-Nahda reflected a moderate political orientation by accepting political pluralism in society, cooperating with other political forces—including the leftist parties—and insisting on gaining official recognition in order to operate as a legal political party.

Tunisia's Socialist Development

The first stage in the development of al-Nahda in Tunisia can be characterized as one based on movement formation. Although the manifestations of organized and active Islamic movements in Tunisia began to take shape in the 1970s, the roots of such movements can be traced back to the 1960s and the reaction to the political and socioeconomic policies of the regime. These policies aimed at the rapid transformation of society, yet created socioeconomic strains and a legitimacy crisis for the system that brought Bourguiba's model of development into question and triggered the rise of a counter-elite with a rival ideology and a different orientation.

During the 1960s, Ahmed Ben Saleh, a strong union leader appointed in 1961 by Bourguiba as minister for planning and finance, led the drive for a planned socialist economy. He wanted to achieve a higher per capita income for the Tunisian people through increasing agricultural productivity and the construction of a national industry that would in turn minimize the country's dependence on foreign sources. To fulfill this objective, Ben Saleh designed an ambitious labor-oriented ten-year plan, for which he secured the full support of Bourguiba. The party was renamed the Destourian Socialist Party (PDS) in 1964 as a sign of commitment to this new transformation. Ben Saleh proceeded by collectivizing the lands that were formerly dominated by the French landowners and restructuring them into farming units. A cooperative system—consisting of agricultural units of 500 hectares each, commercial cooperatives, and credit banks—was created and included one-third of the country's cultivable land and one-third of the rural population. The new system also affected the industrial and commercial activities in the cities. In the late 1960s, the collectivization process was expanded to include the holdings of the large and even small landed peasants.

Although the industrial sector witnessed some expansion, particularly in the phosphate, steel, and oil industries, by 1968 it became clear that Ben Saleh's experiment was facing severe difficulties and growing opposition. Agricultural productivity decreased, per capita income did not rise, and urban unemployment remained high. By 1968, four out of five cooperatives were steadily losing money.[2] Peasants' disenchantment with the cooperatives stemming from their loss of property and decline in real income, as well as complaints of mismanagement, waste, and corruption, added to the undermining of the collectivization experiment. The government was forced to contract foreign loans to finance the cooperatives, but thereby increased the country's dependence on the outside. Ben Saleh's style of centralization of power and alienation of the traditional supporters of the Destour Party—the workers, peasants, and small business people—aroused the fear of party leaders and generated their opposition to the continuation of his program. In 1969, Bourguiba dismissed Ben Saleh as the minister of planning, and a year later he was tried on charges of treason, corruption, and mismanagement. The government backtracked on his socialist economic policies and dismantled the cooperatives.

The devastating collapse of Ahmed Ben Saleh's experiment of state-imposed collectivization in 1969 generated drastic consequences for the Tunisian political system. In addition to inflicting negative economic results and raising social discontent, it shook the credibility of the political regime: Bourguiba's popularity suffered as he was indirectly implicated in Ben Saleh's program. It gave a strong impression that the regime was unable to offer a successful ideological framework for a workable model of development. One of the results was a new phase of political and economic liberalization during which restrictive measures on private enterprise and foreign investment were relaxed and differences in opinion became relatively more tolerated. Though this swift transition from one political orientation to another, socialism to liberalism, was accommodated within the pragmatic and opportunistic tenets of Bourguibism, the fact that it was undertaken by the same leadership and political institutions raised doubts as to its seriousness.

The period of the 1970s can be considered a period of rearrangement of roles within the Tunisian political system, particularly in the beginning, as well as one of a further increase in the state's control over the political process—despite a liberal facade. After Ben Saleh's crisis, the state became concerned with regaining confidence in its policies and alternatives by reversing the socialist measures and promoting more liberal ones. In the 1971 Socialist Destourian Party Congress, elements within the party critical of authoritarian measures and supportive of liberal policies were given the chance to express their views freely. One such person was Ahmed Mestiri, a strong supporter of liberalism, who had resigned as defense minister in opposition to Ben Saleh's policies but was reintegrated into the party and government in 1970. At the same time, to restore its power, the state turned against the leftist opposition and the supporters of Ben Saleh and managed to disperse and repress them through consecutive trials and suppressive measures.

The drive towards liberalism came to a halt three years later, however, depriving Tunisia of its opportunity for true political liberalization. Bourguiba regained his health after three years of putative illness and began to tighten his grip over the whole system once more. In the subsequent Party Congress in 1974 in Monastir, *Mu'tamar al-Wuduh*, the "Congress of Clarity"—an indication that the preceding phase was seen as being characterized by obscurity and improvisation—Bourguiba decided that "it was necessary to eradicate what happened in the last Congress."[3] Some Destourian elements with liberal tendencies made an immediate exit or were simply expelled from the party and the government. This group included political figures such as Secretary General of the Socialist Destour Party Ahmed Mestiri, former Defense Minister Haseeb Ben Ammar, and former Minister of Culture Habib Bouleras. Some, such as Mestiri, later the head of the Socialist Democratic Party, or independents like Ben Ammar, later expressed their disenchantment with the system and declared its bankruptcy; they became part of the state's legalized opposition in 1981.

The lack of a stable political ideology in addition to the oscillation of government policies and positions created a state of apathy and confusion particularly among the young. Salah Eddin al-Jourshi, one of the founders of the Islamic Tendency Movement (MTI), an earlier incarnation of al-Nahda, remarked that "it became clear that the regime had no ideology. In a brief period it moved from socialism to liberalism with the same faces. Some figures had been removed, but under the direction and supervision of the same leadership and the same regime. The young discovered that they were part of a system that possessed no alternatives."[4] This stimulated some of these youth to begin the search for an ideological alternative independent of the state, and indeed they soon formed the nucleus of an Islamic movement, which culminated in 1981 with the formation of *Harakat al-Ittijah al-Islami*, the Islamic Tendency Movement (MTI).

The Islamic Tendency Movement

The beginning of the Islamic Tendency Movement was in al-Zaytouna Mosque, which despite the regime's measures to undermine it, remained a gathering place for traditional scholars seeking refuge from the secularization policies of Bourguiba's regime.[5] These policies generated the discontent of some of the traditional elements and scholars, such as Muhammad Saleh al-Naifar, Ahmed Ben Melad, and Abdel Qader Salama, who adamantly rejected the secularization of the Tunisian society, refused to be incorporated into the state's nationalized religious institutions, and in the beginning of the 1970s supported the nascent Islamic movement in Tunisia.

Starting as early as the mid-1960s, a highly respected Zaytouna scholar, the late Shaykh Ahmed Ben Melad, began to draw into his circle young disciples increasingly at odds with the secular policies of the government. Ben Melad, whose preoccupation chiefly entailed the dispensing of the classic teachings of Islam, voiced strong objections to the lack of Islamic teachings in the secondary school and university systems of Tunisia. In time, these discussions would inspire Tunisian intellectuals such as Rashed al-Ghannoushi to study the conditions of the country in order to seek the revival of Islamic values in society.[6] Ben Melad's circles attracted a number of young followers among whom were Abdel Fattah Mourou and Ghannoushi. They were later joined by Hemida al-Naifar and Salah Eddin al-Jourshi who all became the principal founders of the Islamic Tendency Movement.[7]

There are elements which these founders of the MTI share in common. They all had an early religious formation, a factor not unusual in the traditions of most Muslim families of the region which inculcate in their children at an early age the fundamental precepts and practices of religion. More importantly, though, due to their Arabic-Islamic background, some of them faced early rejection and felt rather alienated in the Westernized educational system in Tunisia.

Abdel Fattah Mourou, the son of a small merchant, was born in 1942. He was raised in a religious family where his parents introduced him to the principles and practices of Islam. He received his primary education in the Sadiki College, a respected bilingual high school established by Khayr Eddin Pasha in the nineteenth century to synthesize traditional and modern education. In addition to the Western curriculum, the school provided him with a religious education. Mourou went on to undertake the study of law, graduating from law school at the university of Tunis in 1971. Mourou's disenchantment with the way that the regime appeared to limit the general practice and overall supervision of Islamic doctrines led him in the beginning of his career to join one of the esoteric Sufi orders, *al-Madaniyya*, a small order established in the beginning of the century and characterized by its rejection of any foreign presence in the country.[8]

Mourou's flirtation with Sufism proved to be short-lived. In time, his training under Shaykh Ben Melad encouraged him to begin giving his own religious lectures on the interpretation of the Qur'an at the Zaytouna and other mosques in Tunis. This course of action was to pave the way for Mourou's eventual ascendancy within the organizational structure of the movement.

Rashed al-Ghannoushi was born in 1941 to a peasant family in al-Hamma, a village near the southeastern coast of Tunisia. Like his counterpart Mourou, Ghannoushi also grew up in a religious household and, in time, established himself as a secondary school teacher in Tunis. His own high school education was pursued in the traditional Zaytouni schools, which the government closed down in the 1960s as part of its secularization of the education system.[9] Lacking French, however, he was unable to pursue his education in Tunisia's francophile university system. So Ghannoushi pursued the rest of his education overseas and headed for Syria in 1964.

In the Syrian capital of Damascus, Ghannoushi joined the Faculty of Philosophy and Letters and graduated in 1968. There, he was exposed to the ideas of Arab Nationalism, still then in its heyday. He started his university years as a member of the Nasserite Nationalist Party of Syria and embraced a secular approach to political expression. It was not long before he discovered, however, that Arab nationalism in the Mashriq (the Arab East) was of a different strand than the kind which existed in the Maghrib. In the East, the bifurcation of Arabism and Islam, designed to accommodate the non-Muslim minorities, conflicted with Ghannoushi's early understanding and convictions of the issue. As he himself recalls: "I had always understood being an Arab and being a Muslim as inseparable realities, such as it is understood among our people in North Africa."[10]

His disillusionment at the separation of Islam and Arabism by the regimes of the Mashriq encouraged him to seek an alternative avenue of political expression. His exposure to the Muslim Brothers and the *Salafiyya* at the university convinced him of the need to cement the demand for social reform within the doctrines of Islam. Indeed, these thoughts bore fruition years later. Having completed his studies and learned French, Ghannoushi went on to pursue a year of graduate work in France before returning home. Back in Tunis, it was through his contact with Mourou that he was introduced to the circle of Shaykh Ben Melad.

Shaykh Hemida al-Naifar, now a professor at the Faculty of Shari`a in Tunis, was born in 1942. He came from a traditional family with a long history in the Tunisian religious institutions, and like Ghannoushi, also continued his university studies in Syria. He too was influenced by Nasserism—until he met Ghannoushi. According to al-Naifar, they both became convinced of the need to relinquish secular ideas and adhere to Islam for "none of those programs, which for so long seemed to offer certain solutions, could provide the answer—neither Arab nationalism nor Tunisian nationalism nor the West."[11]

The son of a civil servant, Salah Eddin al-Jourshi was born in 1954 to a family of Moorish origins. Though not possessing a history in the Tunisian religious institutions, Jourshi's family nevertheless took pride in having been able to maintain its religious commitment to Islam for three centuries in Christian Spain. Jourshi was influenced by the local shaykhs in his community and, though now an independent journalist, co-founded the MTI when he was only sixteen years old.[12]

These four founders all shared a profound alienation to post-independence Tunisian society during their formative years. Ghannoushi shares his memories of those bitter times:

I am of the generation of Zaytouna students during the early years of independence. I remember we used to feel like strangers in our own country. We have been educated as Muslims and as Arabs, while we could see the country totally molded in the French cultural identity. For us, the doors for any further education were closed since the university was completely Westernized.[13]

Moreover, like many young Arabs in the 1960s, Ghannoushi and al-Naifar passed through the phase of Nasserism and Arab Nationalism and experienced their unfulfilled promises and disappointing setbacks. They came to see contradictions within these trends and ultimately abandoned them in favor of Islam.

Having acquired the necessary religious training from Ben Melad, Ghannoushi and Mourou started their activities by delivering religious lectures of their own. They concentrated their activities on two levels, the mosques and the secondary schools in and around the capital, Tunis. At this stage, the movement was still apolitical in its approach. The lectures centered primarily on three basic issues. The first dealt with clarifying the various matters of belief and promoting Islamic principles. This process required the memorization of the Qur'an and the study of the Sunna and other Islamic sciences. The second dealt with demonstrating the discrepancies between Islamic principles and the present "un-Islamic" reality of the Muslims. This reality was perceived to be the product of a Westernized elite, lacking an indigenous vision and influenced by Western values and secular ideas. Using his education and training as a philosophy teacher, Ghannoushi focused on highlighting for his students the contradictions inherent in materialistic ideologies. The third issue dealt with demonstrating the need for changing this reality and eradicating the gaps between what is preached and what is practiced. Lacking a crystallized political consciousness and a cohesive ideology, however, political references were made rarely and only indirectly.

The leaders of the movement began to attract a following and expand their circle. Two special circles were formed in 1970: one for Baccalaureate students, who would soon enter the university and form the movement's base there; and another for women.[14] During this phase, the members of the movement were influenced by the India-based Islamic group *Jama'at al-Tabligh* (Propagation Group). Some members of this group had visited Tunisia in 1966 and 1967, and stayed for three months, as part of their practice of touring and preaching for brief periods throughout the Muslim countries. Influenced by the method of preaching of the Tabligh people, the Tunisian Islamists roamed the cities and countryside urging Muslims to follow their religion and observe its precepts.[15]

In 1969, these young Islamists decided to join the National Association for the Preservation of the Qur'an, which had been established in that year by the government as part of its policies to reverse Ben Saleh's socialist phase and to project a religious image to enhance its legitimacy. The Association was founded as a means for improving and modernizing the traditional primary schools, training numbers of cadres necessary for the dissemination of the Qur'an and its sciences, and educating young Tunisians in the basics of their religion.[16] With its headquarters in Tunis, the Association proliferated through the establishment of various branches in the different provinces. The Secretary-General of the Association, a Zaytouni scholar, Shaykh Habib Mestaoui—also a member of the Destour Party's Central Committee—aspired to play an active role in the party and change its secular orientation from within. In one of the meetings of the Committee, Shaykh Mestaoui received a warm welcome as part of the party's efforts to show respect for Islam.[17] In order to build a base of support, he encouraged Ghannoushi and his group to join the Association. This invitation provided them with the organizational structure that they were lacking and a legal forum from which they could safely carry out and expand their activities.

While in the Association, they organized lectures on a weekly basis, and supplied their audience with Islamic books and materials. More importantly, they expanded their channels of communication throughout the country. In order to enhance his position in the party and advance his reorientation efforts, Shaykh Mestaoui urged the leaders of the nascent movement to join the party and infiltrate its cells. Despite his insistence, however, the leaders of the movement declined. They sensed that their admission to the party would eventually place them on the government's payroll, diminishing their credibility and making them part of the system they criticized.

During this stage, the government followed a policy of toleration toward the Islamic movement, despite occasional tough measures aimed at suppressing its political activities. In the beginning, the extent of the movement's potential threat to the regime was not very clear. It was still very small in number, mainly focusing on moral issues, and its political impulses had not yet been developed. It was viewed as a religious association with reformist tendencies. The government, in addition, was preoccupied with its confrontation with the leftist elements, and, therefore, tolerated the religious activities of the movement within the framework of the Association and in the mosques, schools, and the university as a means to counterbalance the influence of the left.

The fact that the emergence and spread of the movement coincided with the government's suppressive measures against the leftist groups increased the initial mistrust between the left and the nascent Islamic movement. Still influenced by the radical shift of policy after the failure of Ben Saleh, the left viewed the Islamic movement with suspicion and accused it of plotting and collaborating with the government to undermine its activities.

While this last view was doubtless exaggerated, one could still argue that the toleration of the regime for the Islamists in the beginning benefited both parties. On one hand, it reflected an image that the government was concerned about religion and its values—an image which was very much needed after Ben Saleh's experience and the failure of his socialist policies—and on the other hand, the fledgling Islamist movement seized this opportunity to intensify its activities, spread its base of support, and form broad channels of communication.

In spite of this, though, the relationship was not always tranquil. The government used force to disperse an assembly held by the Islamists in Sousse in 1973. Then, in the same year and as a result of the increasing activities of the movement and their noticeable expansion throughout the branches of the Association, the government became alert to their potential threat and decided to end its relations with the group by expelling them from the Association.[18] This step ushered in a new phase in the history of the movement, which now realized the necessity of devising its own organizational structures to spread its message.

Thus the emergence of an Islamic movement in Tunisia can be traced to the political and socioeconomic factors relating to the rapid transformation of the Tunisian society along foreign models and the presence of educated sectors of society at odds with the available intellectual and political alternatives. These sectors may be characterized as a counter-elite in search of a more culturally authentic alternative. At this stage, the movement lacked political consciousness and a clear plan of action and focused mainly on the promotion of religious practices as the main content of its message. The movement's stand of adhering to religion and emphasizing the importance of its principles as guidelines for society, however, implied a political message that contradicted the regime's secular orientation. As the movement was still in a process of formation, the number of its adherents was limited, and its leaders attempted to use the resources at hand, the mosques and the schools, the preaching methods of the Tabligh group, and the National Association for the Preservation of the Qur'an, to spread its message. As a group of ardent activists who journeyed across the country to preach the Islamic doctrines, they may identified as lay-intellectual activists, having received a limited education but still aspiring to a greater understanding of Islamic values. They were activists because they were eager to reform the institutional stagnation of Islam. At the same time, they lacked cohesive guidelines on how to impress these Islamic values on the policy makers of the regime.

Gaining Ground (1973–1979)

As developments in the 1960s carried the impetus for the emergence of an Islamic movement in Tunisia, several factors in the 1970s provided the Islamists with opportunities for expansion. These factors could be identified as, first, the continued dislocating effects of the economic policies pursued by the state during this period; second, the outbreak of massive demonstrations in 1978 attesting to the widespread social discontent and the weakening of other popular forces in Tunisian society; third, the increasing disenchantment of students and youth; and, fourth, the outbreak of the Islamic Revolution in Iran in 1979.

During the 1970s Tunisia maintained a mixed economy in which different economic sectors—public, cooperative, and private— coexisted. However, the liberalization policies of the state resulted in an unequal emphasis on these sectors and the private sector began to receive more encouragement from the state. The 1972 and 1974 laws granted tax exemptions and other fiscal advantages to foreign and private enterprises producing export goods and employing indigenous labor. The Tunisian economy benefited from the new policies and was actually reviving. From 1973 to 1976, Tunisia's aggregate GDP witnessed an annual increase of 7 percent, and continued to grow till 1980, when it began to decline. Generally, the cautious management and rational planning of Prime Minister Hedi Noeira, who possessed an extensive knowledge of finance and banking, contributed to the improvement of the state of the economy. In addition, the economy was boosted by an unusual favorable harvest in 1972, an influx in the number of tourists attracted by the increase of the government's investments in the tourism sector, and the rise in the international prices of such natural resources as petroleum and phosphate, which constitute Tunisia's main export commodities.

However, by the late 1970s the country began to face economic difficulties resulting from declining agriculture, a decrease in the international prices of exports, restrictions imposed by the European Economic Community on Tunisian exports, and the return of thousands of Tunisian workers from Europe and Libya. Unemployment constituted a serious problem as it reached 25 percent with a higher percentage among seasonal workers and young people. According to official sources, in the period from 1970 to 1976 prices of consumer goods witnessed a sharp increase amounting to 47 percent, which was accompanied by a decline in wages and purchasing power. The balance of trade showed a considerable deterioration resulting from the increase of the prices of imported goods and the failure of exports to pay for more than 51 percent of imports; a huge deficit in the country's balance of payments resulted.[19]

The earlier expansion in economic activities had led to an increase in the number of workers through migration from the rural areas to the capital and the industrial cities. In the period from 1966 to 1975, urban growth reached an annual rate of 4.2 percent.[20] With the slow-down of the economy in the late 1970s and the decline in its absorptive capacity, rural emigrants and university graduates were struck by severe unemployment. The sight of fancy resort hotels, tourists ignoring the traditions and values of a Muslim society, an apparent official lack of ideological direction, changes in the patterns of consumption, and increasing signs of social inequality, exacerbated the situation. These developments offset the benefits of many earlier economic gains, and created a feeling of discontent among the less fortunate sectors of society.

The workers and the young were among the elements which suffered most in society. The former agitated through their powerful and well-organized union, headed by Habib Ashour, for the improvement of wage standards and social conditions. After a series of negotiations, strikes, and violent clashes, the government cracked down on the union in January 1978, arresting many of its members and replacing its elected leadership. The suppression of the union benefited the Islamists in many respects. To this point, the movement had been apolitical and preoccupied with the moral and religious aspects of reform. Al-Jourshi recalls that "the Islamic movement observed the 1978 incidents with indifference and were surprised by them as everybody else was. We were concerned with other issues. Later, we began to realize the significance of the social dimension and the importance of bread."[21] The violent conflict between the government and the union brought to the attention of the movement the fact that other issues, in addition to matters of belief and disbelief, existed in society. This was reflected in its later discourse and in the language which it began to use, as will be discussed in chapter six.

The Islamists began to pay attention to the workers as an important social force in society and to the need for activism among their ranks in the union. In response to the government's repressive measures, the Islamists in the university issued a statement in which they announced their objection to these measures and declared their support for the workers' struggle and the independence of their union.[22] The blow against the union deprived the workers of an important channel for articulating their demands and expressing their grievances. The Islamists took advantage of this vacuum by advancing their message among the workers, and thus they began to address issues of concern to the workers, such as the value given to work in Islam and the Islamic economic perspective. When the UGTT was restored, the Islamically-inclined workers also joined the union and participated in some of its elections.

The disenchantment of Tunisian youth was another factor explaining the growing popularity of the Islamic movement during this period. Indeed, in recent years, the young have represented a major problem for the Tunisian government and a serious potential source of instability. Figures show that an estimated 60 percent of Tunisia's population are young people under the age of 20.[23] In a country where the rate of unemployment reaches 25 percent, the majority of these young, whether rural migrants or educated students, are struck by a blockage in the system which is no longer able to incorporate them. Some analysts, furthermore, describe a generation gap between the old elite and the younger generation which sees a system geared wholly to the benefit of this old elite and remaining closed to the young.[24] With new graduates coming out of the universities every year, the number of educated young people has consistently exceeded the number of available jobs. The government's ability to provide employment for them has become more limited, a problem which has required a reduction in the number of secondary school and university graduates.[25] Large portions of high school and university graduates are joining the ranks of the unemployed and becoming a marginalized element in society.

Student unrest in the universities and high schools has been a recurring phenomenon in Tunisian life. It takes the form of boycott of classes, strikes, and sometimes violent demonstrations. Students have expressed their discontent over university regulations, examination policies, cafeteria food, transportation facilities, or government policies. Student demonstrations during the 1967 Arab-Israeli war led to the arrest and trial of many student leaders and young intellectuals on a charge of political dissidence. In 1971-72, student unrest resulted in the closure of the University of Tunis for several months, and the disbanding of the General Union of Tunisian Students (UGET). In 1975, a general one-day strike was organized by young secondary school teachers and recent university graduates. Following the workers' general strike in January 1978, university and high school students joined in a major strike protesting the violent response of the government against the workers. The government ended the strike by arresting a large number of students and expelling others. The government, moreover, put forth a conscription plan whereby unemployed young people between the ages of 18 and 30 went into a special labor corps in which they were treated as soldiers and received minimum wages.[26] Deprived of their union since 1972, in addition to the weakening of the left by the arrests and trials of its elements, the university presented a fertile ground for the Islamists to spread their ideology and recruit a wide following.

During this phase the movement concentrated its activities on two levels: the mosques and the secondary schools and universities. The mosque, as a place of congregation, provided a safe haven for political expression and recruitment. This, however, prompted the government to take drastic countermeasures in order both to keep the mosque attendants under strict surveillance and to limit its use to prayer times.

At the second level, the active recruitment measures of teachers affiliated with the movement bore fruit as thousands of students enlisted. The fact that many of the movement's leaders were secondary school teachers provided them with direct and continuous contact with the students and assisted them in attracting and mobilizing the young to their movement. Moreover, starting in the 1970s, the government allowed the factories and schools to establish mosques on their premises. The Islamist teachers began to use these mosques for their purposes, gathering students and workers around them.[27] Over time, high school students affiliated with the movement began to join the university and form a strong base there. At the university, these students were exposed through their dialogue and conflict with the leftist elements to new political concepts and dimensions, which resulted in the politicization and radicalization of the student members of the movement.

With regard to the nature of the message of the Islamic trend in Tunisia at this stage, developments outside Tunisia had a serious ideological and organizational impact on it. In the beginning of the 1970s, members of the Muslim Brothers Society in Egypt were released by Anwar Sadat and a strong Islamic movement was being restructured. The young Islamists in Tunisia were influenced by the Muslim Brothers and the writings of their intellectuals, particularly Hassan al-Banna and Sayyid Qutb. From them, they adopted some of their views on society and methods of spreading their message, which emphasized the need to educate and resocialize a community of believers that would in the end reinstitute the Islamic values in society.

The activities of the leadership at this stage aimed at generating political and Islamic consciousness among its followers and restructuring their intellectual perceptions. Intellectuals of the movement began to publish their own writings and contributions in the form of articles, pamphlets, and books. These writings, which were published in the 1970s, focused on intellectual and social issues from a philosophical and cultural perspective, and aimed at drawing a clear line between the Islamic value system, on the one hand, and the Western and secular doctrines, on the other. For this purpose, Ghannoushi, the most prolific among the movement's intellectuals, wrote several pamphlets and books, such as *Ma Huwa al-Gharb?* (What Is the West?), *Tariquna ila al-Hadara* (Our Road to Civilization), *al-Islam Bayn al-Mithaliyya wa al-Waqi`iyya* (Islam Between Idealism and Realism), *Wad` al-Mar'a fi al-Haraka al-Islamiyya* (The Status of Women in the Islamic Movement), and *Haykal `am li al-Iqtisad al-Islami* (A General Frame for the Islamic Economic System). The specific themes of these books will be discussed in chapter six.

In addition to individual writings, in 1972 the movement began its own monthly periodical, *al-Ma`rifa* (Knowledge), which disseminated its ideas and views regarding various issues. In its first years, the circulation of the periodical reached 6,000 and by 1979 jumped to 25,000, indicating an increase in the movement's popularity and constituency. For this reason, *al-Ma`rifa* was suspended by the government in 1979. During the nine years of its publication, forty-nine issues came out. The contributors to these issues were mainly the movement's intellectuals, such as Ghannoushi, Naifar, Jourshi, and others, but they also included Muslim intellectuals outside Tunisia.

The writings in the periodical focused on four main topics: culture and intellectual thought; theology and morality; society; and politics. Abdel Latif al-Hermassi noted a change in emphasis in these topics over two periods, 1972-73 and 1979, of the periodical. In the first period, the cultural and intellectual issues represented 43.1 percent of the total number of articles as opposed to 62.6 percent in 1979; the theological and moral issues scored 44.3 percent in 1972-73 and 18.3 percent in 1979; the social issues marked 10.3 percent in 1972-73 and 6.1 percent in 1979; and the political issues increased form 2.3 percent in 1972-73 to 13 percent in 1979.[28] These figures reveal an evolution in the intellectual emphasis of the movement, reflected by the increase in the percentage of articles dealing with intellectual and political topics, and the sharp decrease in the emphasis on theological issues. This change could be attributed to the expansion in the movement's popularity, its increasing concern about its status within the system, and its increasing awareness of other Islamic movements in the Muslim countries.

With regard to the general themes of each of these topics, the theological and moral articles dealt with interpretations of the Qur'an and the Sunna, issues of jurisprudence, *fatwas* regarding religious matters, methods of preaching Islam, and biographies of Islamic personalities. The cultural and intellectual articles focused on general issues such as progress, underdevelopment, religion and science, reform, education, and the values and conditions in the West. They also dealt with the general condition of Muslims throughout the world and the development of the Islamic movement in other Muslim countries as well as in Tunisia. The social articles discussed the issues of family, women, youth, the mixing of men and women and social problems, labor, the conditions of peasants, workers, and immigrants, in addition to social and economic issues in Islam. The political articles dealt with internal issues like the massive demonstrations of January 1978, political liberties, and the formation of a political party. They also raised external political issues dealing with the Palestinian question, conditions in Iran and Afghanistan, the Sahara, China, and Southeast Asia.

The Progressive Islamic Tendency Movement

As the Islamists managed to build a wider constituency of different backgrounds, increase the political consciousness of their followers, and become ready to move to the real and turbulent world of politics, the first split in the movement's ranks took place in 1976 when some of its co-founders, namely Hemida al-Naifar and Salah Eddin al-Jourshi, became concerned about the direction in which the movement was heading and feared that it was jumping too soon into politics without being ready politically and ideologically. They left to form a group, which later became known as *al-Ittijah al-Islami al-Taqadumi* (The Progressive Islamic Tendency Movement—MTPI). The differences between the two groups were based on issues related to the ideological orientation of the movement, the organizational process, and tactics which it adopted. As was mentioned before, during the 1973-79 phase, the movement was influenced by the experience of the Muslim Brothers of Egypt and some of its intellectuals, particularly Sayyid Qutb. Among the Brothers' thinkers, Qutb developed an intellectual paradigm of his own, which could be characterized as more dynamic and militant. This paradigm revolves around a number of concepts: *jahiliyya* (ignorance or decadence), *hakimiyya* (supremacy of God's law), *al-jama`a al-mu'mina* (the community of believers), and *al-infisal al-shu`uri* (ideological separation). Qutb viewed current Muslim societies as *jahili* for not implementing God's law. Therefore, he called for the formation of a community of believers who would separate themselves, ideologically but not physically, from the rest of the society and work for the reinstitution of Islamic values. However, Qutb was never explicit on how this could be achieved, a fact that created difficult problems— concerning the perception of society, the idea and means of change, and the socialization of the community of believers—for the newly emerging Islamic movements in the Middle East, including the Tunisian one.

The members of the splinter group criticized the mainstream movement for its orthodox interpretation of religious texts, its holistic perception of society, and its simplistic ideas of change. They raised a number of questions regarding the criteria by which a society could be judged *jahili*, the status of the community of believers within it, and whether change could be achieved from within its institutions or by the separation Qutb recommended. These members claimed that the main movement lacked a proper understanding of the particularities of the Tunisian society and its dynamics, and, consequently, had failed to devise an independent line of thinking. Instead they hoped to find a more authentic ideology more applicable to the Tunisian context, rather than the radical (and foreign) Qutbist approach.

To address this problem, the MTPI was formed as a coalition of intellectuals, teachers, journalists, and students (but not as a political organization), to discuss specific issues and work on devising a modern Islamic framework of thought capable of meeting the challenges of modernity and understanding the dynamics and characteristics of the Tunisian society from an Islamic perspective.[29] The MTPI issued a magazine, *15/21*, in November 1982, but it was suspended in February 1987 after only 14 issues were published.[30] The name of the periodical refers to the fifteenth century of the Islamic calendar and the twenty-first century of the Christian calendar, indicating a futuristic and a synthesizing attitude for approaching the different issues of concern.

An analysis of the 195 articles which were written in the first 10 issues of the periodical reveals the emphasis and orientation that the contributors to *15/21* maintained that distinguished their periodical from *al-Ma`rifa*. In a corresponding scale to the division of the articles of *al-Ma`rifa*, the number of cultural and intellectual articles in *15/21*—138—occupied a predominant proportion (70 percent). The number of political articles amounted to 15 (7 percent); social and economic, 15 (7 percent); moral and theological, 13 (6 percent); and literary, 20 (10 percent). The cultural and intellectual articles of the periodical contained some components of a political program, though still far from a complete one. They maintained a clear and a positive stand on political pluralism and social liberties and demonstrated a willingness to participate through existing institutions. They also advocated an unorthodox interpretation of the Qur'anic text, that gave primacy to reason in dealing with the text, and stressed the evolution and dynamics of society, the need to understand the nature of these dynamics, and the need to link thought with the existing socioeconomic context in order to produce appropriate and practical solutions in accordance with the interests of the Muslim people and Islamic values.[31]

The Islamic Liberation Party

Among the Islamists in Tunisia, there is another group to which brief attention should be devoted. The Islamic Liberation Party (ILP) in Tunisia stands, ideologically and tactically, to the right of the MTI. The ILP in Tunisia is an offspring of the mother organization, *Hizb al-Tahrir al-Islami*, the Islamic Liberation Party, which was established in Jerusalem in 1948 by Taqi Eddin al-Nabahani, following the defeat of the Arab armies in Palestine. Al-Nabahani was a graduate of al-Azhar

University in Egypt and worked as a judge in the court of appeals in Jerusalem. He was considered to be the most prominent and influential thinker of the group. Over the years, the party managed to spread and form active branches in Jordan, Syria, Lebanon, Iraq, and Egypt.[32] Since its formation the ILP has had an unequivocal political orientation, with a primary objective of establishing an Islamic state and restoring the Islamic Caliphate. The ILP has been critical of contemporary Islamic movements and religious associations for their inability to induce change effectively. It has not believed in their reformist methods for changing the society through the socialization of the individual and the concentration on education as a means for uplifting the moral aspects of society. Instead, the ILP has focused on forming an intellectual leadership and drawing a detailed blueprint for political action to achieve its goal of establishing an Islamic caliphate. This blueprint, which has become an authoritative reference for the members of the party and its branches everywhere, was devised by al-Nabahani and elaborated on by other party thinkers such as Sameeh Atif al-Zin.

The beginning of the ILP in Tunisia was in the 1970s when some Tunisians, while studying in Germany, were introduced to the party's ideas and returned to establish a branch in Tunisia. The founders of this branch were university professors and secondary school teachers, who, starting from 1978, were joined by a number of military officers. They formed clandestine study circles in which al-Nabahani's three major books, *Nidham al-Islam* (The Islamic System), *Mafahim Hizb al-Tahrir* (The Perspectives of the ILP), and *al-Takatul al-Hizbi* (Party Coalition) were thoroughly discussed. In these books, al-Nabahani laid down the objectives and plan of action of the party. The party divided the process of its political activism into three stages. The first stage was called indoctrination, and focused on presenting an internal and intensive program for the collective socialization and indoctrination of members to prepare them for spreading the principles of the party and sacrificing for its cause. During this stage, the cells would maintain a high level of secrecy regarding their formation and location. The second stage was known as interaction and dialogue, during which the members were to be ready to interact intellectually with the masses, convince them of the ideas of the party so that they might become widely-held convictions, and then lead the masses into the final stage, which is deliverance. At this stage the party would take power through the masses, establish the Islamic Caliphate, and restructure society. The transition from one stage to the next would depend on how well the party's ideas managed to gain spread and popularity.[33]

The regime became aware of the activities of the ILP and succeeded in breaking the secrecy of the party in 1983. Twenty-nine party members were arrested and put on trial before a military court in August of that year for the establishment of a clandestine organization with a political objective. Nineteen out of the 29 members apprehended were army officers, five were university and secondary school teachers, two technicians, one an engineer, one a civil servant, and one a student; they ranged in age from 24 to 40.[34] The military personnel received harsher sentences of five to eight years of imprisonment, while each of the civilian members was sentenced to two years.[35] This incident was the first political case since 1962 in which military officers were implicated.

The ILP managed to survive this confrontation with the regime and was able to reorganize its members. Two years after the 1983 trial, however, 44 ILP members, all civilians this time, were arrested, tried in March 1985, and received six months to one year sentences.[36] Based on the official accusations—the formation of a secret political organization—the interrogations of the ILP members, and the relatively light sentences which they received, it seems that the influence of the ILP in Tunisia remains limited. This may be explained by the fact that it was still in its first stage of indoctrination, which requires secrecy and selectiveness and does not advocate interaction with the masses. With regard to its stand towards the MTI and the MTPI, the ILP is critical of both groups for their lack of a clear program of political action and their willingness to work within the system.[37]

Turning Political (1979–1987)

The Islamic Revolution in Iran in 1979 assisted the Tunisian trend in gaining wider appeal and in increasing the level of its political consciousness. This effect was not confined only to the MTI in Tunisia but spread to other movements and countries throughout the Muslim world. The revolution in Iran succeeded in attracting the sympathy of the ordinary Muslim citizen and the support of the activist Islamic movements. It was perceived as having restored to Islam its vitality as a mobilizing force and as a catalyst for change. It succeeded in overthrowing a tyrannical regime and declared Islam the ideology of the oppressed in the Muslim world that would mobilize them in their struggle against tyranny and dependency, achieve social justice, and liberate the Muslim societies from alien cultural influences.[38] The success of the clergy in spearheading the revolution and finally ruling Iran showed that it was possible for the people of the Muslim countries to be ruled by an elite that is not alien or contemptuous of the popular culture of the majority of the masses, could speak their language, and respect their traditional values.

The Iranian revolution considered Islam as a panacea for all problems and so began to structure the society along Islamic precepts. It declared its independence from Western and Eastern orbits and posed a challenge to their interests in the region. In so doing, it reinforced the unfulfilled aspirations of the Islamic movements throughout the Muslim world, and boosted their confidence. It increased their political awareness and contributed to their radicalization as well. They viewed it as a popular revolution under a religious leadership that presented Islam as a comprehensive solution and rejected the bipolarity of the international system.[39] For them, the revolution shattered many fallacies and proved that religion was not the opiate of the people, but rather that it could articulate political and social demands for popular participation, nationalize natural resources, implement land reform, develop national industry, promote self-reliance, and struggle against international imperialism—all the things that the left had promised but never delivered. It also refuted the concept of the separation of politics and religion.[40] The publications of the MTI, *al-Ma`rifa* and *al-Mujtama`* (Society)—which appeared in 1979 following the banning of *al-Ma`rifa*—covered the news of the revolution, published articles on the conditions in Iran, reviewed the writings and ideas of Imam Khomeini, defended the Islamic government in Iran against criticism, warned against the overplay of the Sunni-Shi`a schism, and called upon Islamic movements to support the revolution in Iran.[41]

The political symbols and slogans of the Iranian revolution were reiterated in the writings and speeches of the leaders of the Islamic movement in Tunisia. Phrases such as *al-istikbar al-`alami* (international oppression), *al-mustad`afun fi al-ard* (the dispossessed on earth), and *al-taghut* (oppression) replaced more secular ones like imperialism, the oppressed classes, and despotic regimes. The movement also began to broaden the areas of its concern and acquire a sharper tone and more confident voice. *Al-Ma`rifa* and later *al-Mujtama`*, became much more vocal in their opposition to the regime.[42] The movement organized demonstrations and rejected the system that the government used for determining the beginning and end of the month of Ramadan, and its members sometimes even clashed with those who publicly broke their fast.[43]

By 1979, the relationship between the movement and the government became confrontational. With the coming of an Islamic regime in Iran, the government began to monitor the potential threat of an Islamic movement in Tunisia and launched a severe press campaign against the Islamists.[44] Indeed, the government responded by projecting the state as the main guardian of Islam and portrayed the movement as a subversive one exploiting religion to achieve its political goals. Former Prime Minister Hedi Noeira, in his speech to the Central Committee of the PDS, asserted the Islamic identity of all Tunisians and the members of the Destour Party in particular. He pointed to the role which Bourguiba had played in protecting Islam during the French occupation, and to the government's efforts in increasing the number of mosques and providing religious education. He also warned against a minority cultivating sedition and disunity among Muslims. The former Party Director, Muhammad Sayyah, described the members of the Islamic movement as communists hiding behind Islam.[45] The former Interior Minister, Driss Guiga, explained that "being Tunisians, we are 6 millions Muslims. We are all the Islamic Tendency. No one can accept that certain individuals claim the monopoly of Islam and pretend to act under its name or its sacred values so as to hide their political goals."[46] These stands were echoed even in the words of Muhammad Mzali, who was viewed as sympathetic with the Islamists' cause: "First of all, I dispute the label 'Islamic Tendency', because all Tunisians are Muslims. It is a group that uses religion for political purposes and its action has degenerated into acts of violence."[47]

In 1979, as part of its campaign to discredit the Islamic movement, the official newspaper, *al-'Amal* (Action), intensified its attacks against the Islamists and reiterated the accusations of the state officials. At various times, it described them as: unpatriotic, foreign-inspired, anti-regime, disgraceful, ignorant, misguided, distorters of religion, communists, political failures, fanatics, reactionaries, terrorists, against the interest of the Muslim nation and its unity, agitators, disbelievers in Tunisia and its nationalism, and opportunists.[48] A researcher of the MTI in Tunisia noted that "the official campaign against the movement was characterized by improvisation, superficiality, and contradiction. It had no purpose except for defaming the movement by every possible means, which reduced the effectiveness and credibility of the campaign."[49]

The MTI responded to this campaign by pointing to the contradictions within the regime's claims. It referred to the government's general secularism and recalled the measures which it had taken against the traditional and historic religious institutions. It further juxtaposed its own indigenous stands with the alien orientation of the ruling elite and its submission to foreign influences. It also pointed out the regime's apparent weakness by denying recognition and freedom of expression to the Islamists, and also reasserted that politics was part of the MTI's Islamic program.[50]

The movement became increasingly concerned about the regime efforts to marginalize it, and worked to prove its moderate nature and rejection of violent means. It also tried to regulate the activities of its members and protect them against the government's attacks. In early 1979, it applied for a license to form a religious association under the name of *al-Wa`i al-Islami* (Islamic Awareness). However, the government turned down the movement's request.

The leaders of the movement secretly held a conference in September 1979 in Tunis, which was attended by forty of its most active members, aiming at building its organizational structure and preparing its members for participation in national politics as a well-organized political body. The conference convened for twenty-four hours during which the attendants, headed by Ghannoushi, discussed the political conditions in Tunisia and the possibilities of securing wider support for the movement. The members of the conference agreed to form an organization by the name of *al-Jama`a al-Islamiyya fi Tunis* (The Islamic Group in Tunisia), and elected Ghannoushi as its chairman. It also established the infrastructure of the movement by creating six organizational bodies, electing their members and heads, and assigning each specific tasks. The 1979 conference was very important to the movement because it was able to lay down its organizational structure, draw its institutions and policies for the next phase, and reach the decision of publicly announcing itself as a political organization.

After the conference, the movement began to behave as a well-organized political party. When Bourguiba declared his acceptance of the emergence of other political parties in the Destour Party Tenth Congress in April 1981, the movement held a conference during which it terminated the Islamic Group in Tunisia and declared itself the Islamic Tendency Movement. In June 1981, it formally applied to the government to become a legal political party and held a press conference to declare itself.

During the June Conference, the MTI announced the establishment of a political bureau consisting of five members, headed by Ghannoushi, and issued a communiqué in which it declared its views on the conditions in the Muslim world in general and Tunisia in particular, its objectives, and the means to achieve them. The communiqué referred to the state of underdevelopment, alienation, and submission from which the Muslim world suffered to the benefit of an imperialist West and its own ruling elites. It lamented the marginalization of Islam in guiding the affairs of Muslims in present day Tunisia, despite its historic role in shaping the national character and resisting foreign domination. It described Tunisia as being beset by intractable crises that created social conflict and hindered the achievement of comprehensive development, due mainly to the authoritarian policies of the one-party system. It criticized the regime's increasing domination of power and control over the political institutions, its lack of well-conceived economic and social policies, and linkages to international interests which contradicted the national ones. The continuation of these problems, the communiqué explained, reinforced the legitimate feelings of the Islamists that they had a sacred, national, and humanitarian responsibility to continue and refine their efforts for the liberation and the progress of the country on the basis of just Islamic principles and an indigenous framework. The MTI asserted that it did not consider itself the sole representative of Islam in Tunisia, while preserving the right to adopt a comprehensive vision of Islam that would constitute the ideological bases from which its political, economic, and social perceptions would emanate.[51]

With regard to its objectives, the MTI stated five general themes. The first focused on the resurrection of the Islamic identity of Tunisia in order to restore it as the basis for Islamic culture in Africa and to terminate the present state of dependence and alienation. The second aimed at the renewal of Islamic thought in accordance with its fundamental principles and the necessities of modern life, and purifying Islam from the remnants of the decadent age of Westernization. The third was the restoration of the legitimate right of the people to decide their fate independently of any internal control or foreign influence. The fourth focused on the restructuring of the economy on humanitarian bases and the fair distribution of national resources according to the Islamic principle of granting "a man according to his effort, and according to his need."[52] The final objective stressed the need for the resurrection of the cultural and political Islamic entity on the local, Maghribi, Arab, and international levels in order to rescue the Muslim people and humanity from psychological submission, social injustice, and international dominance.

To achieve these objectives, the MTI specified a number of means which centered on using the mosque as an indigenous mobilizational institution, reactivating the dormant process of Arabization, accepting political pluralism and rejecting violence, and presenting an Islamic alternative. The communiqué detailed these means in the following thirteen points: (1) restoring the vitality of the mosque as a place for worship and popular mobilization; (2) reactivating intellectual and cultural life; (3) supporting the process of the Arabization of the educational system and administration while maintaining openness to foreign languages; (4) rejecting violence as a means for inducing change while resolving conflict in society through *shurawiyya* (consultative) principles; (5) rejecting the concept of a one-party system, confirming the legal rights of all popular forces of political expression and assembly, and collaborating with all national forces in order to gain these rights; (6) clarifying the Islamic social concepts in a modern context and analyzing the condition of the Tunisian economy to determine the causes of inequality and to arrive at alternative solutions; (7) allying with the dispossessed workers and peasants and others in their conflict with the *mustakbirin* (oppressors); (8) supporting the struggle and independence of the labor unions; (9) approving the comprehensive perceptions of Islam and moving the conduct of politics away from secularism and opportunism; (10) liberating the Muslim mind from cultural defeatism; (11) demonstrating a contemporary model of an Islamic system of government to guarantee the presentation of national issues in relation to the historical, cultural, and objective contexts of the Maghribi, Arab, and Islamic societies and the world of the oppressed in general; (12) reviving links with all Muslims in the world; and (13) supporting liberation movements elsewhere.[53]

The MTI did not have to wait long to get a response to its demand for recognition as a political party. On the 18th and 19th of July 1981, 61 MTI members, including their leaders, were arrested and put on trial on charges of forming an illegal organization, defaming the president, and publishing false news. The detention of the MTI members alarmed most of the other opposition parties, including the leftist party, the Movement of National Unity II, and independent organizations. All issued communiqués protesting these arrests for being undemocratic and repressive and demanding the release of the detainees. Regardless of their actual support of the movement, most of these groups were concerned about the possibility that the government might be following a strategy for neutralizing the opposition one by one.

The detained members of the MTI received harsh sentences, cumulatively amounting to three and a half centuries. Ghannoushi and Mourou themselves were sentenced to eleven and ten years, respectively. Mourou was released after two years for health reasons and put under house arrest. The MTI lawyers insisted that the trial was a political one, that the defendants were exposed to torture, and that the accusations against them were not proven. It is worth noting that throughout the trial the government did not press any charges of subversion or violence against the MTI. Following the trial, demonstrations took place to protest the harsh sentences and 43 demonstrators were arrested.[54]

Though the regime went as far as licensing a communist party, it seemed unwilling to accept the challenge of a party formed on an Islamic basis. It argued that the approval of this party would imply that those who did not join it were not Muslims. The MTI regarded this claim to be untrue and asserted that it did not impose any monopoly on Islam, nor did it claim to be its sole representative. In addition, the Islamic label of the would-be party was not exclusive and did not deny non-members the right to be Muslims any more than the national, democratic, or socialist labels of other parties denied non-members the right of being national, democratic, or socialist.

For the next several years, the MTI was continually exposed to harsh press campaigns and more of its members were detained and imprisoned. Despite this, the movement was still able to keep itself active through members who managed to reelect a new leadership, maintain its organizational structure, issue two secret leaflets, *al-Risala* (The Message) and *al-Masar* (The Path), and publish statements in the opposition and independent press, particularly *al-Ra'i* (Opinion). These members were also able to assist the families of the MTI prisoners financially, and keep its contacts with the opposition parties, UGTT, and the Tunisian Human Rights League. In January 1983, however, the government arrested another 40 leading members of MTI in a second major crackdown on the movement. Consequently, the rest of the MTI leaders moved to France and formed a second political bureau and directed the movement from there. Through its student followers in the university, who led demonstrations in the poor quarters in Tunis, the movement managed to play a role in the mass riots of January 1984.[55]

With these direct blows to the movement and its infrastructure, the MTI was temporarily removed from the scene as a potential rival. However, the repressive measures of the government against the movement were perceived by other opposition groups to be in contradiction to the regime's declared commitment to political liberalism and the toleration of pluralism in society. The imprisonment of the MTI leaders became a source of embarrassment for Prime Minister Mzali, who had promised to tolerate the presence of opposition groups. Further, the bread riots of January 1984 brought a major crisis, which forced the government to relax the political situation in response to its inability to resolve the underlying economic and social problems wracking the nation.

A brief mellowing in the confrontational relationship between the regime and the MTI occurred in August 1984 . The massive food riots in January 1984 and the regime's resort to violent measures to suppress the socially discontented masses put the government under considerable pressure. To redress the situation, Mzali undertook a series of policy changes, among which was the obtaining of a presidential pardon for the imprisoned members of the MTI, who were released in August 1984 following the mediation of independent figures and a meeting between Mzali and the Secretary General of the MTI, Shaykh Abdel Fattah Mourou.[56] Mzali futilely urged the movement to change its name and drop any reference to Islam in it. He obtained, however, the agreement of the movement to reject violence as a means of change, comply with the constitutional standards of legitimacy and democratic procedures, and guarantee the absence of links with any foreign country.

After the release of its members, the movement maintained better relations with the regime for almost ten months. The MTI focused on the reconstruction of its bodies and the assessment of its policies in the previous phase and the coming one. A secret conference was held in late 1984 in which Ghannoushi was reelected as the movement's leader, and MTI institutions were reconstituted. With regard to the future activities of the movement, two trends appeared during the discussions. The first advocated the maintenance of a very low profile and the avoidance of any political presence or confrontation with the authorities. The proponents of this view believed that the government would not grant any political recognition to the movement, and, therefore, it should concentrate its activities on purely religious matters. The second trend, which Ghannoushi supported, felt that the denial of this recognition should be taken as an incentive for the movement to speed up its activities, assert its presence, and impose itself on the political scene. Apparently, the second trend managed to gain the approval of the conferees as its views were reflected in the conference's subsequent recommendations and decisions.

These recommendations underscored organizational and political measures for guiding the movement's activities and participation in the political process. They emphasized the need for renewing the activities of the movement in the mosques; the resocializing of the MTI's cadres; reorganizing its active members; granting more attention to female members; finding an outlet of expression for the movement's views during this phase; and keeping in contact with the activities and orientations of other political forces. The conference decided to rebuild the internal structures of the movement; complete studies regarding the movement's Islamic platform and its proposed solutions to the different problems of society; re-proclaim the existence of the movement; and defend its political gains while renewing its support of public liberties. As a concession to the first trend, they decided to avoid any escalation with the regime on the political and social levels.[57]

Organization of the MTI

An analysis of the organizational structure of the Islamic Tendency Movement in Tunisia during the 1980s, which became public after the several trials of the movement's members, reflects a well-planned pyramidal hierarchy that flows from bottom to top in rank formation.[58] The base consists of *usar maftuha* (open cells), each of which is composed of five members. They serve as study groups designed to formulate discussions of religious, political, and economic issues. These open cells provide a testing ground by which qualified members are promoted to closed cells.

Closed cells *usar multazima* (committed cells) are primarily designed to shift the training of the members of the movement from general issues to specific ones, such as the study of other Islamic movements throughout the Muslim world. They also undertake a thorough study of the publications of the leaders of their own movement. At this stage, the member must be prepared to submit to a code of honor based on an oath of allegiance to the leader of the movement. Proclaiming the oath of allegiance qualifies the member to be considered a committed supporter. These closed cells are clustered around 18 regional councils. Each regional council is headed by an *'amil* (governor) who in turn is appointed by the *amir* (leader). The `amil also heads his own organizational apparatus, which is responsible for the religious and political formations of the members of the open and closed cells. Of particular importance is the responsibility of these regional councils to safeguard the well being and social welfare of the members in their respective regions, particularly at times of social unrest (e.g., arrest and incarceration of the members.)

At the same time, a separate category has been established to deal exclusively with the student body of the movement in the secondary schools and university campuses. In the university, the movement succeeded in 1985 in reestablishing the General Tunisian Student Union, which then consisted of 15,000 students.

Beyond the regional circles arises the administrative branch of the movement. This Executive Council (*al-Maktab al-Tanfidhi*) consists of five to six members who are appointed by the *amir* or, in some cases, by the personal representative of the leader. This Council executes the decisions of the Conference and consultative councils of the movement. Its agenda is based on the weekly meetings of its members.

The Executive Council presides over five separate committees: the Organization and Administration Committee; the Finance Committee; the Research Committee; the Social and Da`wa (Call) Committee; and the Education and Formation Committee. The Executive Council is the most dynamic arm of the entire movement. It integrates and streamlines the issues raised in the various committees and is in charge of disseminating and implementing the various decisions and recommendations.

The members of the Executive Council are placed under the supervision of the Consultative Council (*Majlis al-Shura*), the legislative body. This Council is composed of 21 members. Fourteen members are elected by the Conference and the remaining seven are nominated by the elected members of the Executive Council. Members convene every three months unless an exceptional crisis emerges and warrants the holding of an emergency meeting.

As for the Conference (*al-Mu'tamar*), the central committee of the movement, it is composed of 70 delegates representing the various regional branches. They convene bi-annually in order to reelect or depose the leader, and place the overall strategy and tactics of the movement under review. This includes a thorough evaluation of the past record of the activities and performance of the movement on all levels of its operation—financial, ideological, and organizational.

Finally, it is important to highlight the function and capacity of the *amir*. As the symbolic head of the movement, the *amir* receives the oath of allegiance from every committed member of the movement. He is responsible for appointing the members of the Executive Council as well as the heads of the Regional Councils. His authority is checked by the Conference and the Consultative Council. The repeated arrests of the leader, Rashed al-Ghannoushi, however, tremendously reduced his control over the movement, whose organizational affairs were subsequently run by the other elements within the MTI. As he was known to the regime, Ghannoushi was most susceptible to arrest and pressure by the security police. The movement, therefore, agreed not to disclose its active members or their organizational status to Ghannoushi, and he participated in its last conferences, in November 1984 and December 1986, blindfolded.

While these elements of the organizational structure of the movement are a closely guarded secret, the only public organ of the MTI is the Political Bureau (*al-Maktab al-Siyasi*). The bureau is composed of four members headed by the leader of the movement. Its purpose is to follow the political conditions of the country; issue public statements; serve as a liaison to maintain contacts and coordinate activities with other political forces; and hold press conferences.

As for the finances of the movement, the MTI is a self-financed organization. It relies primarily on the mandatory contribution of its committed members. While uncommitted members also provide financial assistance, committed members give five percent of their monthly income. During times of crisis, however, this figure may be raised to as high as 20 to 50 percent.

Social Composition of the MTI

A breakdown of the social composition of the leadership of the Islamic Tendency Movement, based on the first conference in June 1981 of its Constitutive Assembly (*al-Majlis al-Ta'sisi*), differing from the Consultative Assembly, highlighted a number of interesting points. This conference was comprised of a total of 25 members.[59] An analysis of the social composition of these members raises a number of significant observations regarding the age factor and their regional affiliation as well as their general occupation.

Age. Among the 25 members of the Constitutive Assembly, 19 fell in the 24-to-34 age group bracket, representing 76 percent of the assembly members. As for the other six members, four fell in the 40-to-50 age group bracket, and the remaining two were above the age of seventy.

Regional Affiliation. As for the regional affiliation of the 25 members of the Constitutive Assembly, among those who were between the ages of 24 and 34, six were from the north; four from the center; four from the south; three from the Sahel; and two from the capital. As for the other six members of the Assembly, two were from the south while the other four were from the Sahel, north, center and the capital, respectively. These figures clearly reflect the fact that these leaders were scattered throughout the country. One may therefore conclude that adherence to Islamic values takes priority over regional affinity. For instance, even though the predominant gathering place of the members has been Tunis, only three of the 25 members were actually from the capital.

Occupation. As for the occupation of the 25 members of the Constitutive Assembly, among those who were in the 24-to-34 age group, eleven were secondary school teachers; three were lawyers; one, a civil servant; one, a building contractor; one, a doctor; one, a journalist; and one, an engineer. Teachers comprised 58 percent of the membership of this age group. It is important to note two critical factors: first, the predominance of teachers in the Constituent Assembly; and second, the contribution of these teachers in formulating the ideological platform of the movement.

One may draw the same conclusion from those in the older age groups. As evident among the six members above the age of 34, one notes again the overwhelming presence of teachers. Although there was one civil servant and another was the editor of the movement's periodical, *al-Ma'rifa*, the remaining four were secondary school teachers.

In addition, the presence of three well-educated women—one doctor, a secondary school teacher and an engineer—in the founding committee of the would-be party is noteworthy. This signifies a remarkable achievement in a movement which is portrayed by the regime as anti-feminist and reactionary, and especially in a society in which the regime actively promotes the liberal rights of women. Such participation on the part of these well-educated women reflects a possible dissatisfaction with the secular policies of the Bourguiba regime. In the eyes of such Tunisian women, these liberalization policies of social development are bound to disrupt the integrity of the family unit and offend the dignity of women.[60]

Finally, one must note the presence of the two elderly members of the Constitutive Assembly, both of whom are eminent Zaytouni scholars. Their presence in a young movement defies the long-held Bourguiba policy of secularizing the state administration and undermining the formal religious institutions of Tunisia. Most important, they help to provide a sense of continuity between an older generation of Zaytouni scholars and the post-independent generation of young Muslim activists.

To understand the political impact of the MTI, it is important at this point to explore and analyze the social composition of its constituency. Although the MTI claims the support of tens of thousands of Tunisians, the militant core of the movement is estimated to range between 4,000 and 6,000 supporters.[61] Within them, various surveys have placed the size of the student constituency at 40 percent of the whole.[62] The movement cuts across different social segments in society. The diversity of the social composition of its constituency came about as a result of its increasing social awareness and its evolution from an apolitical to a political organization. Field research studies reveal that the average member of the MTI is around 20 years old, well-educated, and of a rural and modest background.[63]

Based on the 1983 field research by a group of Tunisian scholars of 800 MTI members scattered across the country, the average median age is twenty-five, with 39 percent drawn from the Sahel; 30 percent from the capital; 24 percent from the south; and only 7 percent from the north. Concerning their rank and general occupation, it is noteworthy that the bulk of those studied—some 75 percent—were comprised of teachers and students.[64]

An analysis of the August 1987 trial of 99 constituents of the MTI is also revealing.[65] The predominant age factor of this group of detainees—some 77 percent—was under thirty as well. Their geographic affiliation was as follows: 31 percent were from the south; 22 percent from the Sahel; 20 percent from the capital; 14 percent from the north; and 13 percent from the center of the country. As for the rank and general occupation of this group, 27 percent were teachers; 13 percent were students; 12 percent were civil servants; 12 percent were technicians; 12 percent were engineers; 13 percent were shopkeepers; six percent unemployed; four percent lawyers; and the remaining one percent were peasants.

As observed, in both cases, in 1983 and 1987, the teachers and students were the dominant faction. In the sample of the 800 MTI members, they represented 75 percent of the constituents. Moreover, among those arrested and put on trial in August 1987, they constituted 40 percent of the detainees. It also noteworthy that the regional affiliation of the constituents does not represent a determinant factor in the overall composition of the constituents.

Back into Politics

The movement re-entered the political scene considering itself a political party with a widespread constituency. It increased its contacts with other political groups and parties, which recognized the MTI as a force with legitimate rights for legal existence and participation in the political process. On different occasions it issued joint communiqués with these parties, in addition to its own, stating its stands on the general conditions of the country as well as on specific issues. It also resumed its activities in the mosques through lectures delivered by its leaders. The movement directed more attention to the UGTT and its problems with the regime. The presence of MTI members in the UGTT became more noticeable, especially when they defended the right of the released Islamic workers to resume their previous employment. They also organized hunger strikes in January 1985, and managed to gain the majority of votes in some of the Union's regional elections, particularly in Baja and Bizerte.[66]

The MTI's political bureau held several meetings with representatives from the opposition parties—the Social Democrats, the Communist Party, the Movement of National Unity, and the Socialist Alliance—to coordinate their stands on the political and social situations in the country. Joint press conferences were also held in order to protest the government's measures against the UGTT and the suspension of opposition papers, and to condemn the 1985 Israeli raid on the PLO headquarters in Tunisia. They all participated in protest marches against the American raid on Libya, and issued joint communiqués condemning the regime for violating civil liberties and protesting the Press and Associations laws and political detentions.[67]

Alarmed by the increasing appeal of the MTI and its own stained relationship with the other opposition parties, the faction-ridden regime embarked on a two year period of its most vigorous suppression of the movement yet. The regime was particularly concerned about the MTI's insistence on being recognized as a political party and its continued rejection of the government's condition that the movement change its name and choose between functioning as a strictly religious association or becoming a "secular" political party. The MTI refused this difficult condition, which would have deprived the movement of the fundamental characteristic, its Islamic orientation, that distinguished it from the regime and the rest of the opposition groups. The movement regarded other opposition groups as offshoots of the system. In the MTI's view, these parties all shared the same secular orientation, were part of the same system at some point, and were too willing to comply with its rules and limitations for admission to the political process. The MTI leaders understood that if they accepted those rules, it would eventually jeopardize the movement's legitimacy as an independent force and as an alternative to the present regime.

Crisis

During these years, Tunisian political life became characterized by uncertainty and abeyance resulting from the deteriorating health of Bourguiba, who insisted on maintaining a tightened grip over the system and the internal opposition. He permitted the emergence of neither a new generation of political leaders to continue his policies nor an effective counter-elite to revive the system. Therefore, court politics, palace intrigues, and rivalry among the Tunisian elite, whose main concern was reduced to the elimination of each other and the weakening of the opposition groups in preparation for the post-Bourguiba era, dominated Tunisia and paralyzed an already deteriorating situation. This produced many casualties among the elite and among the opposition as well. Bourguiba's closest associates—his wife Wassila Ben Ammar, his son Habib Bourguiba junior, as well as his old time secretary and protégé, Allal al-Uwati—were banished, giving way to a new group, the "palace group" of Mansour Sikhiri, Bourguiba's influential niece Saieda Sassi, and Mahmoud Bel Hussein, who controlled access to the president and greatly influenced him. The ruling PSD, which for long had been considered a model for institution-building in developing countries, had lost its appeal and mobilizational effectiveness.

Anxious of potential rivals, Bourguiba did not permit any official to stay in office long enough to gain popularity and challenge the president's cult of personality, nor any opposition group to become strong enough to play an effective role. He conducted a game of musical "political" chairs in the appointment of his officials. In this game many lost their seats in the premiership, the cabinet, and the party, creating an atmosphere of fear and distrust among Bourguiba's own associates. In the last two years of his rule, authoritarian measures were taken against the different factions of the opposition, secular and religious alike. A strong army general, Zine el-Abidine Ben Ali, was appointed as minister of interior, the first career military officer to occupy a civilian cabinet post. Ben Ali managed to gain the trust of the president and began to engineer the government's onslaught against the opposition and the Islamists. The General Union of Tunisian Workers was dismantled and replaced by a new organization, its leader Habib Ashour was arrested, and its members were harassed. Several opposition leaders, such as Ahmed Mestiri, the head of the SDP, and Khemais Shemari, the Secretary-General of the Tunisian League for Human Rights, were also targeted. Headquarters of the opposition parties were stormed by the police. Opposition and independent newspapers were banned. The police repeatedly penetrated the university to put down and arrest protesting students.

Some noted that the weakening of the secular opposition had made the MTI a viable alternative to the ruling Destourian Socialist Party.[68] To eliminate this possibility, the regime decided to crush the movement. At the end of 1986, the authorities confiscated MTI archives, which contained important documents recording the movement's activities in the country. Consequently, the leaders of the MTI were placed under direct surveillance, and shortly, the third major crackdown ensued in March 1987, marking the most violent confrontation between Bourguiba's regime and the MTI.

On March 9, 1987, Rashed al-Ghannoushi was arrested for delivering a speech in one of the mosques without a license and for causing a disturbance.[69] This was followed by the arrest of forty more MTI leaders. Shortly after these incidents France arrested a group of terrorists, including seven Tunisians, for allegedly planning explosions in Paris, and announced their possible links with Iran. The Tunisian government seized this opportunity to escalate its campaign against the MTI and linked the two incidents without solid evidence. It accused the members of the movement of being "Khomeinists", dedicated to the overthrow of the government and the reconstruction of the country on the Iranian model.[70] Consequently, Tunisia officially broke its diplomatic relations with Iran. The charges for the original incident were overlooked and emphasis was now placed on implicating the MTI in more serious charges that would lead to the possible execution of some of its leaders, particularly Ghannoushi.

Disturbances in the university and demonstrations in support of the MTI broke out during which the demonstrators carried posters bearing the photograph of Ghannoushi and shouted the slogan: "there is no God but Allah, and Bourguiba is the enemy of Allah." The regime responded with further crackdowns, and 3,000 MTI members were arrested within two months.[71] These measures, however, did not stop the MTI from engineering new demonstrations, which it called "the challenge march," indicating its willingness to pursue this confrontation to the end. Explosions in five tourist resort hotels in Sousse and Monastir took place, introducing an unprecedented element in the confrontation between the Islamists and the regime. The MTI denied any responsibility for these explosions.

Later developments, however, revealed the presence of an underground wing of the movement run by some of its most activist elements. The major figures included Saleh Karkar, an economist, Hamadi al-Jibali, a solar-energy engineer, and al-Habib al-Mukni, a journalist.[72] The beginning of the formation of this wing can be traced back to 1981, when the movement was forced to go underground, following its suppression and the arrest of its moderate leaders. Al-Jibali assumed the leadership of the movement and succeeded in rebuilding its organizational structure and reorganizing its members. Following the subsequent repression against the movement, this wing became the vanguard of the MTI, in charge of devising the means for maintaining the secrecy of the whole movement and the cohesiveness of its members. The activities and influence of this wing became salient whenever the original leadership of the movement was imprisoned or put under close surveillance, as was the case throughout 1981 to 1983, and in the beginning of 1987. Based on the methods of organizing the MTI conferences, which involved strictly secretive and precautionary measures, it is possible to argue that the leader of the movement, Ghannoushi, exercised little control over the activities of this wing. In the 1987 confrontation with the movement, however, the regime managed to reveal this wing and put its leaders on trial.

The unfolding of events raised the fear of various elements within the regime, which, given the deteriorating health of Bourguiba and the looming crisis of succession, wanted desperately to put a quick end to the Islamic threat. Marches led by state officials and governors spread throughout the country, and the state-controlled media began to set the stage for the possible execution of some MTI leaders.

In August 1987, 99 MTI followers were put on trial and charged with forming an illegal organization, plotting subversive actions with Iran, and attempting to overthrow the government. In his defense of the movement, Ghannoushi condemned violence, reconfirmed the MTI's commitment to the democratic processes in achieving its objectives, denied any links with Iran, and expressed its reservations on the "disappointing" Iranian revolution.

Seven members were sentenced to death and 69 received sentences ranging from two years to life imprisonment. Ghannoushi received a life term of forced labor. Commenting on this trial, Lewis B. Ware wrote, "The trials that took place in October 1987 failed to produce any evidence that the MTI was revolutionary and subversive, had used violence against the regime, had operated clandestinely, or had, for that matter, bombed hotels in the Tunisian Sahel.

"The October trial," Ware continued, "was an embarrassment for the government in part because Ghannoushi's interrogation and subsequent defense presented a very different image of the movement's activities and political program than that held by the government. ...Ghannoushi's defense convincingly laid the blame for the radicalization of the MTI squarely on Bourguiba in obstinately refusing to acknowledge the indigenous roots of the movement's grievances, and attempting to portray its activities as Iranian interference in Tunisian internal affairs."[73]

Ben Ali: More of the Same (1987–Present)

Many observers consider the deteriorating relationship between the regime and the MTI as one of the factors which led Prime Minister Zine el-Abidine Ben Ali to remove Bourguiba on November 7, 1987.[74] Bourguiba insisted that the leaders of the movement be retried and executed, especially its symbol, Rashed al-Ghannoushi—a step that many Tunisians feared could have led to drastic consequences. Following the removal of Bourguiba, the new president took several measures to stabilize the country and increase the democratization of the political process.

With regards to Islam, Ben Ali, in a reversal of Bourguiba's policies, has made some conciliatory gestures by reasserting the Arab and Islamic identity of Tunisia in his discourse and in several symbolic and practical measures. These include the broadcasting of the call to prayers five times a day on the national radio and television; the restoration in December 1987 of the Zaytouna University as a center for religious learning; his performance of the minor pilgrimage in March 1988, which was repeatedly aired; the formation of a Supreme Islamic Council to oversee the religious affairs of the country; and the assertion of the Islamic character of Tunisia during the discussions on the national charter in April, in which some Islamists were allowed to participate.[75]

Upon Ben Ali's coming to power and the declaration of his new policies on November 7, the MTI declared its full support for the removal of Bourguiba and its willingness to assist the new president in achieving the objectives included in the November 7 statement.[76] It reasserted its adherence to peaceful means, rejection of violence, and insistence on becoming a political party through legal procedures. It also entered into negotiations with the regime to discuss the possibility of becoming a legal party, expressing its willingness to change its name in order to comply with the new party law of April 1988, which prohibits the formation of political parties on the basis of religion, region, or language.[77]

In 1988, Ben Ali released Ghannoushi and most of the imprisoned MTI members. The MTI in turn responded by expressing its support for Ben Ali and his plans for democratization. On November 5, 1988, Ben Ali met with Ghannoushi and conducted talks which were described as "cordial." Two days later, on the anniversary of his accession to power, Ben Ali together with the country's six legalized political parties, the labor union and representatives of the still-unauthorized MTI signed a National Pact, promising consensus, political freedoms, and the right to form political parties.[78]

Ghannoushi, seeking official recognition for his party and participation in the coming legislative elections, agreed to change the MTI's name and remove any reference to Islam from its title in order to comply with the conditions of the party formation code. Subsequently, in April 1989, Ghannoushi changed the MTI's name and redefined its objectives. He announced the formation of *Harakat al-Nahda* (The Renaissance Movement) and applied to the authorities for official recognition. In what came as a surprise to the expectations of many observers, the application was turned down and al-Nahda was forbidden from participating in the legislative elections of April 1989. Insisting on legal participation within the system, al-Nahda's candidates took part in the elections as independents.

The April 1989 Elections: A Turning Point

The legislative elections were a turning point in the relations between Ben Ali and the al-Nahda Movement. Having succeeded in obtaining almost 15 percent of the total votes, and up to 40 percent in major cities, including Tunis, al-Nahda proved that it was the major opposition force in the country.[79] Combined, the other legal political parties received less than 5 percent of the total votes. The legal Communist Party was not even able to participate in these elections as it could not secure the 500 votes required to nominate a candidate in any electoral district.[80] Confronted with a politically viable Islamist opposition party and alarmed by the stunning victory of the Islamic Salvation Front (FIS) in the municipal and provincial elections in Algeria, Ben Ali decided to eliminate al-Nahda as a potential threat and suppress the movement.

Frustrated by the regime's renewed policy of harassment and continued refusal to legalize his party, Ghannoushi left the country in May 1989 and went into voluntary exile in Britain, where he began to criticize the autocratic nature of Ben Ali's regime. Soon after Ghannoushi's departure, the government's campaign against al-Nahda began in earnest. The movement's publication, *al-Fajr*, was suspended in June 1990 and the pro-Nahda student union was banned in April 1991. Scores of mosque leaders were arrested or prevented from delivering religious lectures. Religious lessons at the Zaytouna mosques were again prohibited. The regime declared a policy of "drying up the sources and cutting off the limbs of Islamic extremism." This policy included the systematic arrest of al-Nahda's sympathizers, denying their family members work or financial support, banning the Islamic-style dress in educational and government institutions, appointing a Marxist as an education minister, changing the curriculum of Islamic subjects in schools, closing the mosques immediately after each prayer, and controlling them through government-appointed imams. Between September 1990 and March 1992 Amnesty International reported the imprisonment of at least 8,000 Nahda followers. Three thousand of these have since been tried and convicted for belonging to an unauthorized association.

The regime used two incidents to justify its harsh measures against al-Nahda and deflect the increasing criticism of its reneging on its earlier promises of political liberalization. The first occurred in February 1991, when three young Islamists, allegedly belonging to al-Nahda, attacked the government party's office in Bab Souika and killed one guard and seriously injured another. The incident, which was officially condemned by al-Nahda, inspired intensive official media campaigns against the movement and led to the arrest of thousands of its followers. According to the Lawyers Committee for Human Rights, the trials of the three defendants in the Bab Souika case lacked evidence to support the government's accusations and were characterized by irregularities. "The prosecution case relied on confessions allegedly made to police officers, although these were retracted when the accused appeared before an examining magistrate."[81] Nonetheless, the Bab Souika incident and the increasing pressure on al-Nahda engendered a split among its leadership. Abdel Fattah Mourou, the movement's second man, and two other Nahda leaders issued a statement in which they denounced violence and announced the suspension of their membership in the movement. Mourou, whose statement came three weeks after the incident and subsequent to his brief detention in the regime's prison, began to adopt a reconciliatory approach, express his desire to form a political party, and apply for legal recognition. Mourou's initiative was briefly welcomed in the official press which went on to describe his group as "the faithful sons of Tunisia."[82] Some in the independent press urged the regime to consider his demands for legal participation.[83] The regime however soon turned against Mourou and engineered a defamation campaign aiming to discredit his personal conduct. The 1991 split had in the end had only a minor impact on al-Nahda as several of those who had followed Mourou subsequently rejoined the movement.

The second incident took place in May 1991 when the Interior Minister announced the discovery of a "plot" by al-Nahda to seize power. Around three hundred al-Nahda followers were tried before two military courts during July-August 1992 for attempting to assassinate the president and overthrow the government. At the end of the trials, which lacked "documentary or other tangible evidence to link the suspects to the weapons that had been seized, or to tie the An-Nahda movement to any wide-ranging conspiracy,"[84] the defendants received harsh sentences.

Describing the nature of the relations between the Ben Ali's regime and al-Nahda, and the authorities' flagrant human rights abuse, the Lawyers Committee for Human Rights explains:

> It is in the context of this single-minded determination to liquidate the Islamist threat to the government's monopoly on power that respect of human rights in Tunisia has declined in the past three years. Supporters

and sympathizers of An-Nahda have not been the only victims of officially sanctioned lawlessness. Tunisia's legal profession has been intimidated; its press freedom has been restricted; and the country's only independent human rights organization has been silenced as political debate has degenerated into a witch-hunt against An-Nahda.[85]

The Tunisian government continued to use the "Islamic threat" as a pretext to maintain its monopoly over political power. Intolerant of any public dissent, Islamic or secular, the authorities suppressed the Tunisian League for Human Rights in 1992 and arrested its former head Muncif al-Marzuqi in 1994 for over three months after he had attempted to challenge Ben Ali's candidacy in the 1994 presidential elections. It detained political opponents, censored the freedom of local press, muzzled foreign reporters, and banned entry to numerous Arab and foreign press. These measures have all made the Tunisian government a target for continuous accusations of human rights violations over the past years. In April 1994, 120 women intellectuals, doctors, journalists, and university professors signed a petition entitled "An Appeal for Democracy," requesting from the regime a greater degree of freedom and respect for individual rights.

Ben Ali's regime still insists on consensus as the basis for political conduct and admission into the political process. Justice Minister Sadok Chaabane summarized this view, "we want to open the door to recognized parties that share the same model of society and same principles."[86] In the last presidential elections in March 94, Ben Ali received the usual 99.91 percent of the votes. In the parliamentary elections, his party, the Democratic Constitutional Rally garnered 97.73 percent (144 out of 163 seats), continuing a long history of a single party, centralized state. While 19 seats in the new parliament were reserved for the opposition parties, the actual number of seats was increased by 38 (from 125 to 163), further diluting the opposition's strength in the legislature. Weak, divided, and lacking popularity, the electoral performance of the legal opposition parties has been poor. They received 3.4 percent of the total votes. While the participation of opposition parties in parliament is no more than a cosmetic change, nonetheless, it still represents a first for Tunisia's 40 years of post-independence politics.

The country's loyal opposition became even more frustrated after the local elections of May 1995. Five opposition parties in addition to a group of independents participated for the first time in nine years in the country's municipal elections. The opposition was able to field candidates in only 47 out of the 257 municipalities. Unlike the case in the 1994 parliamentary elections where 19 seats were reserved for the opposition parties, the ruling RCD this time placed candidates in all the districts. The RCD maintained control over all 257 municipalities and captured 99.9 percent of the contested seats. The opposition parties won only 6 out of the 4,090 seats, a mere 0.1 percent. Though the results of the local elections came as no surprise given the Ben Ali regime's increasing intolerance of dissent, the opposition parties felt betrayed and not duly awarded. After all, they have remained silent over the regime's harsh measures against the Nahda and given their unequivocal support to Ben Ali. In a news conference after the elections, Muhammad Moada, the president of the Socialist Democrat Movement, complained that "the results of the municipal elections are a disgrace for Tunisia and the ruling party." Despite the severe humiliation of his party, which won only two seats in Beni Khiar and Fernina, Moada nevertheless went on to express his "full confidence, absolute, and firm support" for Ben Ali and the country's top leadership.[87] Following the elections, the legal opposition parties attempted to form a coalition front that would establish some balance between them and the ruling RCD. Due to long political and leadership rivalries, however, the new front never came into being as the opposition leaders exchanged accusations and demonstrated mutual mistrust.[88]

The local elections were also challenged by the Tunisian opposition abroad. Several exiled Tunisian opposition figures, including politicians, former government officials, academicians, and Islamists, issued a joint statement in which they described the results as "folkloric..., reminiscent of the epochs of the extinct totalitarian regimes." The opposition figures criticized the continued dominance of the ruling party and the increasingly narrow space for the participation of other political forces. They also called for tangible political reforms that would guarantee the respect of popular will, independence of the judiciary, separation of the ruling party from the state, and the institution of freedom of the press. The statement called for general amnesty and the release of political prisoners and prisoners of conscience.[89]

The May elections were revealing in many respects. First, they demonstrated Ben Ali's determination to ignore the mounting demands for devising a new formula for power-sharing between the ruling party and the opposition. Second, it underscored the political insignificance of the opposition parties which the regime had legalized and allowed to participate in the political process. Chadhli Ennafati, RCD Secretary General, responded to the complaints of the opposition parties by saying that "it was obvious that each party would receive [seats] according to its weight and real presence in the field."[90] Third, it also showed that al-Nahda is the only meaningful opposition force to the regime as it was capable in previous elections of mobilizing votes and gaining a significant influence in many parts of the country.

Realizing the potentials for exercising a future role in the politics of the country, al-Nahda has started a process of renewal and reorganization of its structures and redefinition of its policies vis-à-vis the regime and political forces in society. It has convened several conferences abroad since 1992 for its rank and file in order to probe the movement's priorities at the current phase and design a strategy for the coming decades. Following the movement's general conference in early 1995, al-Nahda renewed its organizational structures, adopted new methods of elections for its leaderships, and elected new leaders for the movement's organizations. Among the policies adopted during the 1995 conference were the assertion of the non-violent nature of the movement and the prevention of political polarization in society (i.e. regime vs. al-Nahda), by continuing to advocate the political rights of the entire society and cooperating and encouraging the other political forces in society.[91]

Conclusion

The steady rise of al-Nahda in Tunisian national politics reflects the evolution of a mainstream movement from a small group in the 1960s to an unlicensed political party since the 1980s. At the present, the leaders of al-Nahda, Ghannoushi in particular, are keen to project a moderate image of their movement. On the part of the regime, the al-Nahda factor can no longer be dismissed from the political scene. Its absence still haunts the regime, especially as it reveals the fragile nature of the political liberalization that has taken place since Ben Ali assumed power in 1987.

While the excessive measures against the movement and its members are eliminating any immediate threat of an Islamist takeover of power in Tunisia, they are bound in the long run to increase the level of polarization in society. At stake here is the issue of identity and the type of Islam the regime wants to maintain. The choice will remain, as is the case in other Arab countries, between a tiny elite that imposes its secular values on society through repressive measures, economic pay-offs, and dependence on foreign support, and an opposition party that associates with the identity and dominant belief-system of the people and attempts to devise a synthesis between Islam and modernity. From its past history, al-Nahda has proven its ability to withstand repression, rebuild its organizational structure, and reemerge as an effective political force. While in exile, Ghannoushi is turning into a symbol maintaining his movement's commitment to pluralism, freedom, and respect for individual and public rights. In a moment of popular discontent of the increasing authoritarian policies of the regime, he and his movement could easily spearhead a new cycle of change.

Notes

1. Al-Nahda has adopted several names throughout its evolution. To avoid confusion, I use the Islamic Tendency Movement (MTI) to refer to the movement prior to 1989, when it became al-Nahda.

2. Perkins, *Tunisia*, pp. 132-5. See also Hermassi, *Leaders and National Development*, pp. 184-91.

3. John Entelis, *Comparative Politics of North Africa: Algeria, Morocco, and Tunisia* (New York: Syracus University Press, 1980), p. 138.

4. Interview with Salah Eddin al-Jourshi, Tunis, January 5, 1986.

5. Abdel Latif al-Hermassi, *al-Haraka al-Islamiyya fi Tunis: al-Yasar al-Ishtiraki, al-Islam, wa al-Haraka al-Islamiyya* [The Islamic Movement in Tunisia: The Socialist Left, Islam, and the Islamic Movement] (Tunis: Bayram li al-Nashr, 1985), pp. 51-6.

6. Interview with Jourshi, Tunis, December 28, 1985.

7. See François Burgat, "Islamistes en Tunisie: La Crise?," *Grand Maghreb*, No. 44, November 11, 1985, pp. 445-51. François Burgat, "Intégristes: La Voie Tunisienne?," *Grand Maghreb*, Nos. 33-4, October 1984; Mireille Duteil, "L'Intégrisme Islamique au Maghreb: La Pause?," *Grand Maghreb*, No. 24, October 3, 1983, pp. 55-7; and "L'Intégrisme Islamique au Maghreb: La Pause?," 2e Partie. La Tunisie, *Grand Maghreb*, No. 26, November 14, 1983.

8. Interview with Abdel Fattah Mourou in *al-Ma'rifa*, Vol. 5, No. 5, May 15, 1979.

9. "No Body's Man-But the Man of Islam," *Arabia*, Vol. 4, No. 44, April 1985, p. 18. See also Abdelwahab el-Effendi, "The Long March Forward," *Inquiry*, Vol. 4, No. 10, October 1987.

10. "No Body's Man," p. 18.

11. Hemida al-Naifar, "How can a Muslim live in this era?", interview by François Burgat, translated by Linda Jones in *Middle East Report*, July-August 1988, p. 25.

12. Interview with Salah Eddin al-Jourshi, Tunis, December 28, 1985.

13. "No body's man," p.18.

14. Fatheya Balgheeth, "al-Haraka al-Islamiyya fi Tunis min Khilal Sahifat al-`Amal: 1979" [The Islamic Movement in Tunisia Through *al-`Amal* Newspaper] (Unpublished Dissertation, the Institute of Press and Mass Media, Tunis, 1979), appendix, p. 4.

15. See Balgheeth, "al-Haraka al-Islamiyya," p. 5, and El-Effendi, "The Long March Forward," p. 51.

16. "L'Association Nationale pour la Consérvation du Coran," *L'Action*, 16 May, 1969.

17. "Dawr al-Haraka al-Islamiyya fi Taghier al-Mu`adala al-Tunisiyya" [The Role of the Islamic Movement in Changing the Tunisian Equation], *al-Sayyad*, No. 2137, October 1985.

18. Interview with Salah Eddin al-Jourshi, Tunis, December 28, 1995.

19. John Entelis, "The Political Economy of North African Relations: Cooperation or Conflict?," in Halim Barakat (ed.), *Contemporary North Africa*, P. 119. See also Mark Tessler, "Tunisia at the Crossroads," *Current History*, Vol. 84, No. 502, May 1985, p. 220. For a critical leftist view, see *al-Nidham al-Bourguibi* [The Bourguibi System] (Beirut: Dar Ibn Khuldoun, 1980), pp. 115-19.

20. Riall Nolan, "Tunisia's Time of Transition," *Current History*, Vol. 80, No. 470, December 1980, p. 407

21. Interview with Salah Eddin al-Jourshi, Tunis, December 10, 1985.

22. Las`ad al-Tunsi, "al-Islamiyyun wa al-Haraka al-Niqabiyya" [The Islamists and the Union Movement], *al-Anwar*, September 9, 1984.

23. Interview with Muhammad Mzali, *al-Mustaqbal*, No. 384, January 30, 1984. PP. 24-7.

24. Nolan, "Tunisia's Time of Transition," p. 409.

25. The fact that only 13 percent result passed the 1986 Baccalaureate examination obviously reflects the continuation of this policy.

26. Nigel Disey, "The Working Class Revolt in Tunisia," *MERIP Report*, Vol. 8, No. 4, May 1978, p.14.

27. Disey, "The Working Class," pp. 11-12.

28. Abdel Latif al-Hermassi, *al-Haraka al-Islamiyya fi Tunis*, pp. 101-7.

29. Interview with Hemida al-Naifar, Tunis, January 11, 1986.

30. *15/21* resumed its 15th issue in August 1988.

31. Salah Eddin al-Jourshi, "Limadha al-Fikr al-Islami al-Mustaqbali?" [Why Is the Futuristic Islamic Thought], *15/21*, No. 2, January 1983, pp. 11-15. See also Salah Eddin al-Jourshi, Muhammad al-Quomai, and Abdel Aziz al-Tamimi,

al-Muqadimat al-Nadhariyya li al-Islamiyyin al-Taqadumiyyin [The Theoretical Basis of the Progressive Islamists] (Tunis: Dar al-Buraq li al-Nashr, 1989).

32. In 1974, members of the ILP seized Egypt's military academy and launched an unsuccessful coup attempt against Sadat's regime.

33. Abdel Hai Boularas, "Hiwar Ma`a Hizb al-Tahrir" [Dialogue with the Liberation Party], *al-Mawqif*, No. 42, March 19, 1985.

34. Rasheed Khashana, "Qadiyyat Hizb al-Tahrir al-Islami" [The Case of the Islamic Liberation Party], *al-Maghrib*, No. 65, August 20, 1983, p. 62.

35. Abdel Latif al-Furati, "`Ala Hamish al-Ahkam" [On the Surroundings of the Sentences], *al-Majalla*, No. 187, September 10-16, 1983, p. 39.

36. *Al-Ra'i*, No. 313, March 22, 1985. See also "Ma Huwa Hizb al-Tahrir" [What Is the Liberation Party], *al-Batal*, No. 40, July 8-14, 1985.

37. Al-Dimni, "Na`am li al-Hiwar al-Fikri" [Yes to Intellectual Dialogue], *al-Ra'i*, No. 334, August 16, 1985.

38. Rashed al-Ghannoushi, "al-Thawra al-Iraniyya Thawra Islamiyya," [The Iranian Revolution Is an Islamic Revolution], *al-Ma`rifa*, Vol. 5, No. 3, February 12, 1979. See also interview with Ghannoushi in *Kayhan al-Arabi*, No. 955, December 12, 1987.

39. Interview with Abdel Fattah Mourou in *al-Ma`rifa*, Vol. 5, No. 5, May 15, 1979.

40. Salah Eddin al-Jourshi, "In`ikasat al-Thawra al-Iraniyya" [The Repercussions of the Iranian Revolution], *al-Ma`rifa*, Vol. 5, No. 4, April 1, 1979, pp. 3-5.

41. See *al-Ma`rifa*, Vol. 5, No. 3, February 12, 1979, p. 3.

42. Rashed al-Ghannoushi, "Min Jadid: Nahnu wa al-Gharb" [Once More: We and the West], *al-Ma`rifa*, Vol. 4, No. 9; August 1, 1978; Vol. 4, No. 10, October 1978; and Vol. 5, No. 1, November 20, 1987. See also Ghannoushi's article "Da`wa ila al-Rushd" [Call to Guidance], *al-Ma`rifa*, Vol. 5, No. 2, January 1, 1978.

43. Abdel Latif al-Hermassi, *al-Haraka al-Islamiyya fi Tunis*, p. 158.

44. Fatheya Balgheeth wrote her dissertation on the press campaign which the party's newspaper *al-`Amal* launched against the movement in 1979. See "al-Haraka al-Islamiyya."

45. Balgheeth, "al-Haraka al-Islamiyya," p. 51.

46. "Islam's Challenge to Authoritarianism," *Arabia*, May 1983, quoted from *Le Monde*, August 1, 1981.

47. *Le Monde,* January 27, 1982, quoted in *JPRS*, No. 80310, March 12, 1982.

48. Balgheeth, "al-Haraka al-Islamiyya," pp. 44-55.

49. Abdel Latif al-Hermassi, *al-Haraka al-Islamiyya fi Tunis*, p. 161.

50. Rashed al-Ghannoushi, "al-`Amal al-Islami wa Quta` al-Turuq" [Islamic Action and the Bandits], *al-Ma`rifa*, Vol. 5, No. 5, May 15, 1979. See also

interview with Abdel Fattah Mourou in Balgheeth, "al-Haraka al-Islamiyya," pp. 15-22.

51. "The Statement of the Declaration of The Islamic Tendency Movement," in *Haqai'q Hawl Harakat al-Itijah al-Islami* [Facts on the Movement of Islamic Tendency] (Tunis: MTI, 1983), p. 10.

52. This statement is related to Omar Ibn al-Khattab, the second Muslim caliph.

53. *Haqai'q Hawl Harakat al-Itijah al-Islami*, pp. 11-12.

54. *Haqai'q Hawl Harakat al-Itijah al-Islami*, pp. 38-58. See also "Islam's Challenge to Authoritarianism," *Arabia*, No. 21, May 1983, p. 21.

55. *Al-Sabah*, September 2, 1987.

56. Jim Paul, "States of Emergency: The Riots in Tunisia and Morocco," and David Seddon, "Winter of Discontent: Economic Crisis in Tunisia and Morocco," *MERIP Reports*, Vol. 14, No. 8, October 1984. For the mediation between the government and al-Nahda, see Abu Bakr al-Sagheer, "al-Ifraj `an Qiyadat al-Itijah al-Islami" [The Release of the Leaders of the MTI], *al-Ra'i*, August 10, 1984.

57. *Al-Tali`a al-Islamiyya*, Vol. 5, No. 31, October 1987, pp. 30-2.

58. The following sections are based on "Qadiyyat al-Muntasibin li al-Itijah al-Islami" [The Trial of the Members of the MTI], *al-Sabah*, September 1, 2, 3, and 4, 1981; "L'Acte d'Accusation," *La Presse*, September 2, 1987, pp. 6-9; "al-Shaykh Rashed al-Ghannoushi Uhakim Sajjanih" [Shaykh Ghannoushi Tries his Captives], *al-Tali`a al-Islamiyya*, Vol. 5, No. 31, October 1987, pp. 26-38; and Hassanin Kouroum, "Madha Wara' al-Ahkam" [What Is Behind the Sentences], *al-Wafd*, October 1, 1987, p. 5.

59. *Haqai'q Hawl Harakat al-Itijah al-Islami*, pp. 8-9. See also "Demandes de Visa: Le Mouvement de la Tendance Islamique," *Démocratie*, June 1981.

60. As one of the leaders, Jourshi, commented on the reasons for the participation of women in the MTI: "The regime made the woman feel as if she is endlessly indebted to its benevolence for liberating her...with the implicit understanding that she in turn would defend its policies." Interview with Jourshi, Tunis, December 10, 1985. See also S. Belhassan, "Femmes Tunisiennes Islamistes," in Christiane Souriau et al., *Le Maghreb Musulman En 1979*, pp. 77-94, and Susan Waltz, "Islamist Appeal in Tunisia," *The Middle East Journal*, Vol. 40, No. 4, Autumn 1986, p. 655.

61. Sam Seibert et al., "The Worst Has Been Avoided," *Newsweek* (October 12, 1987).

62. Steven Greenhouse, "Radicals Seen as New Peril for Tunisians," *New York Times*, October 1, 1987, p. A-9.

63. Elbaki Hermassi, "La Société Tunisienne au Miroir Islamiste," *Maghreb-Mashrek*, No. 103, Spring 1984, p. 43.

64. Aziza Medimegh and Elbaki Hermassi, *Essais pour une Sociologie Religieuse* (Tunis: Centre de Perspective Sociale, 1983), pp. 79-99. Hermassi, Ibid., pp. 39-56. Kamal al-Ghozzi, "al-`Awamel al-Maudu`iyya li al-Inti`asha al-Islamiyya bi al-Sahel al-Tunsi," [The Objective Factors for Islamic Revival in the Tunisian Sahel] (Unpublished Dissertation, Faculty of Literature and Social Sciences, Sociology Department, Tunis, 1984).

65. "Qa'imat al-Muttahamin" [The List of the Accused], *al-I`lan*, September 1, 1987, pp. 2-4.

66. *Asharq al-Awsat*, June 6, 1985. See also *al-Majalla*, No. 283, July 10-16, 1985.

67. *Al-Tali`a al-Islamiyya*, Vol. 5, No. 31, October 1987, pp. 33-4.

68. Sam Seibert, et al., "The Worst Has Been Avoided," *Newsweek*, October 12, 1987, p. 52.

69. *Wall Street Journal*, August 12, 1987.

70. Selim Nassib, "Manipulation Intégriste: Tunis," *Liberation*, March 27, 1987.

71. Edward Cody, "Dissidents' Trial Tests Tunisia," *Washington Post*, September 26, 1987, p. A.15.

72. François Soudan, "Verdict Pondere en Tunisie," *Jeune Afrique*, No. 1396, October 7, 1987, pp. 17-20.

73. Lewis B. Ware, "Ben Ali's Constitutional Coup in Tunisia," *Middle East Journal*, Vol. 42, No. 4, Autumn 1988, pp. 588 and 591.

74. See for example Simon Ingram, "Why Ben Ali Ousted His President," *Middle East International*, No. 313, November 21, 1987, p.6; Edward Cody; "Tunisia's Course Unclear under New Leader," *Washington Post*, November 9, 1987; and Paul Delaney, "Senile Bourguiba Described in Tunis," *New York Times*, November 9, 1987.

75. See *Christian Science Monitor*, September 7, 1988, p. 2.

76. Al-Nahda's statement, *Asharq al-Awsat*, November 11, 1987. See also interview with Abdel Fattah Mourou in *Asharq al-Awsat*, November 11, 1987.

77. "Khalfiyyat al-Ifrag `an al-Ghannoushi" [The Backgrounds of the Release of Ghannoushi], *Asharq al-Awsat*, May 17, 1988. See also interview with Mourou in *Asharq al-Awsat*, May 21, 1988; and Muhammad al-Hashmi al-Hamdi, "Mushahadat min Tunis" [Scenes from Tunisia], *Asharq al-Awsat*, September 3, 1988.

78. The MTI was represented by the Tunisian lawyer Noureddin al-Bihiri.

79. This figure was confirmed by Prime Minister Hamid al-Qaraoui in an interview with Raouf Shahouri in *al-Watan al-`Arabi*, No. 140, November 17, 1989, p. 25.

80. Salah Eddin al-Jourshi, "al-Ittijah al-Islami Tahawal ila Haraka Fa`ila" [The Islamic Tendency Turned into an Effective Movement], *al-Muslimun*, April 14, 1989.

81. *Promise Unfulfilled: Human Rights in Tunisia Since 1987* (New York: Lawyers Committee for Human Rights, October 1993), p. 32.

82. *Al-`Alam*, April 20, 1991, p. 23.

83. Abdel Fattah Mourou in an interview with Najeeb Likanji and al-Mouncif al-Mahrouk, "Talab al-T'ashira Qareeb" [Demand for a License Is Soon], *Realities*, No. 294, April 18, 1991. See also Salah Eddin al-Jourshi, "Mubadarat Mourou Fursa Jadida Law" [Mourou's Initiative Is a New Opportunity, If], *Realities*, No. 295, May 2, 1991, pp. 12-13.

84. *Promise Unfulfilled*, p. 10, see also p. 36. The Committee recommended that "All defendants convicted in the Bab Sa`adoun and Bouchoucha trials before military courts in August 1992 should be released, or given a fair re-trial in accordance with minimum standards of international law," p. 39.

85. *Promise Unfulfilled*, p. 13.

86. *Christian Science Monitor*, November 9, 1993.

87. *Reuter*, May 25, 1995. See also, *al-Hayat*, May 27, 1995.

88. *Al-Hayat*, June 12 and June 24, 1995.

89. The Joint statement was signed by former minister Ahmed Ben Saleh for the Popular Unity Movement; Rashed al-Ghannoushi for the Renaissance Movement; former prime minister Muhammad Mzali, Faisal Kaabi for the Nasserite Arab Socialist Forum; Younis Ben Othman for the Democracy Now Society; Najmeddine Hamrouni for the Tunisian Students Union; independent researchers Ahmed Manna`i, Mezri Haddad and the Geneva-based Tunisian journalist Noureddine Amdouni. See *al-Hayat*, May 29, 1995.

90. *Al-Hayat*, June 1, 1995.

91. Interview with Sayyid Ferjani, London-based Nahda official, Virginia, June 8, 1995.

4

From Silent Protest to Political Ascent:
The Islamic Movements in Algeria

In 1990 political analysts were taken aback when a political party based on Islamic principles swept the municipal elections in a country long held to be the model for progressive Third World states. Algeria offers one of the few instances where an Islamic party was actually allowed to compete in electoral contests. The emergence of the Algerian Islamist trend seemingly from nowhere and its impressive performances in both municipal and parliamentary elections mask the long-term presence of an Islamist movement in the nation. While not always as organized as its Tunisian counterparts, Islamism in Algeria has firm roots in the independence struggle. Now, of course, the democratic experiment is at an end and the country is dissolving into bloody chaos.

The Islamic movements in Algeria evolved from repressed groups during the 1960s and 1970s to popular movements on the verge of assuming political control in the early 1990s. Only a few years before, such a transformation would have been highly unlikely. Compared to Tunisia and Morocco, Algeria appeared to have a more centralized state apparatus, a dominant party system, a watchful military, and a secular technocratic elite committed to the modernization of society and to achieving comprehensive development. In fact, it is the interplay of these very elements that led to the emergence of popular Islamic movements and produced the current political turmoil and uncertainty. The Algerian Islamic movements have particular characteristics that distinguish them from their North African counterparts. Among these are historic continuity, the support of the country's historic `ulama', the emergence of several strong Islamist trends, and a determination not to cut links with the country's legacy of the war of liberation. These traits worked together to give them strength and popularity.

This chapter traces the origins of the Islamic movements in Algeria and the political and social factors that led to their prominence. It analyzes the evolution of the Islamic movements within four distinct phases: silent protest (1960s); mobilization and recruitment (1970s); political ascent (1980s); and armed path (1990s). Under each phase, several Islamic groups and intellectual figures are examined with regard to the main actors, their structure and organization, and their political orientation. These include the al-Qiyam Association, the Islamic intellectual Malik Ben Nabi, Hamas and al-Nahda (the Algerian Muslim Brothers), al-Jama`a al-Islamiyya bi al-Jaza'ir (The Islamic Group in Algeria or what became known as the Algerianization Trend), and the Islamic Salvation Front (FIS). The events that followed the 1992 military coup and the growth of armed resistance to the incumbent military-backed regime require a discussion of the Islamic armed groups, their origins, and their structure.

The Nation's Turbulent Beginnings

The eight-year war for liberation and the exodus of the French colonial settlers left deep impressions on Algerian society, which had descended into paralysis. The exiled and imprisoned leaders of Algeria's independence movement returned to the country and began implementing their ideas of a progressive state based on scientific socialism. By the time of the Party Congress of 1964, it had become clear to the rest of the country that Algeria's new rulers were committed to a Leninist orientation for the country. These proponents of a Leninist line of scientific socialism drafted "an avant-project of a party program heavily laced with Marxist jargon and tending to play down the Arab-Islamic heritage of Algeria."[1] During the meetings of the Party Congress, Shaykh al-Bashir al-Ibrahimi, the president of the Association of Scholars, declared his opposition to these leftist ideas and issued a statement in which he expressed his disappointment in the path Algeria was taking. He warned that the country was sliding into a civil war, suffering from an unprecedented spiritual crisis, and facing insurmountable economic problems. He also urged in his statement that the new leaders consider the national interest of the people and their aspirations for unity, peace, and prosperity. Shaykh al-Ibrahimi demanded that "the theoretical foundation of their [the elite] policy should emanate from our Arab and Islamic roots, not from foreign doctrines."[2] A compromise was apparently reached, as was later reflected in the Charter of Algiers, which toned down the idea of scientific socialism—while still confirming socialism as the ideology of the state—and re-asserting the country's Arab and Islamic heritage.[3]

The assertion of the Arabo-Islamic national identity, the choice of socialism, and the achievement of comprehensive development were three state-declared goals that guided the dynamics of political life in post-independence Algeria. They constituted the basis on which the legitimacy of the regime rested. However, Algeria's first president, Ahmed Ben Bella's style of rule was often characterized as hasty and improvising, and created a chaotic situation that did not lead to a solid revolutionary transformation nor assist Algeria in its post-independence economic, political, or ideological recovery. Therefore, the twin issues of state-building and economic revitalization were urgent priorities of his successor, Houari Boumedienne. The importance of these issues were highlighted by Boumedienne's determination to avoid any political differences that might hinder the state from pursuing its socioeconomic objectives. Instead, Boumedienne elevated the military and the administration to a higher status while ascribing the party to a minor role where it would remain subservient to the state. In one of his early speeches on July 7, 1965, he defined that role by stating that:

> the FLN would be a dynamic avant-garde revolutionary party, functioning according to the rules of democratic centralism, and consisting of tested militants. Its task will be, in conformity with the Tripoli Program and the Charter of Algiers, that of orienting, animating, and supervising, but not administrating or substituting itself to the state."[4]

This conception of the party's role was typical of the ruling style of Boumedienne, who preferred to run the country through a small civil-military oligarchy and remained reluctant until the mid-1970s to accommodate mass political participation and expand the decision-making process. He feared that active and vigorous political institutions would slow the process of state building as they might pose a challenge to the emergence and performance of a strong centralized government. In the meantime, Communists from the tolerated opposition Parti d'Avant-Garde Socialist (PAGS) were allowed to hold key posts in the official Trade Union (UGTA), the youth organization (UNJA), the party, and the state apparatus.

After independence, all rival political groupings were banned. The Association of Scholars was the first to be dissolved in 1962. The dissolution of the association came as a shock to the Algerian `ulama' who had played a nationalist role throughout the colonial phase and enjoyed popular respect and legitimacy. They had expected to exercise some influence in the post-colonial phase. The decision to ban the association was driven by several factors. It came as part of the process of establishing a single-party state and eliminating actual and potential rivals of the new regime. Immediately after Algeria became independent, the scholars issued a statement on August 20, 1962, in which they demanded that Islam become the source of reference for the ideological orientation and political structure of the new state.[5] The association's disbanding was also necessary, from the viewpoint of the new state, in order to assert the state's monopoly over the interpretation of Islam in such a fashion as to legitimate its secular policies and its adoption of socialism. In this manner, the new elites felt that they could silence any opposition to their policies on religious grounds. Equally important, Ben Bella himself did not trust the scholars and began to accuse them of not having wholeheartedly supported the armed struggle and of being reactionaries because they did not endorse the ideological choices of the new state. Although a few scholars of the association did cooperate with the regime and were incorporated in the state's religious bureaucracy, others were harassed, imprisoned, or placed under house arrest. Chief among these was the association's leader, Shaykh al-Bashir al-Ibrahimi, who opposed the banning of the association and criticized the new regime's socialism.

Shaykh al-Ibrahimi, who remained under house arrest until his death in 1965, was not sounding a false alarm. The country suffered from political instability and severe dissent that continued until 1970. Following his election as president in 1963, Ben Bella had to declare a state of emergency and quell the uprising of the Kabyle Berbers led by Hussein Ait Ahmed. Less than a year later, another uprising was staged by Colonel Chaabani, who was executed in September 1964. Military coups were not uncommon and Ben Bella was finally unseated by Boumedienne in June 1965. Two years later, Boumedienne found himself a target of another attempted coup, this time led by Colonel Tahir Zubairi. Boumedienne escaped an assassination attempt in April 1968. The regime responded by eliminating opponents abroad, such as the case of Muhammad Khider and Karim Belkacim.[6]

Silent Protest

Al-Qiyam Association

After the banning of the Association of Algerian Scholars, other founding members of the association tried to resurrect it by establishing a new one to continue the reformist message of the scholars. Jam`iyyat al-Qiyam (The Association of Values) was established in 1963, at al-Taraqqi (Progress) Club—the same place where Ben Badis's association had been announced thirty years earlier—by eminent scholars such as Abdel Latif Sultani, Ahmed Sahnoun, Omar al-Arabaoui, and Mosbah al-Huwaiziq, and was headed by al-Hachemi Tidjani. Tidjani was the secretary-general of the University of Algiers, and was influenced by the ideas of the Egyptian Muslim Brothers and the Islamic intellectual Malik Ben Nabi.[7] According to William Quandt and Mohammad Arkoun, al-Qiyam found support among some political leaders, notably Muhammad Khider, one of the historic leaders of the war of liberation and later the head of the FLN during Ben Bella's term.[8]

Al-Qiyam advocated a reformist orientation that sought to reassert the Arab and Islamic identity in post-colonial Algeria. Its members affirmed their link with the reformist line of Ben Badis's association and that of the Salafiyya movement in general, as conceived by historical Islamic thinkers Jamal al-Din al-Afghani and Muhammad `Abduh. Compared to the earlier founders, however, most of the new reformist elite were bilingual intellectuals, well-versed in foreign cultures as well as in the Arabo-Islamic traditions. The association's mouthpiece, *Humanisme Musulman*, articulated al-Qiyam's ideological orientations and demands. The title of the periodical reflects the modernist perspectives of these Muslim intellectuals towards Islam as a humanistic message still relevant to contemporary society. Al-Qiyam focused on the sociological and cultural dimensions of post-independence Algeria. The issue of de-colonization and the reconstruction of the national components of the Algerian identity were recurring themes. It devoted several of its articles to the question of Arabization, Islamic and national education, decolonization, and the cultural and sociological aspects of independence.[9]

The regime did not tolerate al-Qiyam for very long and soon began to fear that it was undermining its legitimacy. The activities of the association were restricted in 1966, following a demonstration by its members protesting the execution of Sayyid Qutb of the Egyptian Muslim Brotherhood; eventually, in 1970, al-Qiyam was outlawed.[10]

The dissolution of al-Qiyam Association did not prevent some of its founders from expressing their opposition to the socialist policies of the regime and continuing to spread Islamic education among the youth. The most prominent of these scholars were shaykhs Sultani (d. 1983), al-Huwaiziq (d. 1973), al-Arabaoui (d. 1984), and Sahnoun, who refused to be associated with official Islam and incorporated into the state's bureaucratic institutions. All of these scholars were members of Ben Badis's original association and had played an active role in fulfilling its objectives during the colonial period. Huwaiziq, Arabaoui, and Sahnoun were all imprisoned during the war of liberation for their activities in supporting the FLN and encouraging the Algerians to join the front in its armed struggle against the French. Sultani was charged with raising funds for the *mujahidin* from the very beginning of the revolution. The preliminary meetings of the Soummam Congress in 1956 were held in his house. Through active careers of preaching, teaching, and establishing free schools, these scholars gained popularity and their lectures at the mosques of Algiers drew a large following. During the 1960s, the mosques at Lahrache, Bab al-Ouad, Belkour, and Qasbah became centers for recruiting and educating young Algerians and for expressing criticism to the regime's policies. For that reason, all of these scholars were harassed and intimidated by the regime. Huwaiziq was banned from the country's main cities and exiled in 1970 to the south.[11] In 1974, Sultani wrote a book, *Masdakism Is the Origin of Socialism*—banned in Algeria and published in Morocco—in which he directed a scathing criticism of the country's ruling elite and secular intellectuals for their deviation from the true Islamic principles and adoption instead of foreign and non-Islamic ideologies. Sultani viewed this as a clear betrayal of Algeria's martyrs and the sacrifice the country had offered in order to preserve the Arab and Islamic identity of its population. He also criticized the regime for its intolerance of dissent and defended the country's scholars against attempts to marginalize them and the harsh criticisms of conservatism and stagnation.[12] As will be later discussed in detail, Sultani was under house arrest from 1982 till his death in 1983 for co-signing the "Statement of Advice" along with Sahnoun and Abbasi Madani.

Malik Ben Nabi

In addition to the active historic scholars who attempted to maintain the reformist message of Ben Badis alive among the Algerian population, a mainly French-educated intellectual, Malik Ben Nabi, played a significant role in forming a well-educated elite of Muslim intellectuals in the mid 1960s. Ben Nabi was born in 1905 in Constantine to a family of modest means. He received his early education at French-administered schools in Algeria and graduated from France in 1935 as an electrical engineer. Due to his predominantly French education, Ben Nabi mastered the Arabic language at a relatively late age. He moved to Egypt in 1956 during the war of liberation and returned to Algeria in 1963. Upon his return, Ben Nabi assumed the post of Director of Higher Education, a position from which he resigned in 1967. Till his death in 1973, Ben Nabi held a weekly cultural meeting in his house that was frequented by university students and intellectuals. Through these meetings, a group of Muslim intellectuals was created that would go on to play a significant role in the evolution of contemporary Islamic movements in Algeria.

Ben Nabi's ideas have influenced a segment of Algerian intellectuals who later became known as *Tayar al-Jaz'ara* (The Algerianization Trend) in the Islamic movement. Due to their impact, their ideas merit some discussion. A prolific writer, Ben Nabi issued all his books under the series title of "the problems of civilization." He strongly believed that the current problems of the Muslim world were related to the issue of civilization in the first place. Unlike many Muslim intellectuals at this period who viewed the relations between the East and the West through the lenses of conflict and polarization, Ben Nabi took the more difficult task of attempting to understand the phenomenon of civilization and its dynamics. Building on the Khaldounian cyclical perception of the rise and fall of states and influenced by Arnold Toynbee's concept of challenge and response, Ben Nabi viewed civilization as moving in cycles: it is first driven by a religious idea; then by reason; and in the final cycle, by instinct. Civilizations evolve through the interaction of a religious idea with three elements: human beings, matter, and time. The dominance of instinct marks the downfall of civilizations.

The strengths of Ben Nabi's thought lay in his great ability to generate original ideas and transform them from the level of abstracts into a dynamic framework that has a powerful interpretative and practical capacity. While clearly admiring Afghani and `Abduh, Ben Nabi was critical of them for focusing on the symptoms of Muslim decline rather than on its core causes. Ben Nabi's dynamic framework explains the reasons behind decline and the ways to progress through the interaction between ideas, individuals, and objects. Ideas have a central place in Ben Nabi's thinking; they are vital in understanding the current crisis of the Muslim individual and of modern civilization in general. He distinguishes between two types of ideas: correct and effective. An idea could be correct but ineffective, and likewise, an idea might be effective but not correct. The mission of the Muslim in the last part of the twentieth century, according to Ben Nabi, is to transform the correct idea into an effective one and the effective idea into a correct one. This way, civilization will maintain a healthy balance. In order for the Muslim individual to achieve this task, he must reconstruct himself internally, that is, he must change the conditions of "colonizability," and then elevate himself to the high standards of civilization. Thus, Ben Nabi's ideas do not confine themselves to the realm of theory, but are meant to be reflected in the behavior and practices of Muslims.[13]

Abdel Latif Abada, a professor at Amir Abdel Qadir Islamic University and a student of Ben Nabi, summarized the effects of Ben Nabi's weekly meetings on the future of the Islamic movement in Algeria. According to Abada, three active currents evolved from the meetings. The first was a theoretical or intellectual trend concerned with the idea of change and the conditions for realizing it. The second focused on simplifying the Islamic doctrines and disseminating knowledge about the different aspects of modern Islamic thought among the Algerian population. This was achieved by holding annual seminars for Islamic thought, that, according to Abada, began in 1968 at the initiative of Ben Nabi himself. The third trend took the form of an active movement to spread Islamic ideals and practices. It began from the students' mosque at the university campus, which Ben Nabi helped establish in 1968 during his tenure at the University of Algiers.[14] The group that formed around the students' mosque (and later became known as the Student Mosque group) became an active nucleus that in the mid-1970s played an important role in the evolution of the Islamic movement in Algeria.

Mobilization and Recruitment: 1970s

A remarkable characteristic that distinguishes the Islamic movement in Algeria from its counterparts in Tunisia and Morocco is the diversity of its currents and the clear continuity of its historical roots. This continuity has been maintained through the remaining scholars of Ben Badis's association, al-Qiyam Association, and Malik Ben Nabi. The 1970s witnessed the formation of Islamic political groups, particularly al-Jama`a al-Islamiyya bi al-Jaza'ir (the Jaz'ara Trend) and other nascent organizations, mainly influenced by the Muslim Brothers of Egypt, that later became known as Harakat al-Mujtam`a al-Islami (HAMAS) and al-Nahda Party.

The Jaz'ara Trend

Al-Jama`a al-Islamiyya bi al-Jaza'ir is the actual name of what became termed as the Jaz'ara trend. The term jaz'ara was coined by outsiders, particularly Mahfouz Nahnah and his group, to distinguish al-Jama`a from other movements that maintained links with the Egyptian Muslim Brothers.[15] The term is also used to describe the group of students and university professors who were influenced by Malik Ben Nabi. The names of the founding members of the group, primarily university professors, became known only in the late 1980s and included Rashid Benissa, al-Tijani Boujelkha, Moustapha Brahmi, Muhammad Said, Moulai Said, Abdel Razzaq Rajjam, and others. Many of them have played and are still playing a significant role in the FIS or the Armed Islamic Group (GIA). The Student Mosque group began its activities in the university and from there evolved into an intellectual and activist trend. Al-Jama`a's members lectured on Islamic issues at the country's high schools, educational institutes, and mosques. As they gathered strength, they formed a student movement, "the Revolutionary Students," which was led by one of Ben Nabi's students, Rashid Benissa. They attempt to counter the influence of the leftists students at the university. This nascent group adopted a strategy of "clandestine organization and public propagation." In other words, the names of the group's leadership and members were kept from the authorities in order to avoid harassment while engaging in public activities that focused on cultural and intellectual aspects of Islam. These activities included the establishment of mosques throughout the country's universities, participating in the annual conferences on Islamic thought (held since the 1960s at the university campus and academic institutes) and holding Islamic book exhibits. Al-Jama`a insisted on avoiding any confrontation with the regime during the 1970s in order to achieve certain objectives: recruiting and preparing a well-educated Islamic elite; forming a popular base through advocating Islamic doctrines as a way of life; infiltrating the educational and state institutions; and establishing a stronghold in the country's mosques, particularly the free ones.[16] The group seized the opportunity of the public discussions occasioned by the draft of the national charter in 1976 and the nation-wide forums held for that purpose to disseminate their own views. They displayed the incompatibility between Islam and socialism, and focused on Islam as an alternative to the state's proposed ideological orientation. Al-Jama`a avoided any confrontation with the regime throughout the process by not expressing their rejection or acceptance of the draft and focusing mainly on advancing their Islamic argument on its articles. By the early 1980s, the members of the Jama`a felt strong enough to participate in the student elections and, indeed, won most of the seats.[17]

The Algerian Muslim Brothers: Hamas and al-Nahda

The influence of the Muslim Brothers in Algeria is reflected in two parties: Hamas and al-Nahda. The origins of Hamas date back to the mid-seventies, when its founder, Shaykh Mahfouz Nahnah began his career of Islamic activism. Nahnah, a professor of religious sciences at the University of Algiers, was born in 1942 in Blida. He was educated at one of the schools established by the Messali's MTLD, and graduated from the Algerian university with a degree in Arabic Language and Literature in 1970. He participated in the establishment of the student mosque.

Nahnah was influenced at an early age by the ideas of the Muslim Brothers. The influence of the Muslim Brothers was introduced to Algeria through some members of the association of Scholars such as Shaykh Na`im al-Nu`aimi, who had contacts with the Brothers while he was staying in Egypt, and al-Fadeel al-Wartlani, who had contacts with the Brothers after Algeria became independent. Several Egyptian teachers were employed during the 1960s and 1970s at the country's educational institutes and many of them were associated with the Muslim Brothers.[18] Nahnah studied the literature of the Egyptian Muslim Brothers and introduced it to his audience during his lectures and preaching. In the mid-1960s he began forming an organization that would work for the establishment of an Islamic state in Algeria. Based on the Brothers' experience, the new organization focused on the education and socialization of the individuals of society. The first phase, which lasted from 1964 to 1975, was a clandestine one dedicated to the recruitment and socialization of the group's core leadership. As state socialism began to acquire deeper manifestations in the country's laws and institutions—the Agricultural Revolution Law of 1971, the proposed Personal Status Code of the same year, the process of nationalization, and the Charter of 1976—the group emerged publicly under the name of "*al-Muwahidun*" (Believers in One God).

In fact, many Islamic groups found an opportunity in the nation-wide discussions of the draft of the Charter to express their anti-socialist sentiments and emphasize the Islamic ideals among the public, particularly since the draft neglected to contain a statement making Islam the state religion. Whether this was a mere oversight or a deliberate omission, it was interpreted by Islamists as a stark example of the regime's indifference to Islam and of the influence of Marxist and leftist elements on the draft of the charter and in the state administration. It was indeed an opportune moment to mobilize and alert the people and criticize the regime's policy towards Islam. Contrary to the position of al-Jama`a, which preferred to avoid confrontation with the regime by declaring its outright public opposition to the draft of the Charter, Nahnah and his group took a different course. They saw this occasion as an opportunity to declare themselves publicly and seek direct confrontation with the regime. The group issued a public statement that was signed by "al-Muwahidun" and addressed to President Boumedienne.

In its statement, which was presented as an open letter to the president, the group staged a scathing criticism of the current policies of the regime and articulated several demands. It rejected the Charter altogether as a creation of communists and a means to institutionalize an already illegitimate regime. It refused the adoption of socialism as the state ideology and its doctrines of nationalization, the dictatorship of the proletariat, and class conflict. It also criticized the infiltration of communist elements in the state administration and the impromptu policies of the regime in the different branches of government. The statement, on the other hand, included the group's demands for adopting Islam as a way of life and as the basis of legislative, economic, and political systems in society. Immediately after issuing their statement, some members of the group were arrested, including Nahnah who was tried and sentenced to 15 years in prison. Following the death of Boumedienne and the change of the system, Nahnah was granted a presidential pardon and released in 1980. In February 1989, Nahnah formed a social and cultural society, Jam`iyyat al-Irshad wa al-Islah (the Association of Guidance and Reform), which after the adoption of a new constitution permitting the formation of political association, became a political party in November 1990 under the name of Harakat al-Mujtama` al-Islami (the Movement of the Islamic Society), with the Arabic acronym Hamas.[19] Hamas's constituency consists of students, teachers, and professionals and is spread throughout the country. The results of the 1991 legislative elections demonstrate that Hamas has some degree of popularity since it secured 450,000 votes.

As a new political party, Hamas devised a political program under the title "Islam is the Solution." In this program, it explained the reasons behind its formation of an Islamic political party, its objectives, the current problems in the country, and its platform on the different aspects of society. The program viewed the post-independence period as characterized by the adoption of imported ideologies that contradict the religion and values of the Algerian nation; the authoritarian style of government and absence of consultation, dialogue, and transparency; the conflict of the various trends/wings within the system at the expense of stability, development, and national interest; the absence of a good example and the adoption of regionalism and personal loyalty, instead of merit, integrity, and ability, in assigning responsibility; the lack of confidence between the people and the government as a result of totalitarianism, tyranny, corruption, and the exploitation of influence to achieve personal, regional, and party gains; the stark failure of the socialist system in industry, agriculture, and culture; and the adoption of an educational and cultural system that ignored the cultural values of the people and its blessed struggle (for liberation). The program prescribed specific reforms for the political and constitutional system; the economy; scientific research and technological development; education; social system; cultural and information policy; the army and military affairs; and foreign policy. The program emphasized that the party's approach to change be based on gradualism, objectivity, and realism. It was a comprehensive program that suggested specific solutions for the various problems in society. It also reflected moderation by accepting the popular achievements of the past and by not attempting to impose its alternatives on the rest of the society.[20]

Harakat al-Nahda al-Islamiyya

The evolution of al-Nahda Party followed to a large extent the same course as that of Hamas. Like Hamas, it dates back to the mid-1970s. It was founded in 1974 as al-Jama`a al-Islamiyya (The Islamic Group) on the university campus in Constantine by Shaykh Abdullah Jaballah, who was a law student at the time. Jaballah was born in 1956 in Skdida, in eastern Algeria, and was imprisoned twice in 1982 and 1985, for one and a half years and fourteen months, respectively, for his participation in the events of 1982 at the Algiers University campus and for his Islamic activities. In its initial phase, Jaballah's group was secretive and thus remained limited in influence until the mid-1980s. The members of the group focused their activities on the students (public lectures, exhibits, and camps) and at the mosques (speeches and sessions). Regarding the influence of the Egyptian Muslim Brothers on the movement, Jaballah acknowledged that "our movement adopts the method of the Muslim Brothers for social change. This method is based on education and gradualism in presenting the comprehensive perspectives of Islam. Such perspectives consider religion as a system of beliefs, worship, morality, and a way of life and reject the separation between these aspects."[21] When the regime permitted the establishment of non-political association in 1987, the group became public and in December 1988 named itself The Nahda Association for Social and Cultural Reform. And when the new constitution of 1989 approved the formation of political associations, Jaballah's group was announced in December 1990 as a political party under the name of *Harakat al-Nahda al-Islamiyya*. Al-Nahda draws support from students, teachers, and professionals. Despite its presence in 38 of the 48 *wilayas*[22] (provinces), it remains more influential in the eastern parts of the country.

Addressing issues similar to those of the political program of Hamas, al-Nahda's program is less specific and reflects a general reformist outlook. The preamble of the program highlights the Algerian people's crisis of confidence:

> The only way to address this problem is through restoring the confidence of the Algerian citizen in himself, his system, and his leadership. The resolution of the crises of society and the achievement of progress require a comprehensive and realistic approach, a wise and firm leadership, and a righteous society confident in its leadership, approach and system and cognizant of its rights and responsibilities. These conditions are best met

not through changing the members of the parliament but by [changing] the constitution.

The program then goes on to detail al-Nahda's views on the aspects that need reform on the political, economic, social, cultural and educational, informational, and legal levels. Al-Nahda's program can be distinguished by its emphasis on, among others things, the issues of independence, national unity, sovereignty of God and the authority of the people, and the protection of individual and public rights.[23]

To sum up, several new Islamic organizations began to emerge during the 1970s. Al-Jama'a al-Islamiyya bi al-Jaza'ir in the universities, Jaballah's group in the east, and Nahnah's group throughout the country have been the main active groups, focusing on the mobilization and recruitment of advocates of Islamic doctrines as the basis for the reconstruction of society. By the end of the decade, other Islamic groups, although marginal ones, began to emerge and were influenced by foreign currents such as the Egyptian-style al-Takfir wa al-Hijra, the Jihad, the liberation party and the salafi movements.

Political Ascent: 1980s

In September 1989, Chadli Benjedid's regime approved the formation of the Islamic Salvation Front (FIS) as a political party. This raised concerns not only among secular parties in Algeria but in all the North African countries, which have adamantly refused to recognize their Islamic opposition. The secular opposition and many western analysts insisted on the unconstitutionality of the formation of the FIS as a political party. This argument became more vocal particularly after the FIS had won the local elections of June 1990. Some even interpreted it as a conspiracy between the regime, particularly Benjedid and his government, and the FIS in order to weaken the FLN.

Constitutionality

Despite the frequently repeated argument that the Algerian Constitution does not permit the formation of religious political parties, the fact is that the 1989 Constitution does not address this issue specifically, nor state any qualifications with regards to the conditions of who has or has not the right to form political associations. Article forty of the Constitution stipulates that "the right to form political associations with a political character is recognized. This right cannot be invoked to attack the fundamental liberties, national unity, territorial integrity, the independence of the country, and the sovereignty of the people."[24]

It is the Code of Associations with a Political Character of July 5, 1989, and not the Constitution, which addresses this issue. According to Article 5 of the Code:

> Any association with a political character cannot found its creation or its actions on a base and/or objectives that include:
> - sectarian or regionalist practices, feudalism and nepotism;
> - the establishment of relations of exploitation and links of dependency;
> - a practice contrary to the Islamic morals and to the values of the Revolution of November 1, 1954.
>
> Within this frame, the association with a political character, moreover, cannot found its creation or its action exclusively on a confessional, linguistic, regionalist base, affiliation to a specific sex, to a specific race or to a specific professional determinant.[25]

The language of the article raises two points. The first is the use of the word "confessional," and not religious, as a restriction on the formation of a political association. The second is the use of the world "exclusively" as another restriction. In light of the language of the article, the FIS cannot be prohibited on either ground because it is not a confessional party nor has it based its platform on an "exclusively" confessional or religious basis. Moreover, the issue of the unconstitutionality of the formation of the FIS was not raised in regards to the other less successful Islamic political parties; nor against Berber-based parties, which were also covered by the restrictions of the article. Even if this article is broadly interpreted to exclude the FIS, then it has to be universally implemented. This means that the more than ten Islamic political parties, such as Hamas and al-Nahda, and the Berber-based parties, such as Hussein Ait Ahmed's Socialist Forces Front (FFS) and Said Saidi's Rally for Culture and Democracy (RCD) should be considered illegal and therefore be banned. Of course, this issue has never been raised or even contemplated. From a procedural point of view, the FIS applied for recognition as a political party in March 1989, one month after the adoption of the new Constitution which does not state any restrictions on the formation of political associations, and before the issuance of the Code of Associations. It received approval in September of the same year. In any case, the FIS was dissolved on the basis of articles 33, 34, and 35 of the 1989 code, which addressed violence, while article 5 was never invoked.[26]

The Road to October 1988

Upon coming to power in 1979, President Chadli Benjedid introduced a number of gradual political and economic changes to the system. Some of these were meant to consolidate the authority of the new president, while others were to relieve the burdens of a socialist economy. These measures included the restructuring of decision-making bodies in the ruling party, shifts of military commanders, pardoning political detainees and exiles, and the partial liberalization of the economy. His efforts, however, were not far reaching enough to redress the problems of the past nor prevent new ones from arising. The state was still dominated by the traditional triad of party, army, and administration. Popular discontent began to mount as a result of shortages of basic commodities, increase of prices, the conspicuous consumption of segments benefiting from the relaxation of socialist measures, increasing unemployment, and party indifference and ineffectiveness. By the mid-1980s it became evident that the entire system needed a thorough overhaul and restructuring. In September 1988, only one month prior to the mass riots, Benjedid mounted scathing criticism of the officials in the party and the administration for resisting reform and, while reaffirming his adherence to the FLN as an institution, expressed his unwillingness to be committed to individuals and groups with rigid ideas. From the beginning, Benjedid's attempts were met by opposition from the party's old guards, stagnant bureaucracy, and conservative military officers who perceived a threat to their privileges and patronage in society. Benjedid now appeared more determined to go on with the reforms, but he needed a trigger, which he indeed found in the popular discontent that was manifested during the October riots.

On October 4-7, thousands of demonstrators, mainly young people, in major cities all over the country protested the harsh economic conditions and the deterioration of the standard of living resulting from falling oil prices, failing socialist economic policies, mismanagement, and widespread corruption. The rioters attacked the symbols of authority, government offices, state-owned stores, and the headquarters of the ruling party. It became clear that the FLN's now vague ideology of social egalitarianism benefited only the few and failed to attract the country's youth, who constituted the majority of the population.

Benjedid called in the People's National Army (ANP) to put down the unrest and maintain public order. A state of emergency was declared and the country was placed under military rule. The Algerian military used harsh and repressive measures against the discontented youth. In seven days, the armed forces killed 500 demonstrators, mostly teenagers, wounded many more, and arrested thousands. The crisis, although placing the army under harsh criticism for their brutal tactics, brought the military back to the center of authority and reinstated it as the guarantor of the continuity of the regime and protector of stability and public order.

The October 1988 riots represented a clear protest against the mandate of the ruling party and the monopoly of power by a small government, party, and military elite. Benjedid seized the opportunity to introduce more ambitious and tangible reforms. He fired the secretary-general of the FLN Central Committee, the head of the internal security, and the prime minister, and reshuffled some army commanders. He gradually began to dissociate himself from the party as he relinquished his post as its secretary general. This, in fact, was an initial signal that the country was moving towards a multi-party system.

In February 1989 a new constitution was approved. The new constitution represented a real break from past ideology and policies as it separated the party from the state, allowed the formation of political associations, and dropped the state's commitment to socialism. A month later, senior army officers, in order to separate themselves from party politics, resigned from the central committee of the FLN, preserving, however, their right to defend "the superior interests of the nation and the free choice of the people," and consequently maintaining their status as major arbiters in the system.

The constitutional reforms reshaped the political landscape of Algeria. Following the approval of a new law on the formation of parties on July 2, 1989, new opposition parties mushroomed challenging the monopoly of the FLN over power. To advance the political and economic program of his government, Benjedid's new reformist prime minister, Mouloud Hamrouche, attempted to change the party from within by placing his supporters in the party's central committee and politburo. This tactic, however, met little success as the party old guards, such as Abdel Aziz Boutaflika, Belaid Abdel Salam, Muhammad Charif Messadia, Muhammad Saleh Yahyaoui, and Kasdi Merbah, managed to get elected to the central committee following the special party congress of November 1989. Ignoring the changes taking place in society and unable to revive the FLN, they expressed harsh criticism of the government's programs and portrayed them as betraying the Algerian martyrs and the values of the revolution. Hamrouche, with the support of Benjedid, was now determined to disgrace and discredit the FLN and its old veterans and responded by unleashing a powerful contender to their continuing domination.

The Rise of Abbasi Madani

The FIS was officially recognized as a political party in September 1989. Under the leadership of Abbasi Madani and Ali Belhaj, it succeeded in three years in gaining wide popularity, winning two elections, and becoming close to assuming power. There are, of course, various reasons for the success of the FIS and a long history that precedes these three years. Madani had become publicly known in November 1982 during the events of the student clashes at the main campus of the university of Algiers. He was born in 1931 in Sidi Uqbah, in southeastern Algeria. The son of a religious teacher and imam, Madani committed the Qur'an to memory at an early age. He then received his traditional Arabic and Islamic education in Biskra at one of the free schools of the Association of Algerian Scholars.

Madani was a former member of the Messali's MTLD and its Secret Organization (OS). He then joined the National Liberation Front (FLN) in 1954 and participated in one of the earliest armed operations against the French occupation. This led to his arrest and imprisonment for eight years by the French. Following his release, Madani resumed his religious and political activism through the al-Qiyam Association, before it was outlawed in 1970.

Despite his Islamic orientations, Madani maintained his membership in the FLN. He was elected in 1969 as a member of the Party's Popular Council for Bab al-Ouad district, receiving 67.32 percent of the electoral vote. In 1974 he resigned from the party as he grew increasingly critical of the FLN's socialist orientation. Deciding to continue his education, he obtained degrees in philosophy and psychology. In 1978 he received a British doctoral degree in comparative education and was appointed professor at the University of Algiers.[27]

After student elections which Islamist students won in November 1982, violent clashes erupted between the Islamist and communist students at the main campus of the University of Algiers. The authorities interfered immediately, arresting Islamist students and closing the campus mosque as well as other student mosques throughout the country. These measures provoked some religious scholars and activists, namely Abbasi Madani, then professor at the university, and shaykhs Sahnoun and Sultani, to call for a public gathering at the University campus. Madani delivered a speech before 30,000 demonstrators, in which he protested the closure of the mosques and the violent suppression of the students. At the end of the event, Madani, along with shaykhs Sultani and Sahnoun, signed a fourteen-point statement, known as "The Statement of Advice," in which they criticized the secular policies of the state and demanded the promotion of Islam in government and society.

Twenty-nine people, including Madani, Sultani, and Sahnoun, were arrested and tried. They were charged with forming and participating in subversive organizations seeking to destabilize the state; printing and distributing statements harmful to the national interest; and agitating and staging demonstrations. Madani was imprisoned for two years, while Sultani and Sahnoun were placed under house arrest due to their advanced age. After his release in 1984, Madani continued his Islamic activities by lecturing at mosques and universities.

The events at the university were significant in many respects. It was the first time that an Islamic protest had taken a public dimension since the authoritarian regime of Boumedienne. The leaders of the Islamic opposition came to a realization that they could mobilize large numbers and press for demands. After all, the demonstrations had started with a call from Madani to which thousands responded from different parts of the capital, a tactic that would characterize Madani's style in the future. There were 150 organizers; people dispersed in a remarkable order and peace despite their huge number. Most importantly, the 1982 events were a meeting of three generations representing different currents: the generation of Ben Badis's associates with their religious and historic legitimacy; the generation of the war of liberation, represented by Madani; and the new generation of independence, represented by the students and the Jama'a al-Islamiyya at the university. This alliance would continue to be a source of strength for the FIS.

The Rise of Ali Belhaj

It was a similar event, though on a much larger and more violent scale, that marked the emergence of Shaykh Ali Belhaj as a popular figure. On October 10, 1988, the sixth day of the riots, Ali Belhaj, the young imam of al-Sunna mosque at Bab al-Ouad in the capital, called for a peaceful march, which attracted thousands of participants, to protest the killings of the rioters by the government forces and demand immediate delivery of the bodies of the victims.

A son of a martyr of the war of liberation, Ali Belhaj was born in 1956 in Tunis. His family was originally from the desert city of Ourgala in the south of Algeria. He received an entirely Arabic education at Islamic schools in Algiers and became a secondary school teacher. He was educated by prominent religious scholars such as Abdel Latif Sultani, Ahmed Sahnoun, and Omar Arabaoui. His influences included the writings of the salafi scholars, particularly Ibn Taymiyya and Ibn Qayim al-Juzaiyya, and by the writings of Hassan al-Banna and the Muslim Brothers. Belhaj started his Islamic activities in the 1970s. He was imprisoned from 1983 to 1987 for his membership in the Bouyali armed group (to be discussed later).[28] After his release, he became prayer leader in the mosques of al-Sunna and al-Qubba in the capital. Belhaj's thorough religious knowledge, modest life style, and remarkable oratory skills, particularly in addressing the depressed segments of society, enabled him to gain popularity and build a large constituency of followers.[29]

Many consider Madani to represent the moderate face of FIS while Belhaj reflects its radical side. The Algerian journalist Ihmeda al-Ayachi made a revealing comparison between the two leaders. Due to his long experience in politics, Madani seems more compromising and more tolerant. Ayachi sees Ali Belhaj as not being on good terms with most political forces in Algeria and abroad, the regime, many of the other Islamists (the Algerian Muslim Brothers, the Takfir and Hijra, the shi`i stream, the Jihad Group, the Islamic Liberation Party, and others), the democrats, the Saudis, Iran, and the West. The reason, Ayachi explains, lies in Belhaj's idealism, "revolutionary purity," and reliance on the spontaneity of populism and not on tactical concessions.[30]

The points of difference in the formation and experience of the two leaders of FIS should be emphasized. While Madani is multi-cultural with regards to his educational background and training, Belhaj is uni-cultural, and is moreover influenced by the salafi doctrine which stresses the purity of Islam. Madani's long experience in the MTLD, the OAS, the FLN, and other organizations has made him more of a politician than Belhaj, whose early activist experience was with Bouyali's group in the early 1980s, which sought to change the system through armed struggle. In an interview, Belhaj, who has no official leadership position in the

FIS, explains that he is "a man of religion and not a statesman."[31] This means that Belhaj sees politics from the viewpoint of the Islamic *shari`a* and not through tactical gains. This could explain his views on several issues, the most controversial of which is democracy. Commenting on democracy, Belhaj has stated, "some people might think that when I launch this fierce campaign against democracy that I glorify dictatorship and despotism. The truth is that I do not believe in either of them. I do not believe in despotism the same way I do not believe in democracy." Giving the rationale behind this judgment, Belhaj continues, "western democracy has revealed its true nature when the West dominated the Muslim countries. It suppressed the Muslim peoples and squeezed their resources." Speaking about democracy as practiced by post-colonial Arab elites, Belhaj states, "The truth is that those elites that adopted democracy for example were worse in practice and effect than the score of men who have distorted religion when they unfairly ruled in its name."[32] In his book, *The Decisive Statement on Confronting the Aggression of Rulers*, which Belhaj wrote while in prison and addressed to the members of the Supreme Court, he elucidates the principles of Islamic government. He divided his over 300-page book into six main parts: the necessity of political action to establish the Islamic state; the principles of the political system in Islam and of the selection of rulers; the main features of despotic and dictatorship systems; the resistance to (autocratic) rulers and systems in the West; the resistance to rulers in the Islamic perspective; and he defends the rights of the *mujahidin* to resist the current rulers. According to Belhaj, the political system in Islam is based on consultation, which is the source of legitimacy; people's free choice of rulers; the accountability of the rulers before the nation; and the rule that the state cannot claim loyalty unless it is a legitimate one.[33] Based on these principles, Belhaj asserts that:

> The concept that should be widely spread in the Muslim countries in general is that the seizure of power is not acceptable, even if the usurper plans to rule in accordance with the *shari`a*. The only legitimate way [for government] is through the choice of the people. There should be no hereditary ascension, usurpation of power, repression, or dictatorship. The nation should resist anyone who pursues other means [than the choice of the people] in order to preserve its integrity as a nation and avoid becoming a toy in the hands of oppressors.[34]

The Emergence of FIS

The remarkably quick rise of the FIS can be partly explained by the style which it has assumed since its formation. The FIS has adopted the tactic of articulating demands and pressing for their attainment through the mobilization of the "street." Benjedid's regime adopted the strategy of allowing the FIS to advance in the hope that they would overextend themselves. Both sides, the FIS and Benjedid, however, overlooked an important actor, the army.

In March 1989, the FIS applied for recognition as a political party, and its request was granted the following September. As a political "front," it encompassed elements from most of the Islamic organizations that have existed since the mid-1970s. Specifically, there were three main trends within the FIS: the Islamic populist stream, led by Abbasi Madani; the salafi, led by Ali Belhaj; and al-Jama`a al-Islamiyya bi al-Jaza'ir, led by Muhammad Said and Abdel Razzaq Rajjam. Some former members of marginal groups such as al-Takfir wa al-Hijra, al-Jihad, and Bouyali's also joined the front. Some of them were represented in the FIS's Shura (consultative) Council, namely al-Hashmi Sahnoun, who is considered the godfather of al-Takfir group.

Many of the statements and practices of these groups, which maintained their independence from the FIS, later became a source of embarrassment for the FIS as they were used, particularly by the regime, the Francophone press in Algeria, and the French media, to discredit the FIS. They raised controversial and divisive issues such as the legality of participating in elections and the wearing of the veil. They behaved in an extreme way, such as when they attacked bars and unveiled women. On several occasions, the FIS expressed annoyance that these groups insisted on maintaining their independence and refused to join. This led to the objection raised by the FIS leaders, especially Madani, who repeatedly declared that the FIS would not be responsible for such extremist acts.[35] Hamas and al-Nahda refused to join as organizations in the FIS. Nonetheless, some of their members joined on an individual basis. Prominent names that became known at later stages were Abdel Qadir Hachani, Rabih Kebir, Ali Jaddi, and Abdel Qadir Boukhamkham, all from al-Nahda.

The swift formation and announcement of the FIS as a political party was a source of disagreement among the various Islamic movements. Hamas and Nahda always felt that the FIS leaders adopted a de facto policy with them. They criticized the FIS for rushing to declare itself as a political party without prior coordination with them and carrying out demonstrations without considering their views. They also sensed that the FIS wanted them to acknowledge that it was the most popular party and in control of the "street." Being older and more organizationally tight than the FIS, these parties, particularly Hamas, were not convinced that the FIS was the most popular nor the strongest. Some feared that the FIS was being drawn into a direct confrontation with the military; or, even if it came to power, that this would create a situation where the West would blockade Algeria financially and economically—as it did in the case of Iran and Sudan—and then give it an excuse to claim the Islamic solution was a failure.[36] After several failed attempts to unite all these movements under one political party, Hamas and Nahda later applied separately to the authorities as political parties.

In less than one year, FIS appeared to be the most popular party in Algeria. Its membership base consisted of 3 million followers from various segments of society.[37] As a party, FIS's structure was based on the country's provinces. Each province elected its local consultative council to manage the party's local affairs and elect representatives to the FIS Central Consultative Council. The FIS's Consultative Council consisted of 40 members headed by Abbasi Madani. The Council was the decision-making body of the FIS and approved decisions by consensus. Officially, FIS's vice-president was Shaykh Ben Azouz Ben Zebda[38], and not Ali Belhaj who was a member of the Council. Yet Belhaj was rightly considered as the second man in the FIS due to his popularity and influence. The FIS had several sets of committees at the national, local, and community levels. Some were assigned general tasks such as coordination and organization, information and propagation, and foreign relations. Others, at the community level, were technical cadres in charge of coordinating FIS's activities at the mosques, schools, markets, or providing social services like marriage assistance and furnishing emergency and relief supplies. The FIS's activities were also structured along four specific sectors: women, unions, youth, and culture.[39] The FIS's mobilization and organizational skills appeared very clearly in the demonstration of April 20, 1990, in which one million Algerians participated.

The FIS presented its political program as a draft to be voted on after public debate. Very detailed and comprehensive, the program was carefully phrased in a language that would reconcile the orientations of the different currents within the front, and meantime, would appear attractive to non-followers, without compromising the Islamic commitment of the FIS. On the political level, the FIS "takes into consideration the realities of the phase of the multi-party system so that every party can exercise its right to contribute to the process of reform starting at the National Assembly, Provincial Councils, and Municipal Councils." In its view of the nature of politics, the program states that the FIS adopts the Islamic concept of religio-politics (*al-siyasa al-shar`iyya*), which is based on persuasion and not coercion. To resolve the contradictions resulting from the adoption of imported ideologies, the FIS endeavors to eliminate authoritarianism by adopting the concept of shura; and to end political, economic, and social monopoly by adopting the principle of equal political, economic, and social opportunity. To avoid individualistic tendencies, nepotism, and selfishness, the FIS guarantees freedom of expression and encourages self-criticism. The program defines FIS's style of action as "demand and apply pressure." In other words, the party would articulate its demands to the regime, and if these demands were not met, it would mobilize the people to achieve them. The program then states specific and comprehensive measures for reforms in almost every aspect of state and society: the executive branch, military establishment, internal security, information, economy (agriculture, industry, trade, and financial policy), education, administration, and the judiciary.[40]

An Attempt at Unity: The League of Islamic Call

The multiplicity of Islamic movements, inter-relations, and possible rivalry became major points of concern for Algerian Islamists. In an attempt to coordinate the activities of the FIS and other Islamic movements, the League of Islamic Call was established in March 1989 under the leadership of Shaykh Ahmed Sahnoun, who is highly respected by all Islamic forces in Algeria, and included the leadership of the main Islamic movements. The League was intended to become an umbrella organization and the point of reference for the various Islamic movements. In several meetings of the parties, it was suggested that the FIS become the political representative of all the Islamic movements, who would, in turn, continue their individual activities on the educational and social levels. In return, the FIS would change its name, abide by the decision of the League, and open itself to all qualified cadres and leadership of the other parties. During periods of elections, inter-party competition would be avoided and all candidates would run under a unified FIS list. The League could not get the parties to agree on these points and the possibility of early unified Islamic political action collapsed.[41]

The League, however, continues to exist. Its most noteworthy activity was the organization of an Islamist women's demonstration on December 21, 1989. In response to a campaign of Algerian feminists, calling for a revision of the personal status code that was derived from the Islamic *shari`a*, the League's head, Shaykh Sahnoun, called for a demonstration of Algerian women to express their view on the issue. More than half a million women—veiled and unveiled—responded to the call and gathered in front of the Algerian parliament. The gathering, in which members of all the Islamic movements participated, raised the slogan of the Association of the Scholars—Islam is our religion, Arabic our language, and Algeria our fatherland. One woman delivered a statement reflecting the feeling that these Muslim women's national identity was threatened. She said that "the time of indifference is now over, particularly since Islam is being targeted by aberrant groups that try to deceive the people and the world by claiming that they represent the Algerian women. We want to teach these bankrupted elements a lesson. The Algerian woman is proud of her religion and satisfied with it as a way of life, every aspect of it, and would like it to be as such in all aspects of the society." [42] In a statement which the demonstrators delivered to the parliament, they reaffirmed their commitment to Islamic values and called for the implementation of the *shari`a*.

From the Municipality to the Islamic State

The FIS sought to use the democratic openings provided by the 1989 Constitution to the maximum. Among the opposition parties, the FIS appeared as the most organized, popular, and ready to compete in the country's first multi-party municipal elections. Eleven parties and 1,365 candidates on independent lists competed for control over 1,539 local councils and 48 provincial councils. The elections were boycotted by the Socialist Forces Front (FFS), a secular Berber party headed by Hussein Ait Ahmed, and other secular parties that were not confident of their success in the process. Though government officials expected the FIS to win not more than 30 percent of the votes, the Islamic party scored a decisive victory, capturing 55.42 percent of the electoral votes and managing to gain control over 853 local councils and 32 provinces. The FIS achieved a sweeping victory in the four major Algerian cities: the capital Algiers, Oran, Constantine, and Annaba. Its candidates even won in Benjedid's home province of al-Tarf, and well-to-do districts in the capital, such as Hudre and al-Biar, where FLN leaders reside. The FLN won 31.64 percent of the votes and took 487 local councils and 14 provinces. Independents won 6.87 percent of the votes and control over 106 municipalities; the Rally for Culture and Democracy, a Berber secular party, won 5.56 percent of the votes and control over 87 local councils. Shocked by the FIS's remarkable performance, the FLN announced that it "rejects all attempts to bring Islam back to an era of charlatanism and myth and to make it an instrument of demagoguery and political opportunism."[43]

The FIS's victory exacerbated the conflicts within the FLN party and its relations with the regime. The FLN and government officials directed blame towards each other for the poor performance of the FLN. Hamrouche and members of his cabinet criticized the party for failing to reform itself and act as an independent opposition. The FLN leaders accused the regime of deliberate attempts to weaken the party. The FLN seemed to be falling apart. Large numbers of FLN's members deserted the party and joined the FIS. Some FLN members with Islamic tendencies had already run on the FIS lists during the local elections. Hamrouche and four members of his cabinet resigned from the party's politburo. Rabah Bitat, one of Algeria's historic chiefs and a co-founder of the party, relinquished his post as the president of the National People's Assembly in protest against Hamrouche's economic policies. Former Prime Minister Abdel Hamid al-Ibrahimi resigned from the FLN protesting the lack of democracy within the party, and Kasdi Merbah left to establish his own party.

Since its legalization as a political party in 1989, the FIS has demonstrated a remarkable ability to attract large segments of the Algerian population and to develop impressive organizational skills. It used an appealing language to mobilize followers. The FIS evolved as an opposition force and an alternative to the FLN and its secular and socialist orientations which for thirty years had bankrupted the country and alienated a large segment of the population, particularly the youth (70 percent of Algeria's population is under the age of thirty) who had lost hope in the future and in the current leadership of the country. It perceived itself as capable of reinvigorating the potential of the population, without severing ties with the country's legacy of the war of liberation. Madani explained the message of FIS as follows:

The FIS emerged to rescue what the FLN has damaged since independence. It redeems history since November 1, [by setting as an objective] the establishment of a free independent Algerian state on the basis of Islamic principles. ... [As an organizational front,] the FIS is an umbrella for all the Islamic currents seeking a comprehensive program. It is non-confessional, non-sectarian, and not confined to specific entities. It is a front that extends all over the Algerian territory.[44]

The FIS demonstrated genuine interest in daily concerns and in the people's living conditions. It proposed a nationalistic discourse, rather than a purely religious or partisan one. It was the first opposition party that relentlessly criticized the widespread corruption in the system and insisted on equal opportunity, justice, honesty, and accountability—values much in demand in Algeria. The party's detailed program addressed the issues of housing, unemployment, and reinvigoration of the economy and proposed solutions to these problems. The FIS opposed a state-owned economy and proposed in its place a free-market one, where private initiative and equal opportunity are encouraged. It advocated lower taxes and substantial cuts in military spending and expressed willingness to cooperate with international companies in exploring the country's natural resources.

Through an extensive network of mosques, the FIS dispensed religious and socialization programs as well as welfare and social services rarely provided by the government. When an earthquake hit Algeria in 1989, FIS's trucks bearing the party logo were the first to reach the disaster-stricken scene and distribute food and medical supplies to the countryside. With more than three million followers, the party involved its members in voluntary activities, including collecting garbage, tutoring high school students, and offering medical care services for needy patients.

The FIS's leadership and inner core represents a new generation of Muslim activists. The majority of party officials are well-educated professionals. The FIS's leader, Abbasi Madani, is a university professor, with a doctoral degree from England. His deputy, Ali Belhaj, is a high school teacher. The provisional leader of the FIS, Abdel Qadir Hachani, is a petrochemical engineer and a Ph.D. candidate at a French university. Both Madani and Hachani are fluent in three languages and adequately exposed to other cultures. In both local and legislative elections, the FIS presented high caliber, educated candidates. Seventy-six percent of FIS's parliamentary candidates have postgraduate degrees. In one district in Algiers, of the 17 FIS candidates on its list, all but one were between the ages 25 and 35—in marked contrast to some of the aging members of the ruling party. The list included four engineers— two with doctoral degrees, three teachers, four accountants, one with a doctorate in physics, three administrators, and the rest were professionals. Once they actually took control of the local and provincial councils, the FIS initiated different development programs for each province to suit the provinces' specific conditions.

The municipal and provincial councils have limited powers and restricted authority in addressing the country's major economic and social problems. One observer considered the municipalities as "booby traps" that Benjedid's regime had set for the FIS.[45] Madani himself accused the FLN of adopting the policy of "scorched earth" before handing the municipalities over to FIS's elected officials.[46] Following FIS's victory at the local elections, the regime issued a barrage of laws stripping the municipalities of most of their authority. A new system of districts was created assuming many of the authorities of the municipalities. According to the new laws, the right of the municipalities, particularly at main cities, to appoint their staffs was relegated to the Interior Ministry. The municipalities were also deprived of their authority to distribute land, allocate housing opportunities, and carry out development programs without the approval of the central authorities. In addition, at the time of the FIS takeover, the municipalities were in poor financial and administrative condition. They depended entirely on the government for their funding. The budgets of many municipalities had severe deficits while others were in debt to the central government. They also suffered from clear mismanagement and corruption. Most positions were filled with FLN-appointees, who had no interest in seeing the FIS succeed. Many projects existed only on paper and were never implemented despite the allocation of funds. The municipalities also suffered from corrupt measures of distribution of housing, land lots and commercial licenses.

The FIS's elected local officials held a conference (November 14-16, 1990) to discuss the problems they faced and the means to address them. After reviewing the general conditions of their municipalities and the bureaucratic hurdles they faced, they marched to the president to deliver a statement of their demands. They called upon the regime to put an end to the partisan mentality in issuing laws, remove the bureaucratic restrictions placed on the authorities of the municipalities, provide special funding for immediate housing projects, and forgive the municipalities of their pre-existing debts.[47]

Despite the financial and administrative constraints posed by the FLN's central governors, who in many cases restrained some of the efforts and initiatives of FIS officials at the local councils, the FIS representatives managed to build an impressive legacy of tolerance and honest administration. In the city of Blida, for example, which came under FIS's control, incompetent FLN employees who had been hired for their party affiliation were not fired, but reshuffled. They were trained by FIS cadres to, among other things, use computers, build roads, and plan housing for senior citizens. Upon assuming control over the city council, FIS officials discovered that FLN officials had sold 70 plots of land around Blida that the municipality did not own. The FIS returned the land to its owners. The FIS officials established recreational programs for the young people and provided low interest loans to skilled workers who wanted to open private businesses. Immediately after coming to power, they opened a shelter for the homeless and a soup kitchen for the poor. The FIS party daily fed more than 120 walk-ins and 90 poor families. Before the center opened, many of these had been beggars on the streets.[48]

The performance of FIS-controlled municipalities was not all positive, however. While some municipalities focused on addressing the immediate problems of the people, others were more preoccupied with symbolic and moral issues such as closing down bars, prohibiting mixing at beaches, or imposing the veil. Madani admitted that some excesses were committed in a few local councils, but he attributed this to inexperience and enthusiasm rather than to a national FIS policy to enforce Islamic law instantaneously.[49]

It was FIS's appealing language and image of honest government that made even anti-FIS voters cast their votes for the Islamic party. When a Western-dressed student who opposed FIS's platform was asked for the reason she voted for the party's candidates, she replied that she did so because its leaders were "loyal and honest. ... Who but the FIS was strong enough to clean out the corruption and get the country moving again?"[50] For many young Algerians, who most likely would have stayed unemployed or gone to France to sweep Paris streets, the FIS offered hope and an opportunity for self-fulfillment.

Cutting FIS Down to Size

FIS's bitter experience at the municipalities made it more determined, if it wanted its platform to succeed, to change the parliament and put an end to the manipulation of laws. After a strong showing of his party at the local elections, Madani tried to appeal to other political forces in the country. While promising to eliminate official corruption, he stressed the moderate discourse of his party, assuring the Algerian public of the FIS's commitment to multi-party democracy, freedom of expression, individual and public liberties, and a continued cooperation with France and the West. He also promised that the FIS would respect the free choice of the Algerian people in any future election. In an interview to *al-Watan* newspaper, Madani stated, "we believe that pluralism is necessary for political development, because we are not angels. ... We are human and make mistakes, and we are prepared to impose ourselves on our people even when we are wrong. ... Pluralism is a guarantee of cultural wealth, and diversity is needed for any development. ... We are not tyrants, and we do not monopolize religion. Democracy as we understand it means pluralism, choice, and freedom."[51]

Persuaded by its massive victory, the FIS's leader, Abbasi Madani was convinced that the ruling party, in which he had once been a member during the liberation struggle against the French, had been shattered and had become too corrupt and incapable of leading the country. Calling the FLN the "party of failure," the FIS positioned itself as the only possible heir of the FLN and its secular elite. In fact, this kind of discourse was one point of FIS's strength. Paradoxically, the FIS did not cut links with the historical legacy of the FLN and Algeria's war of liberation. Madani repeatedly asserted that the FLN and the FIS are "two branches of the same origin, the history of Algeria till March 19, 1962. ... If the FLN goes back to its roots, it will find us there, and we will become one thing. If it returns to Islam and the revolutionary principles which it used to uphold, then we will undoubtedly converge. ... The FLN was destroyed when it lost its principles, abandoned them, and lost its leadership. It replaced its doctrines with imported ideologies, its men with opportunists. We and the FLN cannot meet together in this time of opportunism."[52] The FIS appealed to the Algerian people as the continuation of the war of liberation and the embodiment of the principles of the November 1, 1954 revolution. It always presented itself not as a political party, but as a front open to all Algerians. According to Madani, the FIS "is linked with November 1. The call of November 1 meant that we bear arms for the establishment of a free, independent Algerian state on the basis of Islamic principles. The FLN proceeded on these principles. But when it achieved victory, it no longer committed itself to them. An Algerian state was established on a socialist ideology."[53]

The FIS demanded the dissolution of the parliament, which was dominated by FLN deputies, and advocated new legislative elections in which all political parties would compete. The political confrontation began to escalate when the FLN-dominated parliament approved an electoral law that clearly favored the FLN. In an attempt to avoid a future defeat in the legislative elections, the party tried to redraw the electoral boundaries by disproportionately increasing the number of seats in rural and lightly populated areas where the FLN enjoyed popularity. The FIS accused the FLN of constituency gerrymandering, a complaint that was also voiced by other opposition parties. In a BBC interview, Abdel Hamid Mehri, the secretary general of the FLN, admitted that the election conditions were not fair. On May 25, 1991 Madani called for a general strike and peaceful marches—a right granted by the Algerian constitution—to pressure the government to review this law. Hamas and al-Nahda opposed the idea of the strike fearing that it would lead to a violent confrontation with the regime and the suppression of the Islamic movement.

The peaceful marches indeed turned into a violent confrontation on June 4, when the security forces opened fire on the demonstrators in one of the capital's main squares. With seven FIS members shot dead, Madani urged his followers to stop the demonstrations to avoid further bloodshed and a major confrontation with the army. The following day, Benjedid announced a four-month state of siege, fired his prime minister, and postponed the elections indefinitely. Following a June 7 meeting between Madani and the new prime minister, Sid Ahmed Ghozali, the FIS leaders called off the strike, after announcing that an agreement had been reached between the regime and the FIS. The regime agreed to review the controversial electoral law and to schedule presidential and legislative elections within six months.

The June riots reminded the army of its role as the final arbiter of power. Concerned about the growing influence of the FIS, military generals were determined to cut it down to size. Tension had already been growing between the army and the FIS before the June 1991 crisis. Prior to the local elections, the secretary general of the ministry of defense, Moustapha Challoufi, had announced that the army was "ready to intervene to protect the reforms" initiated by the government. *Majallat al-Jaysh*, an Army publication, was critical of the Islamists and their participation in the democratic process, considering them "a menace to the modern and developed democratic systems." To neutralize the army, FIS's followers raised slogans suggesting that the army supported the Islamic party's leader. When the army leadership issued a decree banning female Muslim doctors and nurses from wearing the veil in military hospitals, the FIS harshly criticized the secular orientation of some army leaders, particularly General Challoufi, who was married to a French woman. To restrict the participation of army officers and soldiers who might vote for the FIS in the local elections, the military leadership abruptly transferred the casting of votes for the first time from the military barracks to the district in which the soldier was registered.

After more than two weeks of calm following the end of the strike, violence broke out anew on June 25, when military forces broke into FIS-controlled municipal buildings to replace the party's symbols with those of the republic. The clashes resulted in the death of 8 FIS members. The army led a massive crackdown to weaken the FIS and break its structural organization: thousands of middle-level cadres and adherents were arrested throughout the country. On June 30, the party's leaders, Madani and Belhaj were arrested on charges of fomenting, organizing, triggering, and leading an armed conspiracy against the state security. Two days earlier, Madani had announced that his party would be obliged to call a *jihad* if the curfew did not end and the army did not withdraw its troops from the streets. The Algerian League for the Defense of Human Rights announced on July 7 that since the state of siege had been declared and the military had taken charge on June 4, eight thousand FIS followers had been arrested and three hundred killed. In a televised statement to the Algerian people on June 28, Ghozali strongly defended the army and the tactics it used to "defend the citizens' security which was threatened; to protect the institutions whose normal functioning was endangered; and to safeguard the future of democracy that some wanted to harm."[54]

FIS Splits

The May strike caused major splits within the FIS. Three trends emerged within the leadership of the party. The first, led by Hachmi Sahnoun (Head of FIS's Call and Guidance Committee), Said Guishi (Head of the Organization and Coordination Committee), Faqih Bashir, Ahmed Mrani, and Muhammad Karrar, declared their initial opposition to the strike and Madani's style of leadership. Some of them appeared on national television and issued a statement in which they accused Madani and Belhaj of not consulting the members of the Shura Council before staging the strike. They also met with Ghozali, who later appointed in his cabinet Said Guishi and Ahmed Mrani as minister of Local Administration and advisor to the prime minister, respectively. Both Bashir and Mrani were fired from the FIS's Shura Council. The second, headed by FIS's vice-president, Ben Azouz Ben Zebda, preferred to stay neutral and not express support or condemn the strike. The third trend was that of Madani and Belhaj who wanted to pursue their populist style and pressure the regime through the mobilization of the street. Following the arrest of Madani and Belhaj, the rifts between these trends became more conspicuous, threatening the cohesion of the party and its ability to secure victory in the legislative elections. The Shura Council was severely split between two views and between two leaderships. Contrary to what has been reported elsewhere, the split was not between the mainstream and radicals, but rather it was between those prepared to accommodate with the regime and those loyal to Madani and Belhaj. The former, represented by Said Guishi, enjoyed an initial majority, favored reconciliation with the regime, and accused Madani and Belhaj of hastiness and impatience in trying to establish an Islamic state. Other members, Shaykh Muhammad Said,[55] Hachani, and Rabih Kebir,[56] expressed their loyalty to the FIS's original leaders and asserted their legitimacy as the party's historic leaders. To reconcile the differences between the two camps, a nation-wide conference was called. The FIS leadership held a conference at Batna in July 1991 mainly to resolve the issue of leadership, restructure the party, and reach a decision on the issue of participation in the coming legislative elections. The conference was attended by representatives of 45 of the 48 *wilayas* (each *wilaya* was represented by three members). The representatives of the *wilayas* remained loyal to Madani and Belhaj and agreed to continue with the plans of their imprisoned leaders. Having now succeeded in securing a majority, Said and Hachani proposed to restructure and expand the current Shura Council by including new members, who were loyal to Madani and Belhaj. They also formed a Provisional Executive Council, headed by Hachani. As Guishi and his group realized that they had become a minority, Guishi offered his resignation, which was immediately accepted.[57] Following the conference of Batna, the FIS succeeded in maintaining its cohesion under a new leadership and asserted the legitimacy of Madani and Belhaj. The conference also marked the ascendance of Shaykh

Muhammad Said and his group, al-Jama`a al-Islamiyya (the Jaz'ara Trend), which constituted a majority in the newly established Executive Council.

The Legislative Elections

In the intervening period between the June crisis and the December 26, 1991 parliamentary elections, the military continued its crackdown on the FIS. It occupied the party's headquarters on July 1, raided its offices in the capital, banned its newspapers, arrested its provisional leader Abdel Qadir Hachani for a month, and harassed its members, particularly at Friday prayers. Armed Islamic groups, with no evident links to FIS, clashed with the army in several incidents. On October 13, a new electoral law was approved. Like the preceding one, it also favored the FLN as it was designed to improve its chances for winning a majority in the parliament. With its leaders in jail, thousands of its members arrested, its headquarters seized, and publications banned, the FIS decided to participate in the legislative elections only ten days before the elections were held. On the final day of campaigning, it held a rally in Algiers which was attended by more than 100,000 supporters, indicating that the party had not lost its mobilizational abilities and popularity despite the repressive measures taken against its followers. The FIS placed candidates in all electoral districts.

In the first round of the elections, the FIS captured 47 percent of the total valid votes, winning 188 out of the parliament's 430 seats. This number represented 81 percent of the 231 seats already decided in the first round. Its candidates were leading in 175 out of the 199 seats that were to be decided in the second round. The Socialist Forces Front (FFS) won 25 seats (10.8 percent), and the FLN took 15 seats (6.5 percent). It became clear that the FIS, which needed only 28 seats to win an outright majority, was on the way to forming an Islamic government in Algeria.

Setting the Stage for Army Intervention

Since the democratic process began in Algeria, the possibility of a growing Islamic influence in the North African country had raised concerns among Algeria's secular elite, Algeria's neighbors, and among several Western countries. Algerian national and Western press became rampant with doomsday scenarios of an Islamic take-over. On the eve of the local elections of June 1990, Italy, Spain, and France, where 4 million Muslims reside, adopted restricted immigration measures. Following the FIS's victory in the elections, which was very minor given the limited authority of the local councils, France's then Youth and Sports Minister, Roger Bambunck, lamented, "It is with great sadness that I see the rise of fundamentalism in Algeria." Treating Algeria as a southern province in France, he added that the results of the municipal elections "will be a source of worry of Algerians and will create difficulty for our Algerian friends in France."[58] Michael Vauzelle, the Chairman of the French Parliament's Foreign Affairs Committee, urged for a partnership with North Africa, warning that, "fundamentalism's threat can create a zone of instability, insecurity and even hostility at our southern borders."[59]

Before and after the first round of the legislative elections, the Algerian and Western press launched a vigorous press campaign against the FIS. On election day, the newspaper *Quotidien d'Algérie* proposed a scenario of "chaos final" in case the Islamic front achieved victory, predicting a cancellation of the second round of elections and an army intervention. *Le Figaro* considered Algeria to be moving from "a military to a religious dictatorship." The campaign, which aggravated the already precarious condition in Algeria, reflected anxiety and fear of the results and their consequences on the country, its secular elite, and its relations with its neighbors and the West, particularly France. Some reports related that France began to receive families or "boat people" of Algerians escaping a future Muslim rule.

The leaders and adherents of FIS were exposed to severe criticism accompanied by a relentless war of words by the regime. Members of FIS were described as chauvinist pigs, fanatics, uneducated, undemocratic, and extremist. These attacks were often extended to include Islam by perpetuating misperceptions in order to portray the FIS as anti-democratic and anti-modern. To prove his point that democracy is incompatible with Islam, Henrick Bering-Jensen wrote, "The mere notion that God and his representatives could be thrown out of office is sacrilegious."[60] In the same vein of suppressing any moderate images of Islam, when the track and field coach of Algeria's Olympics team appeared on a televised interview and stated that Islam was not incompatible with sports, he was detained by the army, tortured, and threatened that his wife would be raped. Commitments of FIS's leadership to democracy, respect of freedom of expression, and individual and public liberties were frequently ignored. Instead, statements by some FIS members, not representative of FIS's national policy, were frequently overemphasized.

As the legislative elections approached, Ghozali, who was presumed to head a caretaker government to ensure neutrality in the elections, called Madani "a liar who lived wholly on deceit." He expressed his convictions that "the FIS could not win a majority in a free election." He also declared that the FIS posed "a very serious threat to safety, stability and national unity."[61] After the results of the first round, Ghozali considered the FIS's victory a defeat for democracy. In an interview with French television, he mentioned that the fundamentalists could still be denied power.

On January 2, an anti-FIS demonstration was attended by 135,000 people, protesting the Islamic party's victory. It was organized by secular, leftist, and feminist forces in the country. Said Saadi, the head of the Rally for Culture and Democracy, called for the cancellation of the elections, the banning of FIS, and the intervention of the army. To cast doubts on the FIS's triumph, on the day following the demonstration the government announced that there had been irregularities in the election process, which it had described earlier as being conducted in freedom and "total transparency," and that the FIS had won one-third of the parliament's seats through terrorist tactics.

As a result of this precarious and unstable atmosphere, the stage was now set for the intervention of the army. The military had never hid its concern about legalizing an Islamic party and its opposition to an Islamist rule. It had vowed that it would never allow the democratic process to bring the FIS to the helms of power. During the election campaigns, army generals had been giving statements to the foreign press warning of the FIS threat and blaming the government for "tolerating fundamentalist excesses." Defense Minister Khaled Nizar announced that if the elections were not conducted in an atmosphere of peace and tranquillity, the army would be ready for all possibilities. On January 11, the army generals forced the resignation of President Benjedid, who in his resignation letter described the democratic process as "riddled with irregularities...and characterized by numerous excesses and tendencies clashing with one another." Benjedid's resignation was intended to provide grounds for the intervention of the army in the government and to block the FIS from taking control. Following Benjedid's resignation, Ghozali, to give a civilian façade to the coup, appeared on television to assure the Algerian public that he was in charge and invited the army "to take the necessary measures in order to contribute to the public security and the safety of the citizens."[62]

The timing of the coup was obviously miscalculated. Had the coup taken place before the legislative elections were conducted, it would have deprived the FIS of the legitimacy that was granted to it by its sweeping victory. On the other hand, the army generals could have moved after the FIS had spent some time in power, attempted to change the Constitution or the institutions of the country, showed some kind of intolerance, or proved incapable of solving the country's staggering economic and social problems, as was always alleged. In either case, the military coup might have enjoyed a greater degree of "legitimacy" and support.

The military generals ousted Benjedid on the same day that the Constitutional Council was supposed to announce its ruling regarding the complaints about election irregularities that, if proven, would have deprived the FIS of some seats. The Council ruling has never been announced to this date, probably suggesting that it would not have affected FIS's triumph. Contrary to the claims of the military-backed regime, there was no immediate threat to the normal functioning of the institutions of the state. On its part, and despite agitation against its victory, the FIS remained calm and avoided provocation to other political forces. Following the results of the first round, Abdel Qadir Hachani, the moderate leader of the FIS, dropped the party's demand for an early presidential election and announced its willingness to coexist with Benjedid. In several press conferences, he also assured the Algerian public of the FIS's intentions on coming to power. Hachani vowed that "there will be no blood-bath or boat people in Algeria." He asserted, "It must be clear that we are coming to government to solve the problems of the Algerian people. ... We guarantee freedom of opinion in Algeria. ... Our purpose is to persuade, not to oblige people to do what we say. I challenge anyone to prove that so far we have repressed any other political tendencies. You must remember that we won control of some 800 municipalities in elections more than a year ago. We have a record of tolerance that no one can deny."[63]

In fact, a few days before the military took over power, and amidst reports of massive army deployments throughout the country, there was a heated debate among government and military officials concerning the measures to be taken against the FIS. Despite differences on tactics, they all agreed on a veto to a permanent Islamic rule. Ghozali's entourage and the army generals urged President Benjedid to interrupt the democratic process, cancel the first round of elections, and resign in order to provide the army with the grounds for intervention. Benjedid, concerned about a popular upheaval, seemed convinced that he could use his broad constitutional powers to keep the FIS in check. In fact, the Algerian Constitution grants the president extensive powers. He appoints the prime minister, controls defense and foreign affairs, can dissolve the parliament, veto any laws passed by the assembly (even when they have a two-thirds majority), issue decrees that have the effect of law, amend the Constitution (the assembly cannot), and declare a state of emergency and call in the army.

These constitutional guarantees, in addition to the existence of several bodies that are assigned the task of protecting the Constitution, such as the Constitutional Council and the military, would have made it almost impossible for a FIS-controlled government to introduce major legal, institutional, or structural changes to the Algerian system, without the approval of the president and these bodies.

The Quest for Legitimacy

By all measures, the military coup was a clumsy one that, despite its attempts to shroud itself in legitimacy, lacked any constitutional basis and failed to generate the support of the significant political forces in the country. The army generals and their alliance of government officials reflected a demonstrable confusion in the first days of the coup. In two days, three governing bodies were announced: the Constitutional Council, the High Security Council (HSC), and the High State Council (HSC). Prior to his resignation, Benjedid discreetly dissolved the parliament, thus creating a constitutional vacuum. As the chairman of the disbanded assembly could not assume the presidency, the chairman of the Constitutional Council, Abdel Malek Benhabyles, was designated as the interim president. As a result of Benhabyles's refusal to assume this role, a High Security Council was formed. It was dominated by military generals, including Defense Minister General Khaled Nizar, Interior Minister General Larbi Belkhair, and Army Chief-of-Staff General Abdel Malek Guenaizia. The civilians on the council were Prime Minister Ghozali, Minister of Justice Hamdani Benkhalil, and Foreign Minister Lakhdar al-Ibrahimi. The Council's first decision was to cancel the second round of the parliamentary elections. This act was denounced by the leaders of the FIS and the FFS, who both considered the coup and the ruling High Security Council as unconstitutional.

According to the Constitution, the HSC is an advisory body to the president of the country and cannot assume executive or legislative powers. In the face of such criticisms, the military-controlled government on January 14 announced the establishment of a five-member High Council of State that would assume presidential powers until December 1993, the end of Benjedid's term. The High Council of State consisted of only one army general, Khaled Nizar (as opposed to three in the HSC), Ali Kafi, the head of the National Organization of War Veterans, Tijani Haddam, the director of the Paris mosque, and Ali Haroun, former Human Rights minister. To shed an aura of legitimacy on this Council, the leaders of the new regime brought back Muhammad Boudiaf, a historic chief and an independence-war hero who had been in self-imposed exile in Morocco for the previous 28 years. Due to his long absence from the Algerian scene and opposition to the previous regimes, Boudiaf was a figure only vaguely known to the majority of Algerians.

Boudiaf's Term: Promises Only

When Boudiaf returned, it was presumed he would act as a conciliator. During the short period of his term, however, he did little to heal the country's wounds. After coming to power, Boudiaf's main objectives were to reinstitute the authority of the state and build a support and legitimacy base. The achievement of these objectives entailed the continuation of a massive clampdown on the FIS, building new political institutions, and waging a campaign against corruption. Boudiaf approved and supported the military's repressive measures to destroy the FIS as a political force. In his first statement to the Algerian people, he sent a clear warning to the Islamic Front stating that, "we will not permit any individuals or group to claim a monopoly on Islam and use it to threaten the country," and "all those who cause trouble to public order will be put in the [detention] camps."

To dismantle the FIS, the military-backed authorities adopted a strategy aimed at provoking violent reaction from the FIS's angry and frustrated followers and thus creating the reasons for the dissolution of the party; and decapitating its moderate leadership to break its control over party adherents, invoke splits within its ranks, and give radical elements a free hand to carry out violent operations against the regime that would justify harsh military measures against the party and its continuation in power. After the coup, the FIS maintained a two-day silence, during which the party's leadership was debating its strategy vis-à-vis the new regime. Concerned about the survival of the FIS as a party and preserving its electoral gains, the FIS leadership advocated working through legal channels to confront the new regime. They were counting on the legitimacy that their party had achieved after the first round of the elections, possible splits within the army, and on cooperation and alliance with other political forces. While denouncing the coup as unconstitutional, Hachani urged FIS's followers to remain calm, "exercise caution, and not to respond to any provocation from whatever source." He vowed that "FIS will remain within the legal framework without renouncing its plan for an Islamic state," and announced that the FIS was intending to file a suit to contest the legality of the newly-formed High Council of State.[64] Until the end of January, FIS leaders kept appealing for calm, despite mass arrests of its members and outright provocations of FIS followers gathering for Friday prayers. Throughout January, the military arrested hundreds of FIS's leadership, banned gatherings around mosques and political activities inside them, and suspended the FIS's two newspapers. As a result of the army's harsh measures, Hachani complained that, "if the junta goes too far, it will be impossible for us to keep the people under control. ... They are doing everything so that it explodes. We are doing everything so that it does not."[65] On January 22, Hachani, who had been a moderating influence on the FIS members, was arrested for inciting army mutiny, a charge that was later dismissed by a civilian court. On January 27, Rabih Kebir, the FIS's foreign affairs spokesman, called for a dialogue with the government. He was arrested the following day (he was later acquitted by a civilian court).

Throughout February and March, the army escalated its crackdown on the FIS. It clashed with demonstrators throughout the country protesting the arrest of FIS's leaders and the military's continued seizure of power. It also battled radical Islamic groups that had by then engaged in armed resistance and attacked police and military posts and personnel. The armed forces seized the FIS's headquarters. They detained more than 10,000 FIS members, including 200 FIS mayors, 28 regional assembly leaders, 109 parliament deputies, and 34 women. They were held in desert camps in the South. On March 3, the FIS was banned by a court ruling.

After coming to power, Boudiaf was critical of the established political parties and rejected their repeated offers for national reconciliation. He sought to create an independent base of support by building new political institutions. In April, Boudiaf announced the establishment of the Consultative Council to fill the legislative vacuum created by the dissolution of the Parliament. The main objective of the Council was to offer advice on laws proposed by the High Council of State. The 60-member Council consisted of individuals outside the established political parties, and was dominated by leftist, feminist, and anti-Arabization elements, some historical figures, independents, and former ministers who had served under Boumedienne. Boudiaf's attempt to pass laws through the Council had little success as it was met with rejection from the leaders of major political parties who questioned the Council's legitimacy and criticized it as being a front for a military rule. In fact, the only significant law that the Council members readily passed was the cancellation of the 1991 Arabization law which was to be in effect in July 1992.

Boudiaf also proposed the establishment of a new political party, the National Democratic Rally (DRN), to replace the FLN and the banned FIS and "lead the democratic change in the country." In fact, the Rally was created to support Boudiaf's candidacy for the presidential elections in 1994, and also to nominate and back the High Council of State's candidates once the new legislative elections were to be held. Major political parties opposed the creation of the Rally, which they perceived as an attempt to return to monolithic politics. Twelve small parties with no influence or popularity accepted to join in the new party.

In his pursuit of legitimacy, Boudiaf considered the issues of economic reform and fighting official corruption as major objectives of his regime. He promised the Algerian public economic reform, housing, and the creation of new jobs. Prime Minister Ghozali proposed an economic reform program that was based on foreign aid and loan credits, devaluing the Algerian dinar, cutting subsidies on basic commodities, and selling shares in the country's oil sector to foreign investors. During Boudiaf's term, Algerians were struck by spiraling prices of basic commodities, a continuing shortage in housing, and increasing unemployment.

The issue of corruption has been raised several times in Algeria since its independence. It was sometimes used to discredit and eliminate political rivals. One year after coming to power, Benjedid established the Accountability Council to look into corruption cases. The Council directed blame at former officials who had served under Boumedienne, such as Boutaflika, Yahyaoui, Belaid Abdel Salam, and Sid Ahmed Ghozali, who was removed from his position as chairman of SONATRACH, the state petroleum company, after being accused of embezzlement. In the summer of 1988, former Prime Minister, Abdel Hamid al-Ibrahimi, had revealed that Algerian officials charged 10 percent commission on every economic or trade transaction, which resulted in the embezzlement of $26 billion over 20 years.

Promising to punish the corrupt, "whatever their social position of hierarchical rank," Boudiaf requested the study of a legislation providing criminal punishment for fiscal fraud and a special tax on those who failed to clarify the source of their wealth. He also approved the indictment of the former secretary general of the Ministry of Defense, General Moustapha Beloucif, for misuse of public funds, and promised to pursue cases with other senior officials who had served under Benjedid. This seems to have angered well-entrenched officials in the army and the government, who became concerned about the possibility of an extended anti-corruption campaign. On June 29, Boudiaf was assassinated in the city of Annaba, the hometown of the indicted General Beloucif. With no evidence to accuse the FIS or militant Islamic groups, the Commission investigating the assassination of the president charged the government in its preliminary report with "blameworthy and criminal instances of negligence" in failing to protect the president. It considered the assassination a result of "complicity at the highest level of decision-making."[66]

Dashed Hopes

Following the assassination of Boudiaf, hopes were renewed for ending the political crisis in Algeria and for reaching a reconciliation with the political forces in the country. However, these hopes were quickly dashed as the newly appointed President Ali Kafi and his Prime Minister Belaid Abdel Salam maintained a hard-line approach towards the opposition and insisted on excluding the FIS, the country's most popular force, from any future discussions. The HSC's choice of Kafi was met by disappointment from many Algerians. Kafi headed the National Organization of War Veterans whose members are accused of having skimmed Algeria's wealth for thirty years. The newly appointed prime minister was an adamant opponent of free-market economy and was extremely critical of Benjedid's policies of economic liberalization. He is known as the father of heavy industry in Algeria and headed its oil nationalization. Upon coming to power, Abdel Salam declared a "war economy" that would implement austere economic measures, reduce imports, and revive the country's failing public sector. He dismissed any attempts to privatize the economy, stating that, "I am not here to provide opportunities for vultures." Abdel Salam was eventually replaced by Rida Malek who, along with interior minister Salim Saadi, pursued a hard-line policy against the FIS and supported the formation of people's militias to fight the Islamists.

Under Kafi, Algeria continued to plunge into chaos and more violence. Government control seemed to be breaking down as armed Islamic groups continued to challenge the authority of the state. Attacks on army and police officials, foreigners, journalists, and civilians, and arrests and killings of Muslim militants became regular occurrences. The new regime increasingly restricted political freedoms and cracked down on the press, suspending several papers and harassing journalists who reported military incidents between the regime and the armed groups. Some state-owned factories closed downed or drastically reduced production because of the shortage of spare parts and cash to pay their workers. The High Council of State replaced Kafi with retired army general Liamine Zeroual in January 1994.

President Zeroual seemed in a better position than his predecessors to achieve some sort of national reconciliation, an objective which he declared upon assuming power. He had not participated in the January 1992 coup and, unlike the coup generals, had never served in the French army. Upon coming to power, Zeroual began the process of consolidating his authority and exercising some political and military control. He sacked the two anti-reconciliation figures, Prime Minister Rida Malek and Interior Minister Salim Saadi, both of whom had publicly challenged the new president's move toward reconciliation. He appointed Mokdad Sifi, a professional technocrat, as prime minister, further enhancing Zeroual's political authority and sending the right signal abroad about the regime's commitment to economic restructuring. The new president has retained the post of defense minister and reshuffled some military commanders, thus creating the image of being able to exercise control over the armed forces. The fact of the matter is that major political and military decisions remain in the hands of a small military oligarchy that include the top generals who engineered the January coup, namely Chief of Staff Muhammad Lamari, who also performs the duties of defense minister; Director of Military Security Tawfiq Madyan; Commander of the Gendarmes Abbas Ghzayel, former Defense Minister Khaled Nizar; and his political advisor, Muhammad Touati. These generals, known as the "eradicationist trend," oppose any reconciliation with the FIS and back elements within the government and some secular parties outside.[67] They appear to continue to exercise great control over Zeroual. When Zeroual issued a decree sending General Ghzayel to retirement, he was opposed by the generals and had to reconsider his decision.[68]

Zeroual's regime has followed a two-track policy of military escalation and political dialogue. The rate of killings since Zeroual came to power has reached a record high, reportedly 400 to 450 per week.[69] Massive military operations, in which the air force, napalm, and intensive bombing were used, were conducted throughout the country to uproot the Islamic militants and drastically weaken the FIS in any future negotiation. The other track was opening rounds of dialogue with the main opposition parties to strike a deal with them that excludes the FIS. Most of these parties insisted on the release of the FIS leaders and urged the government to include the front in any future discussions for any reconciliation to be successful. Despite the failure of the initial phases of dialogue, the process led to the release of two FIS members, Ali Jaddi and Abdel Qadir Boukhamkham in April 1994, and three months later, Madani and Belhaj were released from prison and placed under house arrest. Since their release a series of negotiations has taken place without much success. Contrary to many expectations, Zeroual announced on July 1995 the failure of the last rounds of dialogue with the FIS.

The Armed Path

The FIS was established as a non-violent political party. According to its political program, FIS does not espouse violence as a means of change.[70] Following the cancellation of the parliamentary elections, however, armed Islamic groups began to mushroom and entered in violent confrontations with the regime. The most prominent groups have been the pro-FIS Islamic Salvation Army and the Armed Islamic Group, which became notorious for allegedly killing foreigners, intellectuals, and civilians. In fact, many of these groups were already in existence prior to the formation of the FIS.

The origins of the armed Islamic groups can be traced back to the early 1980s. According to Shaykh Jaballah, the leader of al-Nahda Party, the first armed Islamic group emerged in 1980 and was founded near the capital by a simple worker who was a former member of the Jama`at al-Tabligh. He formed armed groups led by a veteran of the war of liberation to fight the secular Algerian state for not implementing the

Islamic *shari`a*. The group was soon discovered in 1981 and its members were arrested.

In 1982, Moustapha Bouyali formed a more influential armed group, the Armed Islamic Movement. Born in 1940, Bouyali was a war veteran and a former member of the Socialist Forces Front (FFS). In the mid-1970s, he joined the then clandestine Islamic movement and began to lecture in some of the country's mosques. In the early 1980s, the Islamists were suppressed by the regime and their main leaders were thrown in jail, particularly after the events at the University of Algiers. Bouyali believed that the regime had transgressed against Islam and the Islamic leaders and that the only way to change it was through a long armed insurrection. He organized small groups which extended to the capital and other main cities in the east and west of the country. Bouyali's groups staged minor operations against military targets, thus gaining some prestige and respect at a time when any opposition to the regime was severely crushed. In 1987, Bouyali was killed in an ambush and hundreds of his followers were detained. Among those arrested were Abdel Qadir Shabbouti, Mansour Miliani, Ja`afar Borkani, and Izzeddin Ba`a, names which would later become prominent in the violent confrontations that followed the harsh crackdown on the FIS in 1992.

The Islamic Salvation Army

The Islamic Salvation Army was formed in 1993 as a coalition of two main groups: the Armed Islamic Movement in Algeria and the Movement for the Islamic State. In 1990, some members of Bouyali's group benefited from a presidential pardon and were released from jail. Among those released was Abdel Qadir Shabbouti, also known as General Shabbouti, who assumed the leadership of the group. They briefly joined the FIS, which insisted on a non-violence policy in its political activity. By the time they were out of jail, the political dynamics had changed in Algeria. The democratization process permitted the political activity of the Islamic opposition and allowed their organization as political parties. Consequently, Shabbouti, who could not believe that the secular regime would allow a peaceful transfer of power, split from Bouyali's group and began to restructure an armed group, the Armed Islamic Movement, with the objective of overthrowing the regime through armed resistance. The members of the movement organized themselves in the mountains and attacked military targets for the purpose of collecting arms. However, the extent of their operations remained limited until 1992, when they supported the FIS after the military-backed regime began a process of dismantling the front and suppressing its followers.

The other main group in the Islamic Salvation Army is the Movement of the Islamic State. This movement was founded at the end of the 1980s by Said Makhloufi. Makhloufi was an intelligence officer sent by the Algerian security apparatus to spy on the Algerian militants who had fought with the Afghan Mujahidin in their war against the Soviet Union. Makhloufi, instead, joined the Algerian Afghans and returned to Algeria in the late 1980s. Like Shabbouti, Makhloufi briefly joined the FIS. After the 1992 crackdown, he escaped to the mountains to establish the Movement of the Islamic State to resist the Algerian regime. In early 1993, Makhloufi and Shabbouti joined together to form the Islamic Salvation Army (AIS). The AIS attracted many of the FIS's supporters who, after the imprisonment of their political leaders, dismantling of their legitimate party, and closure of political avenues, joined to escape the repression of the regime and fight the military junta. More influential in the east and parts of the west of the country, the AIS has limited its activities to attacking military targets. On several occasions, its leaders have condemned acts of violence against civilians, foreigners, and non-combatant targets.

The Armed Islamic Group (GIA)

Like the AIS, the Armed Islamic Group is an amalgam of various organizations. Its backbone is the Algerian Afghans who opposed FIS's moderate political orientation and its willingness to pursue democratic means for establishing an Islamic state. Since their return to Algeria in the late 1980s, the Algerian Afghans have asserted their presence through quick military strikes (the attack on the military barracks at Guimar in November 1991); infiltrating other armed Islamic groups, such as al-Takfir wa al-Hijra and the AIS; and disseminating their radical ideology of rejecting any settlement with the regime, attacking its supporters, and the continuing armed resistance until it collapses.

The Algerian Afghans were successful in weakening the other armed groups by recruiting many of their members who came in 1992 under one organizational structure forming the GIA. Within three years, six consecutive *amirs* (leaders) of the GIA were killed.[71] This led many to suspect that the group had already been infiltrated by the state security.[72] It has also been suggested that these amirs were field commanders and not the general leaders of the GIA. The GIA has been active in the west (Tirat-Sidi Belabbas), center (Blida-Mtigah-Midia), and in the capital of Algeria. On some occasions, GIA members have clashed with the AIS, which has condemned the group's violent acts against civilian targets.

By 1994, the need to unify the resistance against the regime and avoid violent confrontations between the armed Islamic groups seemed most urgent. The GIA, in addition, was becoming prominent and polarizing the entire Islamic movement. Some of its violent acts and statements, alleged or real, were certainly having adverse effects on the FIS, the legitimacy of its cause, and its control over potential radical rivals. This led two political leaders of the FIS's Provisional Executive Bureau, Muhammad Said and Abdel Razzaq Rajjam, to join the GIA in May 1994. They were also followed by Said Makhloufi's Movement for the Islamic State, which, however, left the GIA three months later. Shabbouti's pro-FIS movement, the Islamic Salvation Army (AIS), refused to merge with the GIA. The merger, which did not replace the FIS as a political entity, aimed at the unification of the military operations of the armed groups and the establishment of a unified Shura Council. This council was dominated by FIS supporters. It comprised the GIA's leader Abu Abdullah Ahmed, Said Makhloufi (FIS supporter), Abdel Razzaq Rajjam (FIS), Muhammad Said (FIS), Abdel Qadir Shabbouti (FIS-supporter, refused to join), Rabih Qattaf (Makhloufi's assistant), Madani, and Belhaj.

The merger of these two FIS leaders with the GIA came as a surprise to many who perceived it as an ill-conceived move.[73] Both FIS leaders, Said and Rajjam, are members of al-Jama`a al-Islamiyya (the *Jaz'ara*), which is known for its moderation. In fact, this merger lends itself to different interpretations. The merger came exactly one month after the regime released from prison two FIS leaders, Ali Jaddi and Abdel Qadir Boukhamkham. The objective behind their release was to prepare the grounds for a dialogue between the regime and the FIS. While enjoying an undisputed political legitimacy among the Islamists in Algeria, the FIS has been drastically weakened since its historic leaders have been in jail since 1992 and its political infrastructure dismantled. More importantly, its image as a non-violent political party has been tarnished by the regime's propaganda and the violent acts of the Islamic militants. This suggests that the objectives behind the merging of the two prominent FIS leaders were multifold: to enhance the FIS's position in any future dialogue with the regime by demonstrating that it still has a military option behind it; prevent polarization and confrontations between the armed Islamic movements; moderate the GIA and exercise some influence or control over the nature and extent of its violent acts; and prepare the GIA for accepting a future political reconciliation with the regime. Another interpretation is that the merger came at the behest of the *Jaz'ara* trend which saw FIS's abilities dwindling and opted to exercise influence through the GIA.

Since January 1995, Algeria has been politically torn between two platforms for resolving the country's crisis: the Rome Accord and the "Presidential Plan." In January, Algeria's main opposition parties and the FIS met in Rome and reached an accord that would set the grounds for a negotiated solution of the country's crisis. Signed by the seven political parties that received a total of 82 percent of the votes in the 1991 elections, as well as the Algerian League for the Defense of Human Rights, the Rome Accord constitutes a common ground that could lead to the formation of real political pluralism in Algeria. It consists of six main parts: a framework of values and principles; measures that must precede negotiations; reinstatement of peace; return to Constitutional legality; return to popular sovereignty; and guarantees. The Rome signatories, including the FIS, have agreed on the renunciation of violence as a means to achieve or retain power; the rejection of dictatorship regardless of its nature or form, the recognition of the right of the people to defend their elected institutions; the respect of political alteration through popular vote and political, cultural, and ethnic pluralism; and the guarantee of both individual and collective fundamental freedoms. They also called for the non-interference of the army in political affairs and the release of FIS leaders.

The Rome platform suffered from one serious problem—it lacked a mechanism to enforce it. Under the current circumstances, the signatories were unable to mobilize popular support for it. The platform in addition received only verbal support from foreign powers that could exercise some pressure on the military-backed regime to accept negotiations. The Accord, however, demonstrated FIS's success in broadening its base of support and forging an alliance with the other political forces, liberal and secular, thus evading the regime's plans to isolate it. The other political parties also benefitted from the Accord. Less popular than FIS and repeatedly accused of not mounting enough opposition to the regime, the secular parties gained some credibility by allying with the FIS, and in case of future settlement, would not be excluded. Some even suggested that the biggest winner in this gruesome ordeal has been the (now in opposition) FLN, which by supporting many of FIS's political demands, was able to accomplish a process of "political laundering" and restore some credibility as an opposition party. In the meantime, however, some of the FLN's men are still in the government, the military, and the administration.[74] Hamas has also benefitted from the suppression of FIS as it has tried to expand its base of support.

To counter the initiative of the opposition parties and ease the mounting pressures on the regime, Zeroual proposed an alternative plan. Zeroual insisted on holding presidential elections before the end of 1995, while pursuing military operations against the Islamic militants and speeding the process of restructuring the country's economy. This has been accompanied by active public relations and diplomatic campaigns sending the message that the military solution is succeeding and that the current regime is worthy of foreign financial assistance and political support. The problem with the regime's platform is that it lacks the endorsement of the major political forces in the country. The main political parties rejected the presidential plan and criticized it for attempting to legitimate an illegal regime and for failing to address the main issues of the crisis or provide a comprehensive solution to the problem. In addition, the security situation in the country makes the possibility of holding free and clean elections remote.

Conclusion

Political Islam in Algeria has its own particularities. It emerged not as a single movement with one structure or a unified leadership. By the late 1960s and early 1970s, it consisted of several movements with different organizations and orientations. All these movements predated the FIS. This, in fact, led Madani and Belhaj, who possessed great oratory skills, to resort to populism and the direct mobilization of the streets as a means to enhance their party's popularity and advance their political program. While generating popularity and influence for the FIS, this style has had major disadvantages. Populism is a two-edged sword. Once a party loses control of the streets, it becomes prisoner to the demands and pressures of the people it had mobilized. For example, prior to the legislative elections, FIS followers shouted at their leaders the slogan "*Ya Ali, ya Abbas, al-jabha rahu Hamas*" [Oh Ali and Madani, the FIS has become like Hamas], complaining that the FIS is not tough enough in confronting the regime.

Islamists in Algeria enjoy uninterrupted organic links with Islamic reformism and the historic legitimacy it generates. The FIS embodies the aspirations of three generations of religious reformers. Contrary to Tunisia and Morocco, the historic reformist religious scholars have associated themselves with the populist Islamic movements more than with the regime. This has been the case of highly respected scholars of the Association of Algerian Scholars such as shaykhs Abdel Latif Sultani, Omar al-Arabaoui, Musbah al-Huwaiziq, and Ahmed Sahnoun. They all refused to join the religious bureaucracy of the regime and instead opposed its socialist policies and supported the new generations of Islamists.

The evolution of the FIS in Algeria provides a unique example for the Islamic movements in the Arab countries. It was the first time that an Islamic political party was close to coming to power through a democratic process. It would have been fascinating to see how the conduct of an Islamic party would evolve under these circumstances. The military coup of 1992, the cancellation of the election results, and the dissolution of the FIS unfortunately cut this process short. The fierce suppression of the FIS and elimination of its moderate political leadership has enhanced the radical elements within the Islamic movement and thrown the country into a vicious cycle of violence.

Notes

1. William Quandt, *Revolution and Political Leadership: Algeria, 1954-1968* (Cambridge, MA: MIT Press, 1969), p. 223. See also John Ruedy, *Modern Algeria*, pp. 202-5.

2. Quoted in Darif, *al-Islam al-Siyasi*, p. 125. A slightly different translation can be found in Quandt, *Revolution and Political Leadership*, p. 224.

3. Ruedy, *Modern Algeria*, p. 204.

4. Quandt, *Revolution and Political Leadership*, p. 249.

5. Darif, *al-Islam al-Siyasi*, p. 123.

6. Darif, *al-Islam al-Siyasi*, pp. 117-9, see also Othman Tazghart, "Assassinations in Algeria," *al-Majalla*, No. 687, April 7-13, 1993, pp. 23-5.

7. Due to its influence by the ideas of Malik Ben Nabi, who indeed contributed to the association's periodical, many thought that al-Qiyam was founded by Ben Nabi. In fact, Ben Nabi was against the formation of religious associations and focused instead on the intellectual aspects of an Islamic revival.

8. Quandt, *Revolution and Political Leadership*, p. 223, and Mohammad Arkoun, "Algeria," in Shireen Hunter (ed.), *The Politics of Islamic Revivalism:*

Diversity and Unity (Bloomington and Indianapolis: Indiana University Press, 1989), p. 172.

9. See, for example, El-Hachemi Tidjani, "Les Composants de Notre Personnalité," *Humanisme Musulman*, No. 8, August 1965; Malik Ben Nabi, "Sociologie de l'Independence," *Humanisme Musulman*, No. 5, May 1965; Ahmed Taleb, "Réflexions sur la Décolonisation Culturelle en Algérie," *Humanisme Musulman*, Nos. 6 and 7, June-July 1965.

10. François Burgat, "L'Algérie: de la Laïcité Islamique à l'Islamisme," *Maghreb-Machrek*, No. 121, July-September 1988, pp. 45-6.

11. Ihmeda Ayachi, *al-Haraka al-Islamiyya fi al-Jaza'ir: Al-Juzur, al-Rumuz, al-Masar* [The Islamic Movement in Algeria: Roots, Symbols, and Path] (Casablanca: Ouyoun al-Maqalat, 1993), pp. 120-3.

12. G. al-Akhdar, "al-Shaykh Abdel Latif Sultani," *al-Mujtama`*, No. 672, May 22, 1984, pp. 30-3. Excerpts from Sultani's book were published in the Moroccan paper *al-Nour*, Jamada al-Awal 1, 1403, p. 3. For a review of Sultani's biography and thought, see Ayachi, *al-Haraka al-Islamiyya fi al-Jaza'ir*, pp. 123-33.

13. Malik Ben Nabi, *Shurut al-Nahda* [The Conditions of the Renaissance] (Damascus: Dar al-Fikr, 3rd ed., 1969), and "The Message of the Muslim in the Last Third of the Twentieth Century," *Asharq al-Awsat*, June 4-5, 1988. See also Ayachi, *al-Haraka al-Islamiyya fi al-Jaza'ir*, pp. 133-48.

14. Ali Bouraoui, "Halaqa Muhimma fi Tarikh al-Haraka al-Islamiyya bi al-Jaza'ir" [A Significant Link in the History of the Islamic Movement in Algeria], *al-`Alam*, No. 426, April 11, 1992, p. 34

15. Moustapha Bouhamza, "L'Opposition Islamique en Algérie ," *La Cause*, Vol. 3, No. 24, July 29-August 4, 1995, p. 5.

16. Interview with Anwar Haddam, President of FIS Parliamentary Delegation in Europe and the United States, Washington, D.C., July 1994.

17. *Al-`Alam*, No. 426, April 11, 1992, p. 34.

18. On the contacts between the Egyptian Muslim Brothers and members of the Association of Scholars, see Nabil A. Blassi, *al-Itijah al-Arabi al-Islami wa Dawrahu fi Tahrir al-Jaza'ir* [The Arabo-Islamic Trend and Its Role in the Liberation of Algeria] (Cairo: al-Hay'a al-Masriyya al-`Amma li al-Kitab, 1990), pp. 83-4.

19. This section was based on the statement of Shaykh Muhammad Abu Sulaiman during the Constitutive Conference of Hamas, quoted in Ayachi, *al-Haraka al-Islamiyya fi al-Jaza'ir*, pp. 177-80.

20. The Political Program of Harakat al-Mujtama` al-Islami (Hamas).

21. Interview with Shaykh Jaballah in *al-Mujahid*, No. 1581, November 23, 1990, p. 2.

22. Interview with Shaykh Jaballah in *al-Salam*, May 21, 1991. See also *al-`Alam al-Islami*, No. 276, April 27, 1991.

23. The Political Program of al-Nahda Movement.

24. *The Constitution*, Algeria, 1989.

25. The Code of Associations with a Political Character, in *Maghreb-Machrek*, No. 127, January-March 1990, p. 201.

26. The statement of the Interior Ministry on February 9, 1992.

27. Aziz Mrimish, "al-Jabha al-Islamiyya li al-Inqadh," *Adwa'*, No. 436, June 25, 1992, p. 4.

28. Interview of Ali Belhaj with Tammam al-Barazi in *al-Watan al-Arabi*, No. 176, July 27, 1990, p. 25.

29. Ayachi, *al-Haraka al-Islamiyya fi al-Jaza'ir*, p.170.

30. Ayachi, *al-Haraka al-Islamiyya fi al-Jaza'ir*, pp. 174-5.

31. Interview with Ali Belhaj in *al-Mujtama`*, June 26, 1990, p. 38.

32. Quoted in Ayachi, *al-Haraka al-Islamiyya fi al-Jaza'ir*, pp. 46-7.

33. Ali Belhaj, *Fasl al-Kalam fi Muwajahat Dhulm al-Hukkam* [The Decisive Statement on Confronting the Aggression of Rulers] (The Islamic Salvation Front, December 21, 1992), pp. 35-4.

34. Belhaj, *Fasl al-Kalam*, p. 44.

35. Jamal Ahmed Khashojgui, "Mushahadat min Dakhil al-Haraka al-Islamiyya" [Scenes From Inside the Islamic Movement], *al-Liwa'*, June 20, 1990.

36. Khashojgui, "Mushahadat," *al-Liwa'*, June 20, 1990.

37. Interview with Abbasi Madani in *al-Majalla*, No. 514, December 19, 1989, pp. 44-5.

38. Azouz Ben Zebda (b. 1944) was in charge of information and the editor in chief of *al-Munqidh*. He has an MA degree in Language and Literature, and is a Ph.D. candidate. He has been prayer leader since he was in high school. See *al-Watan al-Arabi*, No. 177, August 3, 1990.

39. Darif, *al-Islam al-Siyasi*, pp. 197-9.

40. *Mashru` al-Barnamaj al-Siyasi li al-Jabha al-Islamiyya li al-Inqadh*, manuscript, March 1989.

41. *Al-`Aqida*, January 2, 1991, pp. 4-5; *al-Wasat*, No. 76, December 7, 1993, p. 39; and Fadeel al-Amin, "Algeria's Democracy at Crossroads," *al-Amal*, No. 162, August-September 1991, p. 35 and 38. Al-Nahda's perspective on the attempt is in Ayachi, *al-Haraka al-Islamiyya fi al-Jaza'ir*, pp. 186-90.

42. *Asharq al-Awsat*, February 5, 1990.

43. *FBIS*, June 18, 1990, p. 7.

44. Quoted in Nour Eddin al-Tahiri, *al-Jaza'ir: Bayn al-Khiyar al-Islami wa al-Khiyar al-`Askari* [Algeria: Between the Islamic Alternative and the Military Alternative] (Casablanca: Dar Qurtuba, 1992), p. 26.

45. Ayachi, *al-Haraka al-Islamiyya fi al-Jaza'ir*, p. 89.

46. Abbasi Madani in an interview with Youssef Mizyani and Hassan Khalifa in *al-`Aqida*, October 31, 1990.

47. *Al-`Alam*, No 356, December 8, 1990 and No. 357, December 15, 1990.

48. Carol Morello, "City and Resort Show Two Sides of Algeria," *Philadelphia Inquirer*, January 20, 1992, p. 1-A, and Philip Shehadi, "'Islamic Communes' Set about Cleaning up Algeria," *New York Times*, November 11, 1990, p. A-48.

49. Paul Schemm, "Algeria's Return to its Past: Can the FIS Break the Vicious Cycle of History?," *Middle East Insight*, Vol. 11, No. 2, January-February, 1995, p. 38.

50. Howard LaFranchi, "Algerians Test Support for Islam in a Free Vote," *Christian Science Monitor*, June 7, 1990, p. 10.

51. Quoted in *FBIS*, June 27, 1990, pp. 8-9.

52. Quoted in Ayachi, *al-Haraka al-Islamiyya fi al-Jaza'ir*, p. 154.

53. Quoted in Nour Eddin al-Tahiri, *al-Jaza'ir: Bayn al-Khiyar al-Islami wa al-Khiyar al-`Askari*, p. 26.

54. *FBIS*, July 1, 1991, p. 1.

55. Shaykh Muhammad Said was a university professor and the spokesman of the League of Islamic Call. He was one of the influential leaders of al-Jama`a al-Islamiyya bi al-Jaza'ir. In May 1994, he, along with Abdel Razzaq Rajjam, the spokesman of the FIS Provisional Executive Bureau, joined the GIA. Shaykh Said was of Berber origin and used to deliver speeches in the Berber language. In December 1995, both Said and Rajjam were killed by the GIA.

56. Rabih Kebir is a school teacher and a former member of Jaballah's movement.

57. Rabih Kebir in an interview with Jamal Khashojgui in *al-Wasat*, No. 76, July 12, 1993, p. 40. See also, *al-Hayat*, September 1, 1991, and *al-Bilad*, No. 44, August 17, 1991, p. 32.

58. *New York Times*, June 14, 1990.

59. *Washington Post*, June 13, 1990.

60. *Insight*, July 29, 1992.

61. *Washington Post*, July 2, 1992.

62. *FBIS*, January 13, 1992, p. 12.

63. *New York Times*, January 7, 1992.

64. *Philadelphia Inquirer*, January 17, 1992, p. C-17.

65. *Washington Post*, January 20, 1992, p. A-20.

66. Paul Eedle, "Top-Level Algerian Plot Is Alleged," *Philadelphia Inquirer*, July 28, 1992, p. A-3.

67. Othman Tazghart, "Algeria: The Hardliners in the Military," *al-Majalla*, No. 770, November 13-19, 1994, p. 31.

68. Qusai Saleh al-Darwish, "Algeria: The Possible and Impossible Dialogue," *al-Majalla*, No. 759, August 28-September 3, 1994, p. 21.

69. This figure was quoted by Ali Yahiya Abdel Nour, the president of the Algerian League for the Defense of Human Rights, in a speech at the Middle East Watch, Washington, D.C. May 31, 1995.

70. See John Entelis, "Political Islam in Algeria: The Nonviolent Dimension," *Current History*, Vol. 94, No. 588, January 1995.

71. Darif, *al-Islam al-Siyasi*, pp. 240-2.

72. Some Algerians, who have a great taste of political sarcasm, call the GIA the Group Islamique de l'Armée.

73. Paul Schemm, "Hope for Algeria?" *Middle East Insight*, Vol. 10, No. 6, September-October 1994, pp. 44-8.

74. Interview with Sayyid Ferjani, London-based Nahda official, Virginia, July 10, 1995.

5

Under the Shadow of the Imam:
Morocco's Diverse Islamic Movements

Among North African countries, Morocco seems to be the least exposed to the "threat" of political Islam. While there exist several active Islamic groups with different orientations and activities, there is no single mainstream movement spearheading Islamic activism. Rather, two main Islamic groups in addition to scores of marginal associations share this task. The fragmented nature of the Islamic movements can be attributed to the political structure of Morocco and to the particular evolution of the contemporary Islamic movements there. In its relations with the Islamic opposition, the regime has adopted a set of differing measures: suppression, confinement, and toleration, albeit without recognition. How the state treats the movement depends on the movement's acceptance of the political agenda as set by the monarch.

Much like Tunisia and Algeria, the initial proliferation of Islamic groups and activists in Morocco took place in the late 1960s. It was in large measure a result of the perception of inadequacy in implementing basic Islamic doctrines regarding social reforms and economic development policies. Those policies generated crises that overshadowed the Moroccan political system during that period and exacerbated the already harsh socioeconomic conditions of the country. The majority of these Islamic associations are moderate in orientation, constituting a reformist tendency that recognizes the basic legitimacy of the system and seeks to undertake and actualize reform from within and through legal means. They accept the religious legitimacy of the king, who, in turn, refrains from severe repression of these groups.

On the other hand, some of the Islamic groups have been militant, contesting the legitimacy of the system, and pursuing clandestine and sometimes extremist measures to achieve political goals. These groups have been small in number and were usually suppressed at early stages. Also present in Morocco are individual activists who do not espouse organizations but through their prolific writings and personal speeches challenge the legitimacy of the system and demonstrate their opposition.[1]

This chapter presents an analysis of some of Morocco's diverse Islamic activist movements and examines the political, economic, and social factors that contributed to their rise. The discussion then focuses primarily on Harakat al-Islah wa al-Tajdid al-Maghribiyya (The Movement for Reform and Renewal in Morocco—HATM, Arabic acronym) and al-'Adl wa al-Ihsan (Justice and Benevolence) as the two movements that have captured larger followings and enjoy more influence. The nature, objectives, and evolution of these groups will be addressed and their social composition, organizational structures, and relations with the regime will be analyzed.

The Evolution of the Religio-Political Associations

Morocco is dominated by a small, yet fragmented, political elite who come from wealthy and prominent families.[2] It has six major political parties and eight minor ones, all competing for influence and patronage and showing little resistance to co-optation.[3] Actual power is centralized in the king who maintains a clientalist system in which the monarchy is the dominating actor. The king distributes the spoils and appoints his clients to the important political and administrative positions in return for their loyalty. This tactic enables the monarch to exert a considerable amount of influence over the political class by keeping them ever dependent on him. In his relations with the political parties, the king does not allow any party to become strong enough to challenge his authority, nor weak enough to wither away; he has realized the usefulness of parties in the system, particularly when he was left alone with the army in the early 1970s.[4] The king, like his father before him, has practiced a strategy of letting large parties split, new parties emerge, old parties wear down, and weak parties revive.[5] Intermittent violence and repression is also used against the opposition inside and outside the system.

The period from 1965 to 1973, which witnessed the emergence of revivalist groups and associations, was characterized by political uncertainty and social unrest, a confrontation between King Hassan and the different political forces in the polity, and an increase in the king's authoritarian rule. At the beginning of his career, King Hassan sought to consolidate his power and manage the political parties in a way that would insure the preeminence and centrality of the institution of the monarchy in the political process. Lacking his father's charisma and nationalistic record, however, he relied on figures personally loyal to the monarchy and appointed them as his cabinet members. To solidify his legitimacy, King Hassan introduced a constitution in 1962, which was greatly influenced by Charles DeGaulle's Fifth Republic. Though the king gave up some powers, he managed to consolidate his position. The king encouraged the creation of new political parties loyal to him, such as the Front for the Defense of Constitutional Institutions (FDIC) and the Berber party, Popular Movement (MP), in order to counterbalance the historical nationalist party, the Istiqlal (PI), part of which later split off into the National Union of Popular Forces (UNFP).

The king's patience with the participation of the PI and the UNFP grew thin when his supporters were unable to win the 1963 elections; and he did not have full control over the parties. Thus King Hassan resorted to repressive measures against the opposition. In 1965, the bloody Casablanca riots of workers and students over deteriorating social conditions prompted the king to end normal political life. The constitution was suspended, the parliament was disbanded, the parties were reduced to mere pressure groups, and discontented workers and students were severely repressed. The king decided to rule solely by himself and assumed full legislative and executive powers. Left alone, he relied on the most organized forces in the country, the police and the army, but the latter engineered two coup attempts against him in 1971 and 1972. Another alleged attempt to overthrow the government was blamed on the left in 1973, and was followed by the arrest and trials of its active elements. The UNFP was banned and the National Union of Moroccan Students (UNEM) was dismantled. An analyst of Moroccan political dynamics wrote: "After 1973 there was nothing left in Moroccan politics to support the system, outside of the isolated legitimacy and institution of the monarchy alone."[6]

The terrifying experiences of the early 1970s demonstrated the vulnerability of the system and inspired the king to start a new process of reestablishing or reconstructing political life. The king worked on providing an institutional base for his system and on setting a new relationship with the parties. He expanded the social base of the polity and used his political skill in manipulating internal and external issues to enhance further the popularity of the monarchy and outmaneuver the opposition parties.[7] To this end, a new constitution was drafted by King Hassan and promulgated in 1972. It granted more direct representation to the parties. Weak and divided, however, they protested the way the constitution was written, formed a common front, and boycotted the elections. Having strengthened his position after 1973 through police measures, the king announced the nationalization of foreign-owned lands, which were to be distributed to the peasants, and the gradual Moroccanization of some sectors of the economy. This initiative put the opposition parties on the defensive as it deprived them of an old demand, and increased the popularity of the king, particularly among the rural population. He also declared an ambitious five-year plan with a high growth rate of 7.5 percent per annum, and double investment rate.[8]

On the foreign policy front, in a symbolic expression of support for Palestine and Arab issues, the king dispatched a token force of Moroccan troops to the Egyptian and Syrian fronts during the 1973 October war. Yet it was another issue, the Sahara, which tremendously increased the king's popularity. Since independence, the historical integrity of the Moroccan Sahara, which was under Spain's control, was demanded by the Istiqlal and also the UNFP. In 1974, the king reasserted Morocco's historic claims over the Sahara, mobilized all segments of society, and launched an extensive campaign to defend Morocco's territorial integrity. In 1975, the king personally led the Green March of about 350,000 Moroccans across the borders of the Sahara. Indeed, the timing was very opportune. It followed the process of nationalization and Moroccanization that the king had already been undertaking. More significantly, it came after a period of domestic political unrest and an increase in the authoritarian measures of the state.[9] With the Sahara issue, the king managed to introduce an element that would become central to the political agenda and, indeed, a criterion of loyalty to the system.[10] After 1974, entry to the polity was conditional upon two factors: absolute loyalty to the monarchy and outright support of the Saharan policy.

Having secured enormous popularity, the king turned to the political parties and outlined the relation of the monarchy to the other political forces in the system. After independence was achieved, the monarch refused to be put in the same equation with the political parties or have his influence in the polity reduced, and insisted on functioning as a national leader and symbol of the nation's unity.[11] In one of his speeches, King Hassan stated that "Muhammad V, may God's blessing be upon him, had not returned [from exile abroad] in the coach of any of the parties. Constitutional monarchy is an imperative in order to live in peace."[12]

The centrality of the institution of the monarchy, its tactic of playing off one party against the other, and the factionalism of the Moroccan political parties have all reduced the effectiveness of the formal political parties and rendered them unable to mobilize the unorganized, marginal, and socially discontented population. This has been manifested in the sporadic eruption of repeated mass demonstrations in protest against the increasing cost of living and the deterioration of the conditions of the lower classes.

One of the instruments which King Hassan has used to consolidate his authority has been the expansion of the social base of the system by gradually bringing new elites into the government and giving more attention to the middle class in general. In comparison to the old elite, which still dominates the most influential political positions, the new elite, which was introduced during the 1970s, is young in age, highly educated, possesses technocratic training, and is more diversified in its regional background. It is personally loyal to the monarchy and dependent on it. The king's parties, the Rassemblement National des Independents (RNI) and Union Constitutionel (UC), have succeeded in promoting some of these elements to the government ranks.[13]

The middle class in Morocco has undergone a rapid and wide expansion after independence. Its members have joined the civil service and the growing bureaucracy. The number of civil servants at independence was estimated at around 43,000; by the 1980s, this number had increased ten times and reached 450,000.[14] The Moroccanization process and the five-year plan for 1973-1977 helped promote the establishment of a managerial middle class to replace the foreign management of foreign-owned firms and enterprises, and eventually to narrow the gap between the rich and the poor. In addition, several state projects like the distribution of urban land and the housing policy benefited the middle class.[15] Despite the fact that these measures have improved the status of some segments of the middle class, the structure of the Moroccan economy still favors the urban bourgeoisie and the landed rural class, which have long functioned as a middling stratum that maintains the stability of the regime. This order continues, however, to generate the wrath and discontent of the less privileged sectors of the population.

Economic Change

Morocco's economy is based on a free enterprise and private ownership system, notwithstanding a high degree of government intervention and state control. Although the king makes the major economic decisions, it could be described as a mixed economy, in which the agricultural sector plays a central role. Seventy percent of the population live off the land and almost half the labor force is employed in agriculture. Agriculture provides a large portion of the country's food and 50 percent of its total exports, yet agricultural productivity continues to suffer from traditional methods of cultivation, lack of water supplies, and repeated long droughts. Indeed, the severe droughts and deteriorating conditions of the countryside have forced thousands of Moroccans into urban areas. The level of urbanization has increased from 25 percent of the total population in 1960 to 45 percent in 1984, exacerbating the already existing problem of unemployment and the shortage of housing in the cities. Around 20 percent of the urban population live in shantytowns on the outskirts of the urban centers.[16] Unemployment among people of 20 to 40 years of age is very high, amounting to 40 percent of the total unemployed.[17]

During the 1970s the government generally expanded its control over the national economy. A number of major state economic and financial institutions were formed to directly participate in the economy.[18] The state increased its efforts to improve the agricultural sector, health conditions and education, and to diversify the manufacturing sector. However, in reality the Moroccanization and land distribution policies during the 1970s ended up benefiting the already wealthy land-owning families and segments of the newly emerging middle class more than they did the landless and poor classes. As one analyst has noted, "Financial institutions, industry, and agriculture all form a closed sector, bound together by corruption, spoils, inefficiency, and family ties, providing little outlet for the growing young generation and none for the unemployed and landless."[19] In fact, there is a phenomenal concentration of wealth among few families and flagrant inequality in the Moroccan social matrix. More than one-fifth of the national income is controlled by a few thousand families, while more than 50 percent of the population live at or below the level of absolute poverty.[20] The youth and the unemployed have become a major source of unrest and instability.

Origins

Within this context of political hierarchization, factionalism, and social inequality, the current movements of Islamic revivalism have flourished in Morocco since the late 1960s. There are more than twenty underground organizations in Rabat alone, each with its own structure, leadership, and ideology.[21] Some of these are influenced by the teachings of such outside Islamic movements as the Muslim Brothers of Egypt, and the association of Ahl al-Tabligh, or such Islamic thinkers as Sayyid Qutb of Egypt and Abul Ala al-Mawdudi of Pakistan. A few of them are radical and anti-system with a militant political dimension, and are distrustful of the official religious institutions. Unlike in the cases of Tunisia or Algeria, however, the apparent factionalism of the Islamists in Morocco makes it difficult to pinpoint a mainstream or an umbrella organization with a wide following, an enduring leadership, and a developed ideology. Some but certainly not all of these elements may exist in some organizations.

Several factors have contributed to the factionalism of the Islamists in Morocco. The first is the political pluralism of the system. The existence of several political parties with different orientations provides an opportunity and a wider spectrum for expressing discontent and opposition to the policies of the regime. Political pluralism, in addition, divides the potential base of support for the Islamic groups, which in this case are faced with the more difficult task of not only recruiting and mobilizing a following but also converting them first. The second reason could be ascribed to the intensity of religious life and the mystical practices of Islam in the *zawayas* and the Sufi orders in Morocco, which compete, as is the case of the Boutchichiyya order, with the Islamic revivalist movements over the same constituency of middle and lower middle class social elements. The third reason for factionalism among the Islamists is the close surveillance of the regime over such groups and its readiness to employ repressive measures against them whenever deemed necessary to prevent their evolution into influential and popular movements. This has been to the determent of subsequent Islamic movements. The fourth reason is related to the inability of the leaders of these movements to develop a uniting ideology and a mass organization. In fact, the reformist nature of the majority of these groups and associations keeps them divided over the details of reform and the plan of action to achieve them.

A remarkable characteristic of Islamic revivalism in Morocco is the proliferation of several Islamic cultural associations with moderate reformist tendencies. Many of them often include some form of political expression, in most cases reformist, in their activities. Nevertheless, they all accept the legitimacy of the monarchy and acknowledge the official religious institutions, despite harsh criticism of them. This is attributed to the type of legitimacy on which the regime is based. Unlike the case of Tunisia and Algeria where the secular orientation of the regime is more explicit, the monarchy in Morocco refrains from declaring secular tendencies and attempts, instead, to perpetuate the historical and religious basis as a major source of its legitimacy through the production of religious symbolism. These groups cannot, therefore, advocate a total rejection of the values of the system, but propose partial changes that could be introduced to the existing order. In the process, however, they may criticize some of the policies of the regime for undermining certain important and fundamental values.

Most of these Islamic associations are located in urban areas like Casablanca, Rabat, Fez, Oujda, and Tetouan. In March 1975, several of these associations held a conference in Tetouan which lasted for three days. The purpose of the conference was to discuss the condition of Islam and Muslims in Morocco and the means to promote Islamic values in society and to counter leftist influences.[22] The participants at the conference included eleven of the most active religious associations in the country like Jam`iyyat al-Amr bi al-Ma`ruf (the Association of Enjoining the Good), Jam`iyyat al-Ba`th al-Islami (the Association of Islamic Resurrection), Jam`iyyat al-Dirasat al-Islamiyya (the Association of Islamic Studies), Qudama' al-Qarawiyin (the Veterans of Qarawiyin), Jam`iyyat al-Da`wa al-Islamiyya (the Association of Islamic Call), `Ibad al-Rahman (the Worshipers of God), Kharriji Dar al-Hadith (the Graduates of Dar al-Hadith), Jam`iyyat al-`Urwa al-Wuthqa (the Association of the Indissoluble Bond), Rabitat `Ulama' Al-Maghrib (the League of Moroccan Scholars), Majma` al-Shabab al-Islami (the Coalition of the Islamic Youth), and Jam`iyyat al-Thaqafa al-Islamiyya (the Association of Islamic Culture). The conference formed five committees, each assigned with a specific task, such as looking into the conditions of the legislature, mass media, education, and religious propagation. At the end of the conference, a communiqué was issued criticizing some of the social ills in society and proposing recommendations for reforming the aforementioned sectors along Islamic lines.[23] Aside from demonstrating the presence of organized religious associations in the country, these kind of conferences have had limited impact in terms of putting the recommendations, which the associations propose to the regime in a very mild and inoffensive manner, into practice.

In general, the activities of the majority if not all of these associations focus on religious and social reforms. These include the organizing of conferences at which famous Muslim activists deliver Islamic lectures, holding religious ceremonies, and delivering speeches by some of its members in the mosques on Fridays. Most important, these activities include the publication of a newspaper or a magazine that functions as the mouthpiece of the association: it promotes Islamic ideals, offers interpretations on current issues, and engages in intellectual encounters with leftist elements. The periodical usually gives the association more of an organized and a popular facade than it possesses in reality. The following section discusses in greater length two of these associations, the Association of Islamic Resurrection in Tetouan and the Association of the Islamic Call in Fez.

The Association of Islamic Resurrection

The Association of Islamic Resurrection was founded at the beginning of the 1970s by Isma'il al-Khatib. Al-Khatib, a religious scholar, has been a member of the League of Moroccan Scholars since 1968. The League was established in the 1940s to defend the integrity and professional interests of the scholars during the colonial period. Following independence and over time, the League has become more of a pressure group, though an ineffective one, which attempts to safeguard the interests of the *'ulama'* in seeking to formulate reform measures without the need to engage in political participation. As was reflected in its seventh congress in 1979 which proposed a comprehensive program of Islamic reform, the League lacked the power to have these recommendations implemented.[24]

Al-Khatib's father, Muhammad al-'Arabi al-Khatib, was an active member of the *Salafiyya* movement and an advocate of religious, educational, and social reform in Morocco.[25] The first objective of the association is deepening the awareness of the Muslim population, particularly the youth, and emphasizing the need to come forth with "the Islamic solution" for problems in all aspects of life. Second, it aims at asserting the totality of Islam and rejects its compartmentalization. Third, it works for the purification of Islam from folk and traditional mispractices, particularly those of the *marabouts* and Sufi orders. Finally, it attempts to inform Muslims of the conditions of their fellow believers throughout the world.[26]

The association's headquarters is in Tetouan, and has an administrative apparatus to oversee the organization of its members and the regulation of the association's activities. As part of these activities, it holds regular sessions in its headquarters and in mosques for the memorization of the Qur'an and teaching religious subjects, celebrates the different religious occasions, and organizes occasional conferences and cultural seminars. Some of its members deliver Friday sermons in the mosques of Tetouan. The association also extends its activities outside the country. Its director, al-Khatib, traveled to France in 1976 with several members to educate the Muslim expatriates in their religion.[27]

Based on its objectives and activities, the association has a reformist tendency with a sharp political tone. Though sometimes critical of the un-Islamic features in the country, it refrains from directly challenging the legitimacy of the system and prefers rather to work from within to achieve its objectives. In 1975, on the anniversary of the Prophet Muhammad, the association in one of the issues of its periodical, *al-Nour* (The Light), on the one hand, conveyed its congratulations to the Commander of the Faithful, and, on the other hand, organized a celebration for the occasion under the slogan of "The birth of the Prophet...A revolution against poverty, ignorance, and class [society]."[28]

Al-Nour began publishing in April 1974 as an Islamic monthly paper; it turned into a weekly in 1981. The reason for publishing this periodical, as explained in its first issue, was to spread the call for Islam by all possible means, counter religious mispractices, and advocate the return to the Qur'an and the Sunna, particularly "when the Muslim nation is witnessing severe setbacks, struggling with crises, and exposed and besieged by various enemies."[29] Circulating in the major cities, *al-Nour* deals with a wide variety of religious, cultural, economic, social, and political aspects. It is influenced by the views and language of the Muslim Brothers, particularly in its diagnosis of the present conditions of Muslims. The name of the association itself is derived from one of Sayyid Qutb's statements which stresses the need for an Islamic resurrection to salvage humanity from the distress of *jahiliyya* (state of ignorance). Qutb's statement is placed on the paper's front page as one of its slogans. The paper is very critical of the left, and to underline its theses and ideological prescriptions, a special issue was devoted entirely to refuting Marxist economic ideas and promoting Islamic economic principles. Recognizing the predicament of the Islamic movement in Morocco, writings in the periodical repeatedly stress the need for an Islamic organization to unite the unnecessarily scattered Islamic groups and to reconstruct the Muslim individual.[30] The underlying theses that permeate the periodical's topics are as follows: (i) Islam has been confronted with internal and external challenges; (ii) It has been marginalized and removed from conducting the affairs of Muslims, or at best confined to the matters of personal status, and, as a consequence, the Muslim nation has fallen prey to chaos and weakness; (iii) The West, both in its capitalist and socialist form, has gone bankrupt as a source of any ideological inspiration and is unable to offer the Muslim societies solutions for their chronic problems; (iv) Imported ideas complicate the conditions of Muslims and deprive them of attaining their authentic identity; (v) The solution is to implement the doctrine of Islam in its entirety.[31]

In comparison to many Islamic periodicals, the paper articulates these issues in a relatively refined way, projecting some degree of political awareness and a tendency for organized action. The solutions it proposes, however, are in many cases general and sometimes simplistic. In the first four years particularly, they were framed in an idealistic manner that lacked a specific focus. Themes dealing with Islamic economic principles, which were emphasized in the 1970s, began to subside and were replaced by follow-ups on developments of the Islamic movements outside Morocco. In 1979 and 1980, several articles dealt with the news and developments of the Iranian revolution, from which the paper tried to draw "lessons" for the Islamic movements in general. However, this was toned down after the regime's repressive measures against the Islamists in 1980. Since 1984, one can clearly witness a decrease in the intensity of the paper; it began to publish extracts from other Islamic newspapers and periodicals and republish some of its old articles, especially literary articles and others dealing with religious rituals.

The Islamic Call Association

Another publication that reflects a religio-political awareness is the magazine *al-Huda* (Guidance), which is published every two months by the Islamic Call Association in Fez. The magazine was first published in 1982. The purpose of its publication was the association's perception that an unprecedented and fierce onslaught was taking place against Islam. Its editor, al-Mufdel Felwati, wrote in its first issue:

> We are still being invaded, despite the military departure of the colonizer, in our homes, streets, schools, stores, and even in our mosques. We have been conquered intellectually, politically, economically, and morally. We have lost our authentic identity and distinguishing characteristics, because we have become an echo to the voices which vibrate in the West and East.[32]

The paper has thus set its objectives, which reflect those of the association, as clarifying the Islamic paradigm from which the nation has deviated, reinforcing the current Islamic awakening, and closing the schisms between Muslims. It emphasized its reformist orientation by asserting its tendency to resort to peaceful and moderate means to achieve these objectives.[33] The magazine has strong political and social theses, which in some cases are analytical and explicitly critical of the prevailing social injustice and discrimination.[34]

With regard to the evolution of the periodical's themes, in the first two years, *al-Huda* reiterated general ones dealing with issues such as the sweeping Westernization of the Muslim societies, the current Islamic revival, the validity of Islam as a comprehensive system capable of solving the problems of society, and the need to return to its precepts. From 1984, the periodical began to devote special issues to more specific themes pertaining to the condition of the educational system and the media. Concerning the first issue, it called for a total revision of the Westernized and secular educational curricula and the removal of the contradictions inherent in them in order to reflect Moroccan culture and Islamic values.[35] On the media, *al-Huda* highlighted the discrepancy between Islam as officially professed and the disorienting material broadcast on the state-controlled television, which demoralizes Muslims and lures them away from their indigenous values.[36]

In examining the extent and the future direction of these associations and their periodicals, it is possible to argue that within the context of the state's appropriation of symbolism and religious legitimacy, their message will most likely remain reformist in content and moderate in nature, with limited ability to pose a threat to the regime. As these associations are large in number, they divide the potential Islamic constituency, and their influence remains felt more in the regions in which they are located. They are reformist, not militant, and so far have displayed little aptitude for political mobilization. Nevertheless, they still have importance for the movement of Islamic revival in general. Their periodicals deal with a variety of issues from an Islamic perspective that is different from the official one. This in fact provides an alternative view of the issues discussed and reduces the hegemony of the traditional institutions and interpretations. They socialize potential adherents to the Islamic movement and increase the political and Islamic awareness of the sympathizers and would-be Islamists by defending the theses of the more militant Islamic groups. Equally important, they provide channels of communication for the Islamic activists by publishing their statements and communiqués.[37]

The Muslim Brothers Group

Several Islamic groups throughout the Muslim world have been influenced by the Egyptian-based Society of Muslim Brothers (*al-Ikhwan al-Muslimun*), which emerged in 1928. Despite this apparent influence, however, these groups are also influenced by the particularities of their surroundings and therefore differ in their strategies and orientations from one country to the other. In Morocco, the Muslim Brothers group takes a clandestine form. The group is based in Casablanca, although it has a number of underground cells in other major cities. The Muslim Brothers of Morocco adopt the same slogans and socialization methods as their Egyptian counterparts. Their major objective is the establishment of a truly Muslim society and an Islamic state through legal channels of reform—namely, the Islamic education of the individual, promotion of the integrity of the family, and the incorporation of Islamic values into the whole society, which will all eventually lead to the establishment of an Islamic system. The group draws on the secondary students and the dislocated and recently urbanized lower middle class as a major source of recruitment. It concentrates its activities in the poor quarters and the mosques in which the Muslim Brother member makes direct contact with potential recruits and begins to explain the un-Islamic practices in society, the need to return to the true principles of Islam, and the nature of the group's message.

Once recruited, the new member passes through several levels, and after fulfilling the requirements of each, becomes a practicing brother. At this level, the brother gives allegiance in person to the *murshid* (the Spiritual Guide) or the leader of his cell. This allegiance is based on a number of components, such as understanding, fidelity, loyalty, and a willingness to sacrifice and perform the *jihad* (struggle).

The orthodox teachings of the Brothers put them in constant conflict with what they perceive as un-Islamic practices in society. They are opposed to the monarchical system which is based on heredity, a practice that is prohibited in Islam. They also challenge the official religious establishment that justifies the system and its practices and thereby perpetuates its continuation. Likewise, they consider political parties as a divisive element in the *umma* (community) of believers and reject them for their opportunism and secular orientations.[38] The Moroccan Muslim Brothers view the other reformist religious associations as useful in spreading religious awareness, yet ineffective in bringing about the desired change.

The clandestine Moroccan Muslim Brothers are unlike their Egyptian counterparts, who implemented overt methods for achieving their objectives and developed a durable leadership, a well-designed organizational structure, a large constituency, and an appealing ideology. As a consequence, the Moroccan Brothers have reduced their prospects for gaining wide popularity and becoming an influential group. In addition, the group suffers from divisions within its ranks resulting from a disagreement on the method that should be implemented in dealing with the regime. Some advocate moderation and place emphasis on reformist methods in order to avoid possible government reprisals against the group. Others, who constitute a small minority, on the other hand, attempt to precipitate confrontation with the regime to demonstrate the presence and effectiveness of the group. It is possible to argue that if such a confrontation takes place, it is most likely that the group will not be able to contain these differences and will explode into smaller splinter militant factions.

Ahl Al-Tabligh wa Al-Da`wa

Another group which is active in Morocco is Ahl al-Tabligh wa al-Da`wa. It is an offshoot of the India-based Tablighi-Jama`at movement which appeared in the early 1940s. The Tabligh of Morocco began its activities in the late 1960s, after Pakistani members of the mother group toured in Morocco to preach their message. The Moroccan Tabligh gained official status as a religious association in July 1975 with its base in Casablanca. It is also active in Rabat, Nador, Tiznit, Tangier, and al-Kasr el Kebir.[39]

The group's objectives are apolitical and their activities are basically religious and reformist in nature. The members of al-Tabligh disdain politics and the practices of politicians, and they reject the political tendencies of other Islamic revivalist associations, which, they believe, are ignoring the moral and spiritual aspects of the message of Islam. The group therefore aims at spreading the moral and spiritual teachings of Islam and the practices of the Prophet and at attracting followers to undertake the task of *tabligh* (propagation). Their text book is al-Kandahlawi's *Hayat al-Sahaba* (The Life of the Prophet's Companions), which they study thoroughly and on the basis of which they try to imitate the conduct and way of life of the Prophet's disciples. They impose strict disciplinary measures on the personal, moral, and social conduct of their members in order to demonstrate a living example of the path to an Islamic way of life.

To achieve their objectives, the members of al-Tabligh rely on continuous and collective touring of the cities and rural areas where they engage in persistent exhortation. They divide their propagation into three parts: particular, popular, and recollective. In the particular propagation, they monitor their target in advance and approach people who might be useful for the propagation of their message, such as the religious scholars—who in fact rarely respond to their call. The popular propagation is directed to the general public, with no social or professional distinction, and is performed in the marketplaces, assemblies, and private homes. It aims at recruiting new followers to the group. The recollective propagation is a resocialization process for old members who might need additional discipline, and it usually takes place in the mosque.

Ahl al-Tabligh are often opposed by two groups, the `ulama' and the local officials. The former are suspicious of their foreign origin and what they perceive as innovative religious practices. The local officials are often provoked by the activism and vague objectives of Ahl al-Tabligh. Despite the reformist nature of its message, the group in fact competes with the regime in approaching and recruiting the same social elements—the lower class and uneducated populace. Tozy mentions that, indeed, the government tried to prevent Ahl al-Tabligh from approaching and maintaining direct contacts with the masses; a demand which the group rejected on the basis that it was operating in an Islamic country, whose laws did not prohibit preaching among Muslims.[40]

Smaller groups such as these remain politically and socially marginal in Morocco. Substantially more influential and taking a more explicitly political approach are Harakat al-Islah wa al-Tajdid al-Maghribiyya—HATM (The Movement of Reform and Renewal) and al-`Adl wa al-Ihsan (Justice and Benevolence). The two movements are different in size and orientation. Al-`Adl enjoys a larger following than HATM and proposes a more alternative model for the state and society. This model stems from a highly critical view of Morocco's present conditions. HATM, on the other hand, recognizes the historical and religious legitimacy of the institution of the monarchy and considers an Islamic state to exist already in Morocco, notwithstanding some deviations. With both movements rejecting the use of violent means to affect change, al-`Adl's message is clearly more defiant in tone than HATM's.

The Movement for Reform and Renewal (HATM): A Perilous Beginning

The origin of the Movement for Reform and Renewal (HATM) goes back to 1969 when Abdel Karim Mouti` (b. 1936) founded with Ibrahim Kamal Jami`yyat al-Shabiba al-Islamiyya al-Maghribiyya (The Moroccan Islamic Youth Association) in Casablanca. While little is known of the social background of Ibrahim Kamal, except his status as a former secondary school teacher, Abdel Karim Mouti` served for sixteen years as an inspector in the Ministry of Education. A civil servant with long experience as a political activist and a former member of the National Union of Popular Forces (UNFP), Mouti`, for his part, was elected the Secretary-General of the Union of Education Inspectors. During his youth, his religious mentor was Muhammad al-Mukhtar al-Soussi. Al-Soussi was a prominent religious scholar of high esteem, who established and presided over the Association of Scholars in Souss. Al-Soussi integrated modern and traditional subjects in his teachings.[41] Due to his opposition to the French presence in Morocco, al-Soussi was put under house arrest in Casablanca by the French colonial forces. During the national struggle for independence, Mouti`, at the age of sixteen, joined the armed resistance against the French.

Up to the 1960s, Mouti` joined ranks with the leftist-inspired opposition groups among the teachers' union and in the UNFP. The shift from the left to militant Islam arose from Mouti`'s bitter dissatisfaction with the socioeconomic conditions of Morocco, and the inability of the leftist parties to address these problems successfully due to their preoccupation with the rules of political participation set by King

Hassan.[42] In the meantime, Mouti` was exposed to the ideas of Sayyid Qutb of the Egyptian Muslim Brothers and decided to form an Islamic organization on his own, the Moroccan Youth Association (hereafter, al-Shabiba).

After its inception in 1969, al-Shabiba remained a clandestine organization for three years. During this period, Mouti` concentrated on the recruitment of followers, the structuring of an organizational base, and the socialization of members. Through his connections in the field of education, he recruited followers from among the teachers and students in the universities and secondary schools. He organized them into cells and wrote for them several secret studies dealing with the conditions of Morocco and explaining the need for paving the way for an Islamic revolution to reform these conditions and to bring forth the transformation of society.

A book, *al Mu'amara `ala Harakat al-Shabiba al-Islamiyya* (The Conspiracy Against The Islamic Youth Association) which al-Shabiba published in 1984, provides the reasons that triggered the formation of the association. It refers to the general political, social, and economic conditions resulting from ideological deviations in the different institutions—the individual, the family, society, and the structures of the state—and the lack of commitment to the teachings of Islam. It also attributed the emergence of the movement to: (1) the deep dissatisfaction with the stage of apathy which the Moroccan people had reached and their despair of reform by the state or the political parties which monopolized the political process in the country; (2) the experiences of the founder of the movement, Mouti`, who, after a long activist political career, became distrustful of the possibility of achieving reforms through partisan wrangling and political fragmentation; and (3) the absence of any movement to spearhead an Islamic resurrection in Morocco, except for the traditional Sufi orders, which had harmed society with their mystical practices and turned people away from true belief.[43]

Due to the clandestine nature of al-Shabiba, little information pertaining to its organizational structure is available. It appears to have had an underground base organized around closed cells. These cells served two important functions: seeking the active recruitment of members; and indoctrinating them with the writings of Mouti`. As in the case of Tunisia, the induction of members to these closed cells occurred within the secondary schools, the university, and the confines of the mosques. Furthermore, the study of a Moroccan scholar, Mohamed

Tozy, reveals the organizational structure of the association as following the blueprint of a non-Moroccan Islamic movement. In Tozy's analysis, the association appeared to reflect the organizational apparatus of the Muslim Brotherhood in Egypt, which maintains a pyramidal shape. At the top of the pyramid resided *al-Murshid al-'Amm* (the supreme guide), Abdel Karim Mouti', *al-Amana al-'Amma* (the general secretariat), and *al-Maktab al-Tanfidhi* (the executive council). This structure was immediately dismantled by the subsequent arrest and dispersal of its top leaders and activists, following the assassination of Omar Ben Jelloun of the Socialist Union of Popular Forces (USFP) in 1975.[44]

With regard to its constituency, unlike the Tunisian al-Nahda or the Algerian FIS, al-Shabiba did not claim the support of tens of thousands of Moroccans. Among the supporters of the association the students constituted a large proportion (some 40 percent).[45] On the other hand, the majority of the members of al-Shabiba who were implicated in the assassination of Ben Jelloun were workers.[46] Nevertheless, if one looks at the subsequent trials of 71 members of the association, following the riots of January 1984, one sees mainly secondary school students.[47] This indicates that the association drew following from various social segments and not from a specific class.

To understand the rise of Islamic activism on the part of the students, it is useful to refer to the field research of a Moroccan scholar. A tabulation of 400 Moroccan University students concerning Islamic values, carried out by Mohamed Tozy in 1984, revealed that 65 percent believed that there was a need to revitalize the cultural identity of Moroccan society by relying on the precepts of the Qur'an. Another 60 percent agreed that the stagnation of the Moroccan society was due to the inadequate use of Islamic teachings.[48]

In general, Islamic revivalism in Morocco draws its source of strength from the mosques, which, as in the case of Tunisia, served as a center for religious exhortation and a nucleus for the selective mobilization of supporters to various Islamic groups. Attendance in the mosques cuts across the various segments of Moroccan society and provides them with wide appeal.

Going Public

Al-Shabiba obtained legalization in 1972 as a religious society with the objective of "contributing to the social construction of the Moroccan society, spreading moral values and encouraging the Moroccan citizens to enjoin righteousness, virtue, and reform through the implementation of Islam." Al-Shabiba's formation coincided with a precarious phase in Morocco's political history. This period was characterized by severe political and economic crises, popular discontent, spread of leftist influence, paralysis of the political process, and uncertainty of the future of the regime. The two coup attempts on the king's life in 1971 and 1972 obviously reflected this uncertainty. These factors explain the regime's initial toleration of the establishment of an Islamic movement that could defuse the wrath of the discontented youth and counterbalance the leftist threat in schools and universities.

Mouti` adopted for his organization a dual political tactic, public and clandestine. In public, he presented the movement as a legal, apolitical religious association, advocating reform and non-violence as a means of preserving Islamic values and confronting the Moroccan left. In its statute and intermittent statements, al-Shabiba identified itself as a religious and educational organization with a legal status. In this capacity, it claimed to be disinterested and uninvolved in politics. The association was keen to confirm that it represented only its members who were one community, rather than the whole community, of Muslims. The purpose of this confirmation was to deny any exclusivity to its activities and to counter the official claims that accused it of considering those outside it as non-Muslims. It also officially rejected violence as a means for resolving conflict with other groups and for fulfilling its goals.

Al-Shabiba's declared, though vague, objectives were reformist in nature and did not distinguish it from any other religious association. They included the reformation of society, the spread of a proper ethos, and the encouragement of all citizens to pursue virtue and good deeds through the implementation of Islamic principles. Its methods were to include moderate social activities, such as offering Islamic education, combating illiteracy, organizing summer camps and public health campaigns, and socializing youth through educational, religious, artistic, and athletic activities.[49]

In the meantime, Mouti` built a clandestine structure for his organization and propagated a radical position against the regime. He held a critical view of the "un-Islamic" practices in Moroccan life and called for the overthrow of the regime and the total reconstruction of society. In a study which he wrote for circulation among the association's cells in 1970, Mouti` viewed the Moroccan society as passing through a critical historical transition, resulting from the tremendous pressure of social, economic, political, and cultural interactions. These conditions reflected an uneven growth and social inequality among a deprived majority and a well-to-do minority, political division among opposition and loyal parties alike, and various ideological orientations leading to the despair and disorientation of the Moroccan people. By contrasting this context with preceding, yet in Mouti`'s view, similar periods in Moroccan history, he concluded that political collapse and foreign intervention was probably imminent. (Two years later the king barely escaped two coup attempts and the whole system bordered on collapse.)

Mouti` critically analyzed the evolution and political stands of the different political forces in the system, including the Islamic advocates. He warned against the forthcoming conflict between the left, the most organized force, and the emerging Islamic trend, and against the expected attempts of the authorities to liquidate this nascent movement. He therefore deemed it necessary for the militant Islamic movement to reorganize itself into active units to undertake the task of mobilization, socialization, and control.[50]

This dual tactic enabled al-Shabiba for some time to function legally, focus on the recruitment of followers, and work on the socialization of its members. It was meant to provide the association with a legal facade for its activities and to distract the attention of the regime, which had already become concerned about its orientation and potential threat as the members began increasingly to make their presence felt in the university and private mosques.

Another party that was also anxious about the rise of an Islamic activist movement was the left in general and its Marxist elements in particular. The Islamic groups were challenging them in their traditional constituency, the university. In 1973-74, they engaged in several clashes with the members of al-Shabiba in the high schools and the university, and exchanged harsh accusations in the press. Several philosophy teachers were physically attacked, allegedly by the members of the association, who accused these teachers of spreading atheist, Marxist ideas among their students. The Association of Philosophy Teachers published a statement in the Communist Party's newspaper *al-Bayan* (The Manifesto) and in *al-Anba'* (The News), the government's paper, warning against the threat of the Islamic activists and the fundamentalist ideas which they propagated.[51]

After succeeding in monitoring the association and identifying its leadership, the regime avoided early and direct confrontation with al-

Shabiba. After all, it was indirectly playing a useful role, in the eyes of the government, by counterbalancing the pervasive influence of the left. At the same time, however, the government tried to contain the movement in order to keep it under control. But al-Shabiba made the fatal mistake of refusing to declare its support of the king over the issue of the Sahara and declining to participate in the Green March in 1975.[52] Al-Shabiba thereby failed to comply with a fundamental prerequisite for political survival, and, consequently, brought upon itself the wrath of the regime.

In 1975, the regime announced that some members of al-Shabiba were implicated in the assassination of Omar Ben Jelloun, the editor of the USFP (Union of Socialist Popular Forces) paper. This incident ushered in the second phase of the movement's history.

Suppression and Fragmentation

The assassination of Omar Ben Jelloun ushered in a phase of confrontation between the regime and al-Shabiba.[53] The regime accused al-Shabiba of the murder of Ben Jelloun and arrested some of its members. The members of the association were tried after four years, in June 1979. Following the trials, demonstrations broke out in Casablanca supporting the association and condemning the sentences and the leftist USFP. Two members received the death sentence; seventeen, including Abdel Karim Mouti`, who was tried in absentia, received life imprisonment; and two were acquitted, including Ibrahim Kamal, the co-founder of al-Shabiba.[54]

The USFP in turn charged the government with authorizing the assassination of Ben Jelloun and facilitating the escape of Mouti`.[55] Unsurprisingly, to discredit the Islamists and mobilize sympathy for their cause, the left believed the Islamic groups to be the creation of the regime and its tool in counterbalancing the Marxist groups and attempting to eliminate them, even physically, whenever necessary.

Al-Shabiba, for its part, directed a stronger accusation against the government. It emphasized that its leader Mouti` had maintained good relations with the different factions of the opposition, including the USFP. It cited as an example that two months before the assassination of Ben Jelloun, Mouti` had met with the latter and exchanged views on their respective ideologies; they had agreed on a public debate in the USFP's paper, *al-Muharir* (The Editor), in which Mouti` would write a series of studies on Islam, and the members of the USFP would respond.

Al-Shabiba pointed out that the government was the only side benefiting from the murder of Ben Jelloun. It argued that by eliminating him, the government reaped a double benefit: it managed both to weaken a radical wing within the left by direct assassination and to liquidate the Islamic opposition by arrests and trials.[56]

It is difficult of course to verify the accuracy of the view of either the left or the Islamists. However, the issue of Ben Jelloun helped the USFP in many respects. Making it appear the victim of official repression, the incident enhanced the USFP's credibility as an opposition party. The implication of guilt to an Islamic group, moreover, assisted the party in discrediting its religious rival. It might also be true that the Moroccan regime benefited from the Ben Jelloun affair. Prior to the incident, the king was setting the stage for the issue of the Sahara and was undertaking the process of rearranging roles within the system. The king granted some degree of political freedom to the political parties in order to mobilize support for the Sahara, but two trends represented a potential threat—the radical wing of Ben Jelloun within the USFP and the radical Islamic activists.

After 1975, al-Shabiba was outlawed and entered into a period of total disarray and factionalism. The presence of al-Shabiba was reduced to sporadic activities in the university and the distribution of statements in the Islamic periodicals, which attempted to emphasize the non-violent nature of the association, defended it against the charges of assassinating Ben Jelloun, and called for the release of its members and the return of its leader.[57] But as a result of disputes over the leadership of Abdel Karim Mouti` and his policies, the association split into several antagonistic militant groups. Tozy listed four of these groups, the Revolutionary Commission, the Islamic Students Vanguard, the Movement of the Mujahidin, and an anonymous fourth, operating clandestinely in France.[58]

In 1979 and 1980, after the Iranian Revolution and the take-over of the Holy Mosque in Mecca, the regime became concerned anew about the threat of the Islamic revivalists. It tightened its grip over their activities, launched several arrest campaigns against them, and prevented their congregations in mosques.[59] Following the January riots in 1984, King Hassan appeared on television and accused three elements of instigating these riots—Khomeinists, Marxists, and Zionists.

The file of al-Shabiba was reopened in July 1984 when the Moroccan government arrested 71 members of the association and put them on trial. The charges included "the creation of an association of criminals, plotting to overthrow King Hassan and create an Islamic republic, distribution of Iranian-style literature on the eve of the fourth Islamic summit [January 1984 in Casablanca], and belonging to the banned Islamic Youth Association."[60] Thirteen members were sentenced to death, seven of whom were tried in absentia, including once again Abdel Karim Mouti`; thirty-four received life imprisonment; and the rest received sentences ranging from four to twenty years. Representatives of international organizations who attended the trials believed the detainees to be guilty of a "simple opinion offense" that did not warrant such harsh sentences.[61] In October 1985, thirty members belonging to the Mujahidin, a splinter group of al-Shabiba, were tried in Marrakesh for attempting to overthrow the government, and received sentences ranging from one year to life.[62]

While in exile, Mouti` tried unsuccessfully to maintain the organizational structure of al-Shabiba and his control over the group's activities. His leadership style reflected poor organizational skills that led to the eventual disintegration of the entire movement. Mouti` appointed a six-member leadership to run the affairs of the group inside the country. He later replaced it as a result of his concern over its growing independence. Mouti` then selected another leadership, which the deposed former leaders did not recognize. To contain the confusion and disorder within the ranks of the organization, Mouti` finally named a third leadership, which was actually manipulated by another shadowy group selected by Mouti`.[63] This muddle led many members of al-Shabiba to withdraw from or freeze their membership in the organization. The breaking point occurred when Mouti`, following his sentencing, declared his fierce opposition to the regime and produced a publication, *al-Mujahid* in March 1981, in which he called for violence and harshly criticized the monarchy and its policies regarding the Sahara issue.

HATM Emerges

The increasing disagreement over the personalistic leadership style of Mouti` and his radical policies raised uncertainty about the future of al-Shabiba. This led some members to hold a general assembly in 1981 to reconsider the movement's policies and strategy. Concerned about losing control over the movement, Mouti` condemned the assembly and its organizers. While agreeing on dismissing Mouti`, the participants in the meeting differed on the nature of the group's future activity—

clandestine or public—and on the measures to be taken during the transition from the old to the new phase. While this precarious phase lasted for three years for some groups within al-Shabiba and consequently made them subject to periodic arrests, the Rabat group decided to split in April 1981 under the leadership of Abd al-Ilah Benkiran.

Benkiran published a statement in January 1982 in which he clarified the group's position regarding al-Shabiba. He denounced the practices of Mouti` and announced the total separation of his group from the mother movement, while pledging the continuation of Islamic action within legal frameworks.[64] Indeed, a year later, Benkiran declared the establishment of al-Jama`a al-Islamiyya (The Islamic Group) and applied for legal recognition as an Islamic organization. The association produced a charter outlining its nature, principles, objectives, and method of action.

In describing the nature of al-Jama`a, the charter stated that the association is a national group which is not affiliated with any foreign organization or state. It perceives itself, not as the only Islamic group, the only representative of Islam or its sponsor, but as a group of Muslims working on establishing religion in all walks of life in cooperation with others who strive to achieve the same objective.

Reflecting the nature of the association, its principles were multifaceted. The principles of the association include achieving total submission to God, adherence to Islam, and collective organized action; promoting fraternity and trust; following the *shura* (consultation), obedience and discipline, gradualism, and positive involvement; interaction in society and cooperation with others for the well-being of Muslims. Regarding the objectives, the charter states seven main goals: to renew the understanding of religion, call for the respect of individual rights and public freedoms, advocate the implementation of the Islamic *shari`a*, improve the material and living conditions of Muslims, perform charitable works, achieve a comprehensive cultural renaissance, and work on accomplishing the unity of Muslims. In a later statement, the association added "confronting the ideologies and ideas which are subversive to Islam and participating in raising the educational and moral level of the Moroccan people" to its objectives.

Al-Jama`a listed seven legal means through which these objectives could be attained. These included different types of activities: individual, public, cultural, social, economic, political, union, educational, and organizational. It categorically condemned the use of violent means in any way or form. The association also devised a rigorous program for the socialization, spiritual and moral education of its members.[65]

While awaiting formal legalization since 1983, the group has been tolerated by the authorities to conduct itself as an active organization. It was permitted to open branches in different parts of the country. It also began production of a monthly publication, *al-Islah* (Reform) in February 1987, which became the mouthpiece of the group and a significant channel for expressing its views on various internal, regional, and international issues. However, *al-Islah* was banned in 1990. This apparently sent a signal to the group with regards to the limits of the regime's toleration. Al-Jama`a issued another publication, *al-Raya* (The Banner), in June 1990, which appeared first bi-monthly and from June 1993, weekly. Following its ordinary general assembly in August 1990, al-Jama`a asserted its commitment to the "sacred components" of the country: Islam, the Maliki legal school, the constitutional monarchy, territorial integrity, and the Arabic language.[66] In fact, these elements have been set by the king as indisputable constants of the Moroccan nation and as prerequisites for participation in the political process.

Al-Jama`a went a step further in February 1992 by changing its name to Harakat al-Islah wa al-Tajdid al-Maghribiyya—HATM (The Movement of Reform and Renewal in Morocco), thus omitting any direct religious reference from the new name. HATM explained the reasons behind changing the old name as to eliminate any possible misperception of the exclusivity of the group, reassert its status as an Islamic group among many others, reconfirm its willingness to participate and cooperate with other forces in society, and highlight the essence of the group's activities, mainly to reform the conditions of the Muslims and renew their understanding of and commitment to Islam.[67]

The issue of changing the name can be considered an important concession on the part of the group. It reflects a realistic attitude in dealing with the political facts of Morocco. In a reflective statement that translates this realism, Abdullah Baha, the movement's vice-president, stated, "we do not want to politicize Islam, but Islamize politics. We hope to have a political role that matches our size."[68] It is very unlikely that a regime which is anchored in religious legitimacy would allow any political party to challenge this legitimacy on religious grounds. Recognizing this fact, Muhammad Yateem, the newly elected HATM's president, admitted that "Our problem in Morocco is not in establishing an Islamic state. Theoretically and constitutionally, this state already exists. We, on the contrary, support this legitimacy and consider it an asset that should not be given up or disputed.[69]

Having satisfied this condition, HATM intensified its public activities and improved its organizational structure. It issued statements on various domestic and foreign issues; its representatives appeared frequently in cultural and political gatherings held by other parties and even in those sponsored by the Ministry of Endowment; it participated in marches and public demonstrations; it persistently raised the case of the detained Moroccan Islamists and their conditions in prisons; organized national campaigns for health and social services; held special lectures and seminars during religious occasions; and established a student branch in the universities. HATM also revised its bylaws, institutionalizing the practices of collective leadership, consultation, and democracy within its organs. The movement holds regular internal elections for its leadership (every four years). The elections' lengthy procedures combine the practice of consultation and the mechanisms of modern democracy.[70] This process indeed allows for the rotation of different persons in the position of the leadership of the movement. For example, during the period from 1981 to 1985, Yateem was elected the head of the movement; from 1985 to 1994, Benkiran replaced him as head; and in July 1994, Yateem was again elected as president.

In March 1992, King Hassan announced that local elections would take place in October. As its activities expanded and recruitment ability increased, HATM needed to articulate the demands of its constituency and ensure the political participation of its members within a legal framework. The leaders of HATM along with some of its members, hoping to participate in the coming elections, established Hizb al-Tajdid al-Watani (The National Renewal Party—NRP) in May 1992 and applied for recognition.

The party's bylaws stated that the NRP functions within the system of the constitutional monarchy and in conformity with the laws of the country. Its objectives included reasserting and deepening the Islamic identity of the Moroccan people; enhancing the status of the Arabic language and supporting the policy of Arabization; preserving the country's territorial integrity and enhancing its political and economic independence; supporting the democratic process in accordance with the components of the Moroccan society; participating in the socialization of the citizens and in defending their legitimate rights; participating in developing the society through encouraging (individual) initiative, legal gains and working on achieving social justice; enhancing social stability through the achievement of justice, cooperation, and tolerance; reinforcing the historic role of Morocco in cultural achievement; supporting the tendencies of unity among the Arab and Islamic nation; and advocating the causes of the Muslim nation and supporting the freedom movements in the world.

The NRP was formed as the political wing of HATM, which would not be dissolved but keep functioning as a comprehensive Islamic movement. The new party, the bylaws stated, would be open to all Moroccans irrespective of their religious affiliation as long as they abide by the party's policy. The party would participate in the political process according to the guiding rules: respect for democracy, the free choice of the people, accepting the concept of transfer of power, and respect for pluralism.[71]

It is evident that the bylaws of the party and the ensuing statements of its founders are carefully phrased to conform with the laws regulating the formation of political parties and calm the concerns of other forces in society. The innovation of creating a parallel and purely political organization was meant to avoid risking the continuity of the mother movement. However, without any convincing reasons, the request by the founders of the NRP was rejected by the authorities. In addition, the government banned the issue of *al-Raya*, in which HATM published a legal response to the government decision.

HATM had to look for other means of legal participation. It approached the Constitutional and Democratic Popular Movement (MPCD) and formed a federation with it. The MPCD is an old party which broke away from the Popular Movement (MP) in 1967 under the leadership of Abdel Kareem al-Khatib, a historic figure and a well respected politician with Islamic tendencies. This federation is expected to be convenient for both sides. The inclusion of members of HATM into the MPCD would certainly revive the activities of the already dormant MPCD, while at the same time provide HATM's members the opportunity to participate in politics through formal channels. So far, HATM has succeeded in revitalizing most of MPCD's branches throughout the country with its members. It fielded two candidates in Oujda and Tangier in the partial legislative elections of April 1994, though they were not elected.[72]

Al-`Adl wa al-Ihsan (Justice and Benevolence)

Larger in its base of support than HATM, al-`Adl wa al-Ihsan was originally founded in 1979 as al-Jama`a (The Group), using the name of a magazine published the same year by Abdel Salam Yassin. Yassin, the founder of al-Jama`a, is considered to be an influential ideologue of the contemporary Islamic revival in Morocco.

Yassin was born in 1928. Similar to Abdel Karim Mouti`, Yassin is a former education inspector. In his open letter, *al-Islam aw al-Tufan* (Islam or the Deluge), which he directed to the king in 1973, Yassin gave an account of his social background. He was the son of a Berber peasant and was raised in poverty and material deprivation. Despite his modest background, Yassin claims membership of a sharifian family and thus, like King Hassan II, he is a descendant of the Prophet Muhammad.

A son of a traditional peasant, Yassin received an early religious education and committed the Qur'an to memory. He then studied under traditional scholars in one of the religious institutes, which was the dominant type of education prior to independence. Not completely satisfied with his traditional education, Yassin read widely on Western cultures. When independence was achieved in 1956, he became an inspector, later an inspector-general, in the Ministry of Education, a post which he occupied for 27 years. In his letter to the king, Yassin mentioned that his history in both fields gave him the experience to speak of the traditional scholars, as their student and associate, and of administrative corruption in Morocco, as an administrator and an educational expert.[73]

In 1965, Yassin went through what he described as a spiritual crisis. He recovered through a Sufi shaykh from the Boutchichiyya order, a popular mystical order in Morocco, and was content to find truth with the Sufis. He closely followed his shaykh and remained in this order for several years. After the death of his mentor, Yassin started to witness signs of deviation and mis-practices among his Sufi brothers. The rift became irreconcilable when he began to urge them to become more active and defend Islam in Morocco. He parted company with them in order to begin a militant and activist career on his own.[74] He wrote a book, *al-Islam Bayn al-Da`wa wa al-Dawla* (Islam Between the Call and the State) in 1972, which he followed by another huge volume, *al-Islam Ghadan* (Islam Tomorrow) in 1973.

It was Yassin's letter to the king, *Islam or the Deluge*, however, which earned him fame as a political activist and a three-year imprisonment in 1974. Yassin wrote this 114-page "suicidal" letter and printed several copies on his own and distributed them before sending it on to the king. The letter clearly reflects Yassin's elegant style and confident command of the language. Following the publication of this letter, Yassin was detained for three and a half years. Yassin also wrote an essay in French, which he directed to the Moroccan intelligentsia in 1980. His other book in French, *La Révolution à l'Heure de l'Islam* (Revolution and the Hour of Islam) was also addressed to the French-speaking Moroccan intellectuals and was printed in 1982 in France to avoid censorship.

Yassin began publishing his own periodical, *al-Jama`a,* named after his organization, in 1979, after the outbreak of the Iranian Revolution. From the first issue, its militant orientation was clearly expressed. Describing the nature of its message, Yassin wrote, "our work is a call for Allah. This call is general and, therefore, does not exclude the ruler nor the ruled, the oppressor nor the oppressed, the exploiting classes nor the exploited ones."[75] *Al-Jama`a* appeared quarterly and then turned into a monthly, but, after its sixteenth issue, was banned in 1985 for its critical and militant tone.[76]

Yassin tried to issue a new publication, *al-Subh* (The Morning), in 1983. *Al-Subh* appeared as a daily newspaper, but was immediately banned by the authorities, after 7,000 copies had been distributed in two days. Yassin was arrested in December, after the publication of the first issue of his newspaper, for writing articles calling for public disorder. He was sentenced to two-years imprisonment in May 1984.[77] Having served his term, Yassin was released, but was put under virtual confinement in his house. Since 1989, he has been under house arrest, without any court order

Yassin has tried repeatedly to obtain legal recognition for his association. In 1982, he applied for a license for his group under the name of *al-Jama`a.* When his request was rejected, he re-applied in 1983 under a new name, Jami`yyat al-Jama`a al-Khairiyya (The Charitable Group Association), stating clearly in its bylaws the political nature of the movement. Despite the denial of recognition, the association worked on recruiting followers, especially among high school and university students, teachers, civil servants, workers, and peasants. It also built an organizational structure that resembled in many respects that of the Muslim Brothers of Egypt. It consists of a Supreme Guide, Bureau of Guidance, Regional Councils, branches, cells, and specialized and technical committees.[78] From the various lists of arrests and trials of the members of al-Jama`a, it appears that it has succeeded in establishing presence in the different parts of the country. Most of al-Jama`a's constituency, however, is based in the center of Morocco, especially in the main cities of Rabat and Casablanca.

In 1987, the association raised the slogan, *al-`Adl wa al-Ihsan* (Justice and Benevolence), as its motto. Since that date, it has become known by that name. In the movement's view, the concepts of *al-`Adl wa al-Ihsan* summarize the objectives of the association and the means to achieve them. Yassin explains, "these two words were revealed in the Qur'an: God commands justice, doing of good [16:90]...Justice is a popular demand and a divine command. It therefore must be achieved in all aspects of life. Benevolence is an educational program addressing the individual and the community. We thus combine two duties: the duty of the state and the duty of calling [to God]."[79] However, in January 1990, the authorities officially dissolved the association and restricted any activities of the movement, arresting all the members of its Guidance Bureau (later released in January 1992 after spending two years in prison) along with scores of its followers.

Despite restrictions over the movement's members and activities, al-`Adl wa al-Ihsan was able to expand its following and increase its influence. This could be attributed to the charismatic leadership of its leader, Abdel Salam Yassin, who has been able to provide a coherent ideological framework for the members of the group. Moreover, the Sufi influences of Yassin and of the moral and spiritual program which he devised for his followers make al-`Adl attractive to a wider following, especially middle and lower classes, civil servants, peasants, and workers, who are the usual recruits of Sufi orders. This gives it an advantage over HATM, which appeals more to intellectual and student elements. Finally, the long history of suppressing and confining the movement, its uncompromising language, and comprehensive outlook generate sympathy and draw supporters to the association. This popularity was evident when, in December 1989, al-`Adl wa al-Ihsan's student followers were able to organize activities in all the country's universities in support of the Palestinian intifada in its second anniversary. In February 1991, ten thousand members of al-`Adl took to the streets in protest to the Gulf war. Al-`Adl also has a well organized student branch in the universities, which was announced in March 1991. The branch released a charter which was generally inspired by Yassin's ideas.

Conclusion

The often repeated assumption that Morocco has weak Islamic movements is certainly incorrect. Not only are such movements active, but they have good prospects for further expansion and increase in influence. The conduct of these movements, however, is different from that of their counterparts in other countries such as Tunisia and Algeria. In Morocco, they have to conform with the historical, cultural, and political uniqueness of the country.

Apparently, HATM has recognized this lesson and demonstrated a high level of realism and flexibility. It has accepted the political parameters as set by the regime and avoided any unnecessary confrontation. While remaining determined to exercise its right of political participation, it has shown a willingness to give concessions, such as changing its name, choosing not to pursue legal action against the authorities' unfounded decisions against the movement, nominating candidates under the name of other parties, and accepting federation with another party. This pragmatic and realistic attitude will definitely help HATM broaden its base of support and increase its influence, if it does not grow impatient nor exceed the limits of the regime's toleration. On the other hand, this same attitude brings upon HATM the criticism and suspicions of some other Islamic movements that perceive it as co-opted by the regime and compromising the true Islamic values for the political objective of securing its participation in the political process and ensuring the safety of its organization.

Al-`Adl wa al-Ihsan, on the other hand, despite being larger in number and currently more influential, seems to reject the issue of conformity. It still challenges the legitimacy of the regime and is unwilling to give concessions, either with regards to its program or for cooperation with other forces in the country. This makes al-`Adl look more genuine and credible as an opposition force, at least to its followers, but will keep the movement under the regime's confinement for some time. It was not a surprise that the list of political detainees that were granted amnesty by the king in July 1994 did not include any of al-`Adl's members.

In the event of the success of an Islamic movement to gain influence and popularity, Morocco will not turn into another Algeria. For Moroccans, the continuation of the institution of the monarchy is perceived as necessary for the unity and stability of the country, and the pluralistic nature of the political structure is a safeguard against its fragmentation.

Notes

1. Mohamed Tozy and B. Etienne, "La Da`wa au Maroc: Prolegomenes Theoritico-Historique," in Olivier Carr and Paul Dumont (eds.), *Radicalismes Islamiques: Maroc, Pakistan, Inde, Yougoslavie, Mali*, Vol. 2 (Paris: L'Hartmattan, 1986), p. 29.

2. Jean-François Clement, "Morocco's Bourgeoisie: Monarchy, State, and Owning Class," *Middle East Report*, Vol. 16, No. 142, September-October 1986, pp. 13-17.

3. I. William Zartman, "King Hassan's New Morocco," in I. William Zartman (ed.), *The Political Economy of Morocco* (New York: Praeger Publishers, 1987), p. 21. See also Entelis, *Comparative Politics of North Africa*, p. 65

4. I. William Zartman, "The Opposition as Support of the State," in I. William Zartman and Adeed Dawisha (eds.), *Beyond Coercion*, p. 64.

5. Zartman, "King Hassan's New Morocco," p. 18.

6. Zartman, "King Hassan's New Morocco," p. 6.

7. Zartman, "King Hassan's New Morocco," p. 6.

8. Entelis, *Comparative Politics of North Africa*, p. 54.

9. Mark Tessler, "Morocco: Institutional Pluralism and Monarchical Dominance," in I. William Zartman (ed.), *Political Elites in Arab North Africa* (New York and London: Longman, 1982), p.82. See also Mark Tessler, "Image and Reality in Moroccan Political Economy," in Zartman (ed.), *The Political Economy of Morocco*, p. 227.

10. Zartman, "King Hassan's New Morocco," pp. 8-9.

11. Zartman, "The Opposition as Support of the State," p. 64.

12. King Hassan II's speech on November 19, 1972.

13. Tessler, "Morocco: Institutional Pluralism," pp. 76-81.

14. Paul Delaney, "Uneasy Lies the Head that Wears Two Crowns," *New York Times*, December 25, 1987. See also Abdallah Sa`af, "Middle Class and State in Morocco," unpublished paper delivered at Morocco's day at the Johns Hopkins School of Advanced International Studies. Washington, D.C., April 12, 1985.

15. Zartman, "King Hassan's New Morocco," pp. 29-30.

16. Dale Eickelman, "Religion in Polity and Society," in Zartman (ed.), *Political Economy of Morocco*, p. 89.

17. Tessler, "Morocco: Institutional Pluralism," p. 82.

18. See Clement, "Morocco's Bourgeoisie," pp. 15-16.

19. Tessler, "Morocco: Institutional Pluralism," p. 81.

20. Clement, "Morocco's Bourgeoisie," p. 16.

21. Interview with Muhammad Gessous, Rabat, April 5, 1986.

22. "Al-Liqa' al-Awwal li al-Jam`iyyat al-Islamiyya" [The First Meeting of the Islamic Associations], *al-Nour*, No. 12, April 1975.

23. *Al-Nour*, Ibid., p. 5.

24. "Fi Tawsiyyat al-Mu'tamar al-Sabi'" [The Recommendations of the Seventh Conference], *Da'wat al-Haqq*, Vol. 20, Nos. 6-7, June-July 1979, pp. 48-61. See also Mohamed Tozy, "Monopolisation de la Production Symbolique et Hiérarchisation du Champ Politico-Religieux au Maroc," p. 225.

25. *Al-Nour*, No. 100, May 30, 1980.

26. Abdel Salam Yassin, *al-Islam aw al-Tufan* [Islam or the Deluge] (Morocco: n.p., 1973), pp. 4-5.

27. *Al-Nour*, No. 60, June 21, 1978.

28. *Al-Nour*, No. 11, March 1975.

29. "Hadhihi Assahifa" [This Paper], *al-Nour*, Vol. 1, No. 1, April 1974.

30. Abu Qutb, "Hajatuna ila Tandhim Islami" [Our Need for an Islamic Organization], *al-Nour*, No. 19, November 1975. See also No. 69, November 1978 and No. 159, June 1983.

31. These points were raised in many issues. See for example, *al-Nour*, No. 3, June 1974; No. 60, June 1987; No. 69, November 1978; and No. 161-162, July 1983.

32. *Al-Huda*, No. 1, Jumada Al-Thani 1402 A.H.

33. *Al-Huda*, Ibid., p.3.

34. *Al-Huda*, No. 8, Sha'ban 1404 A.H.

35. Abdel Salam al-Harras, "Mulahadhat Hawl al-Tarbiyya al-Islamiyya" [Remarks on Islamic Education], *al-Huda*, Vol. 3, No. 10, November-December 1984, p. 5. See also Muhammad Brish, "Ghiyab al-Tarabut" [The Absence of Coherence], Ibid., pp. 9-10.

36. Al-Mufdel Felwati, "Ama ana li-Tilifizuna" [Is it not about Time for our Television], *al-Huda*, Nos. 11-12, April 1985, p. 2.

37. See for example the statements of the Moroccan Islamic Youth Association in *al-Nour*, No. 43, August 1977, and No. 55, April 1978.

38. Salaman Bekhtir, et al., "Nahwa al-Bahth 'an Kharita Thaqafiyya wa Idiyulujiyya," [Toward a Search for a Cultural and Ideological Map] (Unpublished Dissertation, Muhammad V University, Faculty of Literature and Humanities, Rabat, 1979-80), pp. 85-7.

39. Mohamed Tozy, "Champ et Contre Champ Politico-Religieux au Maroc," (Thése pour le Doctorat d'Etat en Sciences Politiques, Faculté de Droit et de Sciences Politiques d'Aix, Marseille, 1984), pp. 305 and 307.

40. Tozy, "Champ et Contre Champ Politico-Religieux au Maroc," pp. 325-30.

41. *Al-Mu'amara 'ala Harakat al-Shabiba al-Islamiyya* [The Conspiracy Against the Islamic Youth] (Holland: n.p., 1984), P. 8. See also Tozy, "Champ Politique et Champ Religieux au Maroc," p. 105.

42. *Al-Mu'amara*, p. 8.

43. *Al-Mu'amara*, p.8.

44. Tozy, "Champ Politique et Champ Religieux au Maroc," p. 348.

45. Henry Munson Jr., "The Social Base of Islamic Militancy in Morocco," *The Middle East Journal*, Vol. 40, No. 2, Spring 1986, pp. 267-84.

46. *Al-Mu'amara*, p. 52.

47. Munson, "The Social Base," pp. 267-84.

48. Tozy, "Champ Politique et Champ Religieux au Maroc," pp. 248 and 252. On the activities of al-Shabiba's students in the university, see "Nashat Harakat al-Shabiba al-Islamiyya al-Maghribiyya" [The Activities of the Moroccan Islamic Youth Association], *al-Mujtama'*, No. 403, July 11, 1978, pp. 42-4.

49. *Al-Mu'amara*, p. 143. See also al-Shabiba's statement which was published in the League of Moroccan scholars' paper *al-Mithaq*, No. 227, July 13, 1976.

50. Abdel Karim Mouti', "al-Awda' al-Maghribiyya wa Hatmiyat al-I'dad al-Islami li al-Thawra" [The Moroccan Conditions and the Necessity of Islamic Preparation for the Revolution], in Abdel Karim Mouti', *al-Thawra al-Islamiyya: Qadar al-Maghrib al-Rahin* [The Islamic Revolution: The Current Fate of Morocco] (Holland: n.p., 1984). pp. 9-22.

51. *Al-Mu'amara*, p. 10.

52. *Al-Mu'amara*, p. 12.

53. Ben Jelloun, an influential leader and a hardliner in the General Union of Moroccan Workers (UGTM) and the USFP, split from the UNFP in 1974 after disputes over the UGTM's and UNFP's conciliatory policies toward the regime and their moderation in defending the right of the unprivileged classes in Morocco. He pushed for changes and reform within the two institutions and opposed collaboration with the regime.

54. *Al-Nour*, No. 100, May 30, 1980. Mouti' managed to escape to Saudi Arabia, and is now believed to be residing in Holland.

55. Hamid Barrada, "De Rabat à la Mecque," *Jeune Afrique*, Nos. 990-91, December 26, 1979 and January 2, 1980, p. 38.

56. *Al-Mu'amara*, pp. 34-35.

57. See *al-Mujtama'*, No. 403, July 11, 1987; *al-Mithaq*, No. 227, July 13, 1976; and *al-Nour*, No. 43, August 17, 1977 and No. 55, April 9, 1978.

58. Tozy, "Champ Politique et Champ Religieux au Maroc," p. 349.

59. *Al-Nour*, the mouthpiece of the Association of Islamic Resurrection, mentioned that in 1979, the regime arrested a number of scholars in Tangier for breaking their fast of Ramadan a day ahead of that designated by the authorities. In 1980, it also accused the regime, for purposes of monitoring their activities, of keeping list of the names of all veiled girls in the secondary schools; the regime also forced shop-keepers to keep their shops open during the Friday prayers. On May 5, 1980, a violent clash between the authorities and the group of al-Faqih al-Zaytouni, which is very critical of the regime, took place in Fez

and left dead and casualties on both sides. See *al-Nour*, No. 87, September 9, 1979; No. 91, January 19, 1980; and No. 100, May 5, 1980.

60. "... but Morocco says 13 Islamists must die," *Arabia*, Vol. 4, No. 37, September 1984.

61. "... but Morocco says," pp. 24-5.

62. *Al-'Alam*, October 16, 1985.

63. Muhammad Darif, *al-Islam al-Siyasi fi al-Maghrib: Muqaraba Watha'iqiyya* [Political Islam in Morocco: A Documentary Approach] (Casablanca: Manshurat al-Majalla al-Maghribiyya li-'Ilm al-Ijtima' al-Siyasi, 1992), pp. 234-6.

64. Published in *al-Mithaq,* January 6, 1982, see also Benkiran's letter to the interior minister, March 3, 1986, appendix 1 in Moustapha Boutizoua and Abdel Rahim Gannouhi, "al-Haraka al-Islamiyya fi al-Maghrib: Harakat al-Islah wa al-Tajdid Namudhajan," [The Islamic Movement in Morocco: HATM as a Model] (Unpublished B.A. thesis, Faculty of Literature and Human Sciences, Ibn Zuhr University, Agadir, 1991-1992), pp. 116-17.

65. The Charter of Jam'iyyat al-Jama'a al-Islamiyya al-Maghribiyya (Casablanca: Dar Qurtuba, 1989).

66. The Final Statement of the Ordinary General Assembly of al-Jama'a al-Islamiyya: August 3-5, 1990, in *al-Raya*, No. 2, August 18, 1990, p. 6. See also al-Jama'a's letter to King Hassan, October 10, 1987, quoted in Boutizoua and Gannouhi, "The Islamic Movement," p. 128.

67. *Al-Raya*, No. 15, February 2, 1992, pp. 1 and 3

68. Interview with Abdullah Baha, vice-president of HATM, Rabat, November 27, 1994.

69. Interview with Muhammad Yateem, president of HATM, Rabat, November 27, 1994.

70. *Al-Raya*, No. 107, August 16, 1994, p. 2.

71. *Al-Raya*, No 22, May 18, 1992, p. 9.

72. *Al-Raya*, No. 91, April 19, 1994, p. 1.

73. Yassin, *al-Islam aw al-Tufan*, pp. 4-5.

74. Yassin, *al-Islam aw al-Tufan*, pp. 5-7.

75. Abdel Salam Yassin, "'Unwan li 'Amalina" [A Title for our Work], *al-Jama'a*, No. 1, March-May 1979.

76. *Jama'at al-'Adl wa al-Ihsan: Rijal, Ahdath wa Minhaj* [The Association of Justice and Benevolence: Men, Events, and Approach], a special newsletter published by the association, March 1992, p. 5.

77. "The Trials of a Muslim Activist," *Arabia*, No. 32, April 1984. See also *FIBS*, May 31, 1984, p. Q3.

78. On the theoretical aspects on the organizational structure, see Abdel Salam Yassin, *al-Minhaj al-Nabawi: Tarbiyyatan wa Tandhiman wa Zahfan*

[The Prophetic Paradigm: Socialization, Organization, and March] (Morocco: n.p., 1989), pp. 55-77.

79. Quoted in Darif, *al-Islam al-Siyasi*, p. 316.

6

The Ideology of Change

Islamist political ideology persists as part of the internal dialogue of Muslim intellectuals and activists concerned with the task of improving the welfare of the population within their nation-state boundaries and in the Muslim nation as a whole. Proponents of Islamic ideologies operate out of an acute sense of the rational need for change on the individual and community levels: the individual, through a comprehensive process of socialization and mobilization; and the community, through the integration of Islamic values into the political, economic, and administrative structure of society. This chapter examines the political and intellectual thought of Rashed Ghannoushi of the Tunisian Renaissance Movement, Abdel Salam Yassin of the Moroccan al-`Adl wa al-Ihsan, and Abbasi Madani of the Algerian Islamic Salvation Front.

The Islamic themes of change as expounded by Ghannoushi, Madani, and Yassin provide a set of broad guidelines and specific values encompassing the political, socioeconomic, and cultural aspects of the individual and the community. They stress the imperative to break away from the dual circles of capitalism and communism in order to devise an indigenous modern Islamic system. They each provide a critical perspective of the West and a scathing condemnation of the Westernized elites of their respective countries. They are lay critics whose broad objectives are to transform the individual Islam of the people into a collective and practical faith and to change fragmented and weak Islamic states into modern-day societies of economic sufficiency, political independence, and high moral values.

Sources of Discontent

It is useful to present an overview of the various sources of discontent that brought about the revivalist call in the first phase. It will be seen that, as an instrument for the rationalization of social change and the mobilization of the people, Islam becomes an ideology of change aimed at bringing about the reconstruction of society and the transformation of its values.

Perceptions of the West

Rashed al-Ghannoushi is by all measures the most prominent leader of al-Nahda Movement. He is the intellectual architect of the movement and is considered to be its chief ideologue. He edited the movement's periodicals *al-Ma`rifa* and *al-Mujtama`*, and has published several books. The education and intellectual evolution of Ghannoushi, as a philosophy teacher well-versed in Western and Islamic philosophies, is reflected in his writings. These writings evolved over the years from a traditionalist position that lacked a unique line of thinking, yet were firmly and unyieldingly critical of the secularization policies of the regime, into an original rationale seeking to integrate the political developments and ideological needs of his organization into the political and socioeconomic realities of post-independence Tunisia.

Until 1978, a period that corresponds to the physical growth and ideological formation of al-Nahda Movement, Ghannoushi dealt from a strictly Islamic perspective with issues that were related directly with his professional concerns. He wrote about philosophy programs (1973), progress (1974), as well as about literature and ethics (1974). In his article "Philosophy Curriculum and the Generation of Loss," Ghannoushi addresses a broad and fundamental Islamic concern: Do Muslims possess a distinct culture or not? In Ghannoushi's view, the response to such a question is crucial as a starting point in order to enable the Muslims to distinguish the various components of their social culture and religious heritage and thereby manage to identify the various crises plaguing their society. He laments the methods of teaching philosophy subjects in Tunisia: Either students are presented with contradictory answers to their questions while being unable to choose between them for lack of a cultural measure of Islamic dimensions, or they are presented with answers to questions that have been developed in other cultures and societies alien to Islamic thoughts and teachings. Ghannoushi explains that "philosophy subjects deal primarily with the moral and social problems of Western society and their solutions which reflect the religious and social upheavals through which the West has passed."[1] Pointing to the critical approach that the West applies in teaching and studying the different philosophies of the world, Ghannoushi wonders "why do we not study Descartes, Marx, Durkheim, Sartre, and Darwin on the premise that we have a distinct culture that can offer its own solutions to its own problems?"[2] He, therefore, concludes that without reaching an agreement on the type of culture to which one should belong and identifying its philosophical perspective and practical framework, the Muslims will always remain incapable of tackling their problems.[3]

In his article "Progress = Preservation + Transcendence," Ghannoushi devises a general definition of progress, which—based on several Qur'anic verses—is a law of nature, a necessity, and a dynamic process. For Ghannoushi, progress is the evolution from one stage to another through a dual process of preserving essential past experiences (accumulation), and, on this basis, transcending them to achieve new experiences (innovations). Ghannoushi's definition is, in fact, imbued with significant suggestions. He also takes a nationalist stance by declaring that, above all, one must maintain a critical view of the nation's past experience, and that of other nations as well, in order to decide what is essential to preserve. The nation's memory should never be lost in order to preserve its identity and social cohesion vis-à-vis other cultures and to propel its people to achieve further contributions in line of overall human progress and endeavor. Ghannoushi then reaches the conclusion that if the Muslims are serious about developing their culture, they must link the past with the present. They must cherish the true glories of the past without neglecting to study and understand the negative aspects of historical pitfalls that led to their decline and submission under foreign rule and domination. They must also be prepared to deal with Western ideology and culture with an objective and critical mind, absorbing its hard sciences and social gains while submitting its philosophy, literature, and values to the criteria of Islam.[4]

Ghannoushi wrote his "Literature and Morality" article in response to a fellow teacher who advocated a separation between literature and values when the process of evaluating any artistic work is being undertaken. Ghannoushi rose to argue that any artistic endeavor is a reflection of a philosophical or moral stance, which transmits a critical message, and that the relationship between the methodology and pattern (forms of expression) and the substance and content is closely intertwined and cannot be separated. Though he does not advocate imposing an a priori philosophical, ethical, or moral stand on the students, Ghannoushi perceives the problem as one of the absence of an educational policy and of a cultural model for the state.[5]

In his early articles, Ghannoushi appears as a restless intellectual in quest of an indigenous cultural model that does not sever ties with the nation's past, yet maintains the right to view it critically in order to be able to achieve future advancement. Later writings, particularly his 1978 article, "Once Again: The West and Us," reflect more original thought in tackling the issue of the West and the Westernized elites. He attempts to safeguard his followers against false doctrines and disillusionment. He presents an overview of the West which, from an historical perspective, has been an ongoing preoccupation of Muslim reformers since the nineteenth century[6] "when the Muslim world was suddenly awakened by the artillery of the West, demolishing its already collapsing walls, destroying its institutions, and shattering its pride. Hence, the file of the West was opened again." (According to Ghannoushi, the first time took place during the Crusades.)[7]

The West has raised several pertinent questions in the minds of Muslim reformers. These questions attempt to address several fundamental issues, such as the essence of the West's evolution and progress, the nature of its inherent dynamics, the various reasons for its cultural supremacy as expressed through the dispersion of its values at the height of its colonial era, and the relations between the West and the Muslim World.[8] The answers to these questions have varied from one Muslim intellectual to another, leading to a variety of intellectual orientations within Muslim scholarly circles. In many cases, the West and its colonial heritage was viewed with a great deal of fascination and awe, a source for emulation and inspiration, while in fewer cases, it was met with trepidation and ambivalence.[9] In Ghannoushi's view, both orientations fail to address the dilemma of having to respond to Western encroachment while at the same time preserving one's indigenous values. This dilemma still persists, though it has taken new forms of social expressions as manifested in unequal economic relationships, imported secular models of national development, and an uneven distribution of power between the industrialized and developing nations in the international system. Islam is being exposed to direct assault and fierce attempts to subjugate Islamic societies to Western models of law and order. Yet, forced to reckon with the pervasive influence of Islam on the Muslims of the world, the West has changed its method of dealing with Muslims, from one of rejecting basic Islamic values to one of devising parallel forms of legal and constitutional standards.

It comes as no surprise to Ghannoushi that the spearhead of cultural penetration—that is, the Westernized secular intellectuals—is now admitting the prominence of Islam. They describe it as a progressive, socialist, or democratic religion, and call for a liberal Islam and a Marxist Islam. As far as Ghannoushi is concerned, this attests to a number of undeniable facts: (1) populist Islam is a reality, which is hard to deny or change; (2) all attempts to resolve the problems of the Islamic world away from Islam are futile; (3) the technology of Western civilization, despite its partial success in deforming the identity of some nations, is encountering difficulties with the Muslim identity; (4) the ongoing deterioration of the Muslim world on the political and economic levels seems to have reached its lowest point, particularly with the 1967 war and Sadat's visit to Jerusalem in 1977, and the hour of an Islamic take-off thus seems near.

All of the above, Ghannoushi asserts, makes Muslim relations with the West pivotal and gives all the more reason for reconsidering the role of the West in any transformation process in the Muslim world. For several reasons, such a reconsideration should be free of any spontaneous responses. First, the imperialist tide, or at least the direct imperialist tide, has after all subsided, providing the opportunity for a conscious dialogue with the West. Second, the spread of education in the Muslim world has decreased fascination with the West as the new generation has come to realize that the supremacy of the West lies in its technology, which is available now to all peoples: "The West then is not that almighty power which mysteriously controls the world." Third, two world wars have shaken "the dreamers in the Muslim world" awake, demonstrating the limited ability of the West to control even itself. Fourth, the Muslim world has finally regained consciousness of itself and of the other, and this has increased confidence in the Islamic identity and promoted the idea that the need of the West for Islam is no less than the need of Islam for the West. Finally, the Western imperialist experience has generated Muslim disappointment in the humanitarian and egalitarian values which the Capitalist and Communist West preached, but which it was the first to betray. Ghannoushi reaches the conclusion that it is time that the Muslims reevaluated their perception and relationship with the West, without feelings of inferiority or arrogance, in order to devise a modern Islamic cultural model that restores to the Muslims their potency.[10]

In evaluating the West, Ghannoushi raises the issue from a philosophical dimension to an East-West dialogue. He perceives the

West as an ideological counterweight to Islamic doctrines of government, law, and order. The West is considered neither superior nor inferior to Islam. Western values are clearly understood in a different framework of judgment from those of Islamic values. What sets the two worlds apart is the difference in their perception of the fundamental concept, or what Ghannoushi calls "effective ideas," that move their cultures—that is, their perception of the value and place of man in the universe. Citing a large number of Western philosophers, Ghannoushi states that the central idea in Western culture is the belief in man as a master of the universe and in his ability to control it through reason, will, and technology. He is inclined to understand the universe and harness it to fulfill his interests; to understand and improve himself through his efforts and work. "Modern Western culture stimulates man to achieve independence and supremacy over nature; even, if necessary, to rebel against any external force."[11] This perception carries both positive as well as negative consequences.

The positive attributes, which Ghannoushi certainly admires in the West, are the liberation of man from the feeling of inferiority towards nature; the development of a scientific and empirical mind; the evaluation of thought on the basis of its validity; the belief in constant progress and evolution; the spirit of adventure and search for the unknown; the appreciation of the value of time and the values of freedom and responsibility; and the readiness to rebel against any form of tyranny, be it feudalism, the church, the bourgeoisie, capitalism, or communism. The system of democracy has been a direct consequence of this spirit.[12]

The negative aspects, on the other hand, are manifested in the inability of the intellectual mind, despite its outstanding achievements, to provide, on theoretical or scientific basis, a comprehensive perception of the essence of man—a perception which does not exclude the phenomena that lie outside the realm of material life. The failure of science to provide man with a fruitful meaning for life and universal moral standards, free of hedonism and despair, and the loss of the real meaning of democracy so that it has become a mere slogan for justifying exploitation are, in Ghannoushi's view, among the other major failures of the West. Basing his argument on the doctrines of the Qur'an and on Islamic reasoning, Ghannoushi then proceeds to analyze the Islamic perception of man. He sees it as containing all the positive aspects of the Western perception, yet departs when it replaces the "man-god" formula by an Islamic one, "man the successor of God on Earth," which places

God as the ultimate value in the universe, acknowledges the material and spiritual essence of man, and attempts to reconcile them. Man's movement is then directed according to divine regulations and concise values embodied in the *shari`a*. If all this is true, how could the decline of Muslims be explained? Ghannoushi does so by pointing to the deviation from these concepts, resulting from the infiltration of alien ideas such as fatalism and mysticism into the Muslim mentality and society. As these ideas generated the effect of subjugating the will and freedom of the individual, they were welcomed by tyrannical Muslim rulers—by which he means the Umayyads—who transformed "man the successor of God" into "man the oppressed."[13]

Similar to Ghannoushi, Abbasi Madani is a teacher. He is a professor of education at the University of Algiers. He has lived in Britain and studied the West for several years. As an education specialist, Madani wrote his doctoral dissertation on the comparative educational programs in Britain, France, and the Muslim world. He is thus well-acquainted with the Western culture, its intellectual development, and philosophical values. Madani produced several books in which he examined these issues, juxtaposing them with Islamic values in an attempt to devise an indigenous intellectual and educational model.

Madani views modern Western thought as passing through a crisis. As a result of the swift and unprecedented advancement in science and technology, "modern" ideologies are lagging behind and becoming increasingly incapable of resolving the emerging moral and social problems of modern man. This dichotomy, according to Madani, has been inherent in the West's intellectual evolution, in which religion was replaced by rationale and ideologies, and then at a later stage by science. This process had undeniable advantages on Western progress as it led to the pursuit of freedom of thought and its utilization in a broader cultural frame and the rise of political consciousness that in turn generated economic, cultural, and educational awareness. The realization of cultural progress highlighted the need for sciences, technology, and their practical implementations, and a qualified elite in the sciences and all fields to maintain progress. The scientific and technological achievements of the West have energized Western man and expanded his capabilities in controlling his environment.[14] However, the ideologies of the eighteenth and nineteenth centuries, despite their ingenuity, were void of spiritual guidance. They have moved a full circle by the twentieth century and are only providing old solutions for new problems. They could not prevent the West from committing mistakes that have come to constitute the sources of its weakness. These are evident in the marginalization of religion and its substitution by non-comprehensive ideologies; the increasing pragmatism and relativeness especially in the pursuit of justice when Westerners are ruled and its abandonment when they rule others. The imbalance in the priority of values, the establishment of economic and cultural paradigms within a colonial experience that impoverished and enslaved others, and the perpetuation of unequal conditions to maintain economic and cultural superiority over other nations are all proof for Madani of Western culture's moral lapse. Madani's criticism of the West certainly recalls a long history of Western colonialism and its aftermath of foreign-inspired models that still constitute the political, economic, legal, and cultural basis in most post-colonial societies. This raises the need for an indigenous model that avoids the contradictions inherent in modern thought and elevates the contemporary Muslim to the level of high civilization, once again. The components of this model will be discussed in later sections dealing with change and the Islamic model.

Unlike either Ghannoushi or Madani, Abdel Salam Yassin is a passionate thinker, who attempts to inject the anguish he shoulders from observing the sources of discontent in Morocco into the body of the Muslim nation in order to stir it up and revive it. In his view, "no Muslim generation has ever faced challenges as serious as the ones the present generation is confronting."[15] The key concept behind Yassin's ideas is mobilization—that of a leader, a community of believers, a society as a whole—to bring about the transformation of the Muslim nation. He is very fluent in style, with a remarkable command of words. He uses an inflammatory language, yet an eloquent and original one, in which he replaces the un-Islamic terminology of the *jahiliyya* with proper Islamic ones. Unlike many Muslim thinkers and members of the Islamic movements who were influenced by and adopted many of the phrases, symbols, and slogans of the Iranian revolution, Yassin had already used and extrapolated on them long before the revolution.

Despite the precarious situation of his organization, Yassin does not seem interested in appeasing the regime or the secular intellectual elite. He is very critical of the current condition of Muslims as well as of the presentation of their history. For Yassin, who is vastly different in this regard from Ghannoushi, the glories of the past are only for infants to take pride in; history should become a burden for the elders, an incentive for mobilization, and a source for inspiration and activism.[16] Unlike Ghannoushi, Yassin appears more of an optimist although his writings tend to reflect a touch of idealism when it comes to explaining the mobilization aspect of collective Muslims as a social weapon of immense power.

With regard to the West, Yassin seems to have reached an uncompromising conclusion: "The world is divided into two camps: Islam versus *jahiliyya*."[17] Similar to Sayyid Qutb, Yassin uses this term to refer to the Muslim societies that do not conform in their legislation and practices to the rule of God, and to the secular West, which is characterized by a lack of a clear and proper understanding of the value of man and inclined towards violence.[18] Along these lines, Yassin attempts to realign Muslims, with their culture, values, and identity into one camp, and separate them emotionally from the West. After knowing where they stand, Muslims can still learn from the *jahiliyya*, particularly its sciences, technology, and rationale. From the viewpoint of Yassin, "The nation is torn between two worlds, which do not meet in its conscience...However, it wants to reconcile them to preserve its cultural and national values as well as those of human perfection."[19] He explains that:

> the present stagnant mentality of Muslims perceives phenomena in an atomized way; it can not relate causes...Only the critical mind does that. We the Muslims, particularly the Arabs, are emotional and impulsive...If we admire Western civilization, we become submissive, consider it absolute, abandon our own values, and become students of *jahiliyya*. The resurrected Islam is an educated Islam; it learns from the universe in relation to the Creator while relating phenomena to their causes. If we transfer something from the *jahiliyya*, we ought to transfer rationale and techniques but not philosophy or a perception of mankind and the universe.[20]

For Yassin, the steel and iron civilization is a gloomy and violent one, despite the artificial rewards of material happiness. It is a consumerist culture. In capitalist societies, Yassin believes, "a large portion of human life is wasted between the banks and the courts."[21] It turns man into a quantity and reduces his value when it professes that he is the outcome of Marx's dialectic materialism or that his behavior is controlled by Freud's "libido."[22]

Similar to Ghannoushi and Madani, Yassin criticizes the excessiveness of Western culture in overemphasizing positivism and empiricism in dealing with human phenomena, an attitude which often reduces the humanistic qualities of man, overlooks his spiritual needs, and underscores material gains as a mark of grand achievement and progress. Yassin, however, asserts that there are positive values on which Western civilization is based, and which the Muslims need to learn. These values are power, appreciation of the value of time and work, persistence, and the quest for new knowledge, innovation, and organization.

The Westernized Elite

In his criticism of the Westernized elite, Ghannoushi makes an important intellectual contribution by linking Westernization with dictatorship. According to Ghannoushi, there are two common characteristics dominating the political systems in the Arab and Islamic world. The first is Westernization, which he defines as the uprooting of a nation from its cultural origins and the wholesale adoption of alien models. This process involves some degree of violence and political dictatorship in order to persist, and economic dictatorship in order to distribute the spoils on the political, military, and cultural apparatus that protects the system and constitutes the privileged class in society.[23]

Most of these systems, Ghannoushi argues, look up to the West, in its capitalist or socialist form, as a source of inspiration in devising their cultural, socioeconomic, and political models of development. This is in part due to the fact that the educated elite, that led the movement for independence, was formed intellectually and trained in the West. Though modern, this elite was not indigenous. It failed to understand that colonialism was also a cultural, philosophical, and civilizational structure superimposed on Muslim societies, in addition to being a military and political domination. The perception of Islam on the part of the Western educated elites was confined to viewing it as a set of moral and spiritual principles unrelated, if not hindering, social transformation; they failed to view it as a comprehensive ideological and cultural structure. Nevertheless, Ghannoushi acknowledges the fact that at the time this elite was being formed intellectually, the Islamic cultural model was already deteriorating—except for its spiritual part—and could not provide this elite with a social framework. Therefore, it was unsurprising that Europe became the exemplar of development for the Muslim world. This model, however, "is neither [purely] Western, nor, indeed, Islamic, because its initiators are not deeply rooted in Islam; nor are they Western, simply because they are imitators and therefore can not be indigenous...It is mimicry."[24] Ghannoushi warns against the wholesale emulation of this model and its consequences by stating that "the collapse which our nation witnesses on all levels is a result of the failure of the modernization project, the imitation of the civilization of the conqueror, Western civilization...The end result is submission."[25]

Ghannoushi goes on to link the concept of Westernization with the second dominant characteristic of political systems in the Muslim world—the dictatorship of the ruling elite. He argues that as these dominant models were foreign-inspired, they remained a superstructure, incapable of infiltrating into the collective consciousness of the people who remained attached to Islam as their belief system and their social and historical model. Yet this people lost the zeal which they had displayed during their struggle against imperialism, and began to be controlled by bitterness, alienation, and frustration as they grew estranged from the social context in which they operated; they became imbued with the ex-colonialists' arts, customs, administration, and even language.

It was not surprising, therefore, that all development models have failed to promote adequate growth and proper development structures in the Islamic world and that no single Muslim country can be counted among the developed nations. The programs of the elite have ignored the traditional culture of the population, and, more often than not, worked against it, which pushed the people to become desperate, apathetic, and ready to revolt.[26] Ghannoushi concludes that dictatorship is an inevitable consequence of Westernization: due to its alienation from the rest of the population, the Westernized elite has no choice but to resort to violence in order to impose its imported model and perpetuate its rule. As Ghannoushi perceives the situation, "The Westernized elites presently in power in our countries only represent a small minority imposed by the force of the state, the army, and the mass media on a population of Muslim believers. They were educated by the colonizers and from them they inherited power. The future elite that will govern Islamic Tunisia is the new generation that is now persecuted."[27]

Arguing on a more specific level, Ghannoushi explains that the Westernized elite has to rely on coercion in order to prevent the rights of political organization and public freedom of the Muslim community. This process was achieved through the usurpation of civil liberties; the formation of a new privileged class of a small elite linked to the regime to defend its interest and maintain its stability; and the attachment of the elite to the international, financial, and military centers of power in order to be backed economically and militarily, in return for its preservation of the Western model in the Muslim world.[28]

Ghannoushi's analysis leads him to three conclusions. The first is the need to emphasize justice and freedom as the driving forces behind the demands of the people. The second is the need to search for a new cultural model that would evolve not from the degenerated Islam but from the original Islam—which is a comprehensive revolution against tyranny, exploitation, and dependence—and in accordance with the requirements of modernity.[29] The third is that the Islamic movements must "... recognize the legitimacy of the regime as it is elected by the people. However, as long as the state does not rule by Islam, we do not recognize its religious legitimacy, until religion becomes the base for society and legislature...The regime is not Islamic nor legitimate as long as it does not permit the people to express their freedom and will in society."[30]

Like Ghannoushi, Madani holds the secularized elite responsible for the current state of cultural dependency and intellectual confusion in the Muslim world. He links the issue of secularization with the process of colonialism and the educational models it has implanted in the colonies. The educational policies of the colonial powers aimed at spreading their cultural values, detaching Muslims from their own, forming a new cadres of foreign-educated Muslims in the army and the administration. This type of education creates deformities in society in general. It molds its members on submissiveness and undermines cultural awareness and collective action.[31]

Madani, however, makes a distinction between two types of western-educated elite. The first are those who in spite of their Western education remained attached to their indigenous culture and Islamic values. They participated in the national movements, formed political parties, and allied with the reformist Muslim scholars in order to achieve the independence of their respective countries. The second type of elite, whom Madani describes as "the intellectuals of backwardness and dependence," are those who advocated a wholesale adoption of Western values and models. Despite being a minority, they were able to exercise influence as they were aided by the powers of the time. These intellectuals were under the illusion that the West was the source of progress and that religion was the reason for the backwardness of the Muslim peoples. As they lost confidence in their indigenous cultural models, they favored foreign ones, overlooking the countless differences between their own culture and that of the West. They called for change, as an end in itself, without critically examining the validity of the imported doctrines they propagated. They were behind the introduction of new currents such as ethnic, linguistic, and parochial forms of nationalism which eroded the unity of the Muslim nation and its intellectual integrity. As an extension of colonialism, Madani is confident that this elite will soon wither away as did their intellectual mentors before them. For him, the increasing signs of Islamic reassertion is an indication that this westernizing trend is losing ground in the Muslim countries.[32]

Yassin presented a similar case for Morocco when, as noted, he took the daring step of risking persecution by addressing an open letter, *al-Islam aw al-Tufan* (Islam or the Deluge), to King Hassan II at a time, in 1974, when Morocco faced immense political and social problems. The purpose of this letter to the king, as stated by Yassin, was two-fold: to rescue the Muslims of Morocco from *fitna* (disorder); and to assist the king in finding new sources of legitimacy to enhance his rule.

Yassin's criticism took the form of a personal condemnation of the king and his coterie of advisers. Yassin raised the issue of rampant corruption. In a frank and scornful yet eloquent manner, Yassin lodged a criticism of the personal lifestyle and social conduct of the king himself. He condemned the political manipulation of the king and raised doubts as to the sincerity of his religious convictions and practice.[33] In noting that two kinds of people reform or corrupt Islam—the rulers and the scholars—Yassin lodged the bulk of his criticism at the personal conduct of the king himself. Although the king professes to adhere to a religious stand as the Commander of the Faithful, Yassin points out that, nevertheless, he is more influenced by his Western education. As he put it, "The young king has complemented his liberal thought with an Islamic veneer, which he has used as a camouflage."[34] In staging a critique of the Westernized elites of Morocco, Yassin summed up the problem from the top by accusing the king of undermining the true mission of Islam.[35] Noting that corruption is a symptom of decadence in Muslim societies, Yassin declared, "You give a living example that religion is the opiate of the people."[36] Yassin took his argument a step further by criticizing the historical legitimacy of the king. He argued vehemently that the ancestors of King Hassan extracted their legitimacy by force with no consultation with or concession from the Muslim inhabitants of Morocco.

Yassin uses strong language to condemn the secular policies of the Westernized elite in Morocco. He argues that it has become part and parcel of the *jahiliyya* bloc—a *jahiliyya* shielded with Western technology, material power, and anti-Islamic principles of decay and decadence.[37] As he perceives the situation, "We are undoubtedly Muslims, but our Islam is the Islam of *fitna*, and corruption, started by authoritarian rule and assisted by the worms of books, [the scholars]."[38] In his condemnation of the Westernized elite, Yassin elaborates on a set of practical steps through which the king should repent. He should remove and replace his entourage and counselors with men of faith, who will form the nucleus of the community of the faithful; publicly declare his repentance and his covenant to renew Islam and its programs; redeem oppression through a comprehensive program of reforms, disbanding all political parties, and letting the people of *al-da'wa* (the call to Islam) explain to the nation what *fitna* is and the ways to overcome it; and declare his allegiance to a representative council. One of the responsibilities of this council will be to check the function of the army, the only organized force in Morocco. As far as Yassin is concerned, the proper way to withstand *jahiliyya* is by calling on the mobilization of the nation. Such a mobilization can only occur through a restitution of Islamic values, because Islam and only an Islamic solution is the viable alternative to save the country from turmoil.[39]

Yassin views the evolution of secular ideas in the Arab and Muslim world as part of a process of Western domination that began with Napoleon's invasion of Egypt. For him, the secular era introduced alien ideas into Arab and Muslim culture and promoted a secular national consciousness among the Westernized elite. This process led to the emergence of dual identities within the Arab social order: secular national and Arab-Islamic. The relationship between the two has been dominated by mistrust and confrontation, especially after the establishment of the Arab system of nation-states and the control of the secular elite over the political and cultural institutions.[40]

Despite his criticism of the Westernized elite, Yassin does not lose hope for bridging the gap between the Islamists and the secular liberals. He wrote an entire book, *Dialogue with the Virtuous Democrats*, in which he presented the Islamist view of mutual political, social, and economic issues. Yassin disapproves of equating democracy with disbelief. This will necessarily mean that Islam is against democracy and for despotism. This should not be the case for Islam is against disbelief and democracy is against despotism. "We have no conflict with democracy if we understand its essence and if we realize its prerequisites and how it could meet or contradict the Islamic demands."[41] He distinguishes between Western democracy, which despite many shortcomings, is a source of stability, and democracy as practiced in the Arab and Muslim countries. He agrees that a clean democracy is better than despotism and a step towards liberation. However, he accuses the Arab democrats of concealing the true essence of Western democracy which is clearly associated with secularism, and of allying themselves with autocratic regimes, particularly when it comes to suppressing Islamists and exiling Islam inside the mosque. For Yassin, what happened to the FIS and Islamists in Algeria attests to the insincerity of this class of Arab democrats more than any accusation against the Islamists of using democracy in order to thwart the whole process after coming to power.[42] He asserts that "if the people of any country choose at any stage to follow the democrats, we will question our performance in explaining what the Islamic rule is. We will follow all the means permitted by a clean democracy and not despotism to explain to the people, open up to them so that they can understand our true nature and the true nature of the democrats."[43]

Traditional Islam and Co-opted Scholars

Both Ghannoushi and Yassin mount a strong criticism against the submissiveness of the religious scholars and their co-optation by the Westernized elite. They base their criticism on the ground that these Muslim scholars, who were traditionally models of veneration, are no longer fulfilling their duty of upgrading and defending the moral integrity of the Muslim community. The corruption of the Westernized elites has transformed them into nothing more than pawns, employed by the state to legitimize the right of these elites to run the affairs of the country.[44] This policy was in part achieved through a process of coercion and the dismantling and bureaucratization of the religious institutions. The scholars are not free to speak up against and prevent un-Islamic practices in society, and they must serve, moreover, in the capacity of state employees, thus isolating themselves further from the people and leaving themselves no alternative but to defend the regime or lose their job. Ghannoushi recalls the condition of the religious scholars after independence: "Since the time of the so-called 'independence', the authority of the `ulama' had been weakened. If an *imam* dared to speak against the government he was removed from his office and his life made difficult."[45] Though understanding in tone and unwilling to antagonize the `ulama' directly, Ghannoushi displays his disappointment in them by venerating such religious reformers as Hassan al-Banna, Abul Ala al-Mawdudi, and Sayyid Qutb, none of whom was an `alim by profession.

Madani, understandably, presents a more positive attitude towards the scholars. As was discussed earlier, the Algerian religious scholars were associated with Islamic reform during the colonial period and even after independence was achieved since many of them rejected co-optation to the state bureaucracy and joined or supported the emerging Islamic movements. It was thanks to the relentless efforts of the Association of Scholars that Algeria was able to maintain its Arab and Islamic identity despite the French attempts to uproot it. This made Madani place in high regard the scholars, whom he considers to be the true successors of the Prophet Muhammad.[46] Therefore, Madani highlights the significant cultural, social, and political role that the scholars have played in Muslim societies. Madani underscores several standards for the scholars. These scholars were venerated so long as they remained faithful to the source from which they derived their knowledge and judgments (the Qur'an and the Sunna); practiced what they preached; and maintained their independence from the power elite. Therefore, it was not surprising that the scholars constituted a source for reform and for preserving the identity of the Muslim people to confront internal decay and outside challenges. They were assisted in this regard by a decentralized religious, educational, and financial system that enabled them to exercise independence and maintain a leadership status in society. Under the colonial powers and the post-colonial state, this system has been severely dismantled and has become highly centralized under the control of the state. This process has destroyed an indigenous model of education and social endowments and undermined the status of the scholars by turning them into state employees. [47] As religious bureaucrats, many scholars have lost their freedom and independent judgment and their knowledge has become a tool serving the objectives of the political authorities.[48]

Unlike Ghannoushi or Madani, Yassin is far less apologetic in his views of the co-opted scholars. In his judgment, the `ulama' have betrayed their religion by associating themselves with the state apparatus and legitimizing its policies. They have competed for posts and privileges aimed at supporting the interest of the Westernized elite and not that of the welfare of the Muslim community. The end result has been factionalism, corruption, and alienation, a chaotic situation by which these elites have successfully neutralized *al-da`wa*, the character and source of legitimacy of the Islamic way of life.

Yassin also condemns the adroit manipulation of the *`ulama'* by King Hassan. He describes them as "court scholars who corrupted Islam."[49] As Yassin perceives the situation, "The scholar has no choice but to comply and that is the type of corruption based on fear and intimidation that runs through every Moroccan."[50] He, therefore, calls upon the scholars to "look up to the example set by their counterparts in Iran—who have restored to the turban its integrity and glory—in order to liberate the Muslim mind from the domination of imported values and invading cultures, free the people from *fitna*, and rid them from hunger and poverty."[51]

The Secularized Educational System

A specific criticism of the Westernization process is that it has led to the corruption of the educational systems in Tunisia, Algeria, and Morocco. Ghannoushi, Madani, and Yassin, all educators by profession, consider the present system of Francophile education as alien, designed in part to disorient and dislocate the future generations of the country.

Ghannoushi condemns the secular system of education as inadequate in meeting the needs of a Muslim society. He perceives it to be undergoing a severe crisis, manifested in the deformation of the present generation of young Muslims who remain vulnerable to foreign values and unable to confront the encroachments of imported intellectual currents and doctrines. As he points out, the new group of educators who have been delegated by the regime with the task of designing educational programs, forming a new generation of young Tunisians, and bringing about the transformation of society are not fully aware of the particular characteristics of the cultural model and belief-system to which these youngsters belong. As Westernized intellectuals, they have more in common with their counterparts in the West than the indigenous lot of their own students. They therefore lack an educational philosophy that defines the intellectual orientation and determines the moral and ethical components of the new individual they are trying to build. As a result, the education process turns into a process of accumulation of imported information and not a real formation of culturally distinct students.[52]

Madani devoted an entire book to the issue of education and its problems in the Muslim countries. He made comparisons between the educational systems in Britain, France, and the Muslim countries, examining the philosophical backgrounds and the evolution of each system. While sharing many of the criticisms that Ghannoushi leveled against the secularized educational system in the Muslim countries, Madani gives the reform of education a very pivotal role in any meaningful attempt at the reconstruction of Muslim societies. He considers the reform of education as the basis for any successful reform.[53] Madani however realizes that the issue of emulation and borrowing from other cultures is not confined only to Muslim societies and has been an ongoing debate since the end of the nineteenth century. The British and French who admired the Prussian educational system and acquired some of its aspects faced the same problem. Yet the process of reforming their educational systems was well studied and came after long examination and never involved total abandoning of their own native models of education nor undermining of their national identity.[54] Madani, therefore, attempts to devise a detailed plan for educational reform that takes into consideration the cultural components of the Muslim society, its historical, economic, social, and political conditions and the current reality of scientific and technological advancement.[55]

Similar to Ghannoushi and Madani, Yassin strongly criticizes the educational system in Morocco. An education inspector by profession, he assesses the system in relation to the general plans of development designed by the state. He criticizes the orientation of these plans, which focus on progress and advancement in quantitative and not qualitative terms. This orientation affects the policies and quality of education.

Yassin flatly describes the educational system, which is not guided by clear objectives, as "corrupt, backward, and foreign."[56] He agrees with Ghannoushi that the education of the Westernized elites has only served to broaden the gap between them and the people. They speak a different language, not understood by the nation as a whole. It is a system designed by an alienated elite and administered by a group of educators—"with an employees' mentality"—who are infatuated and subdued by the consumerist values of a conquering culture. They transfer these values to their students and turn them into job-seekers, competing to join the service of the state apparatus. In a society in which the unemployment rate is very high, this process increases the frustration of university graduates and generally exacerbates social problems.

Yassin proposes an alternative educational orientation. This orientation should be geared towards change and aim at the mobilization of wills, the development of human intellect, and the liberation of the Muslim mind. He recommends the reorganization of the school system, its administration, and curricula. These recommendations involve the resocialization of school administrators and teachers, changing the relationship between the teacher and the student, and designing indigenous educational programs that combine belief with reason and scientific outlook, while avoiding eclecticism.[57]

Change and the Islamic Model

The Islamist concept of change aims at bringing about the reconstruction of a way of life that ascribes to Islamic doctrines. It is intended to sum up the necessary plan of action and mobilize the people to bring about social transformation and an Islamic order. In doing so, the intellectual route has shifted from the traditionalist call, as voiced by the `ulama', for the reproduction of an early Islamic ideal, to the call for the exercise of *ijtihad* in order to fit Islamic values to the present needs of the Muslim community. In this transition, the biography of the Prophet Muhammad is seen to be particularly suggestive, bearing the imprint of an ideological framework.

Along these lines, Ghannoushi explains the nature and objective of al-Nahda as "a movement for a comprehensive change of the existing order through Islam, and for the reconstruction of an Islamic society."[58] In his view, this movement embodies salient characteristics which distinguish it from other political forces in society. The first characteristic is the holistic nature of the movement's ideological outlook and its belief in the perfection and applicability of Islam as a religion encompassing the personal and social aspects of the individual and combining religion with the politics of the state. This outlook affects the political convictions of the movement, which perceives all Muslims as one entity that should be united and believes in the need to work for the establishment of an Islamic state and its resurrection on the international level.

The second characteristic is the movement's belief in the importance of the issue of nationalism, which represents for the Islamic movement a point of departure for achieving the universalism of Islam. Ghannoushi perceives no contradiction between nationalism and Islam, and confirms that "the Muslim is a nationalist, because he represents the genuine extension of the culture and glory of the fatherland, whereas those who do not adhere to Islam are alien, the left-overs of imperialism."[59] The third, which is a direct outcome of the comprehensive outlook of the movement, is its concern with the social and economic issues in society. The members of the Islamic movement, as Ghannoushi explains, stand against poverty, extravagance, and the squandering of the nation's resources. Whereas they acknowledge the right of private ownership, they, nonetheless, advocate the regulation of this right in order to benefit the collectivity and prevent exploitation. They also advocate economic and political independence from the West and the East. The fourth characteristic that distinguishes the al-Nahda from other groups is the *salafi* nature of the movement in drawing on the Qur'an and the Sunna as the fundamental sources of reference and deduction, rejecting "doctrinal sectarianism," while tolerating differences in opinion.

The final characteristic is the populist nature of the movement, which attempts to draw support from among the various social segments of society regardless of class distinctions. It, therefore, rejects the concept of class conflict, believing in the instrumentality of the Islamic ideology in eradicating any form of exploitation and oppression within the Muslim society. In a society in which Islam is not implemented, however, Ghannoushi states that the movement has to align itself with the ranks of the poor and dissociate itself from the ruling elite in order to liberate Islam from the latter's hegemony and to be able to fulfill promises to the population.[60]

Ghannoushi believes that the existing order contradicts the real meaning of independence as it is characterized, on the economic front, by an increasing dependence on the West and the international financial markets which determine its economic policies, trade relations, and the value of its currency. On the political front, the existing order suffers from deep fragmentation and submissive alignment to the Eastern or Western bloc. On the cultural level, it is dominated by alien cultural models that influence its thought, educational system, arts, and customs. On the level of law and jurisdiction, there is a clear disparity between the doctrines of the Islamic *shari`a*, on the one hand, and the laws and regulations that govern society and its institutions, on the other.[61] He concludes that since the structure of the Islamic state has collapsed and Islam is no longer recognized as the most sovereign force in society, the renewal that is needed should not be confined only to bringing about partial reforms but extended to the reconstruction of society as a whole.[62]

Ghannoushi makes, however, a distinction between the fulfillment of this objective and the take-over of political power. He argues that "politics or power is one dimension, and the fruition of the collective movement of society towards Islam another...The objective behind this dimension is to provide the appropriate framework for cultural and social action."[63] He therefore defines for the members of his movement the fundamental prerequisites for a strategy of Islamic action. These include the need to: determine the movement's stand towards the Islamic heritage regarding what to keep and what to discard in it and its position concerning the West; understand society and the forces that operate in it without any pre-conceived judgments; understand the means and vehicles for bringing about change in society; link the call for Islam with the political, economic, and social demands of the people; achieve a comprehensive education of the Muslim individual to develop a critical and objective mind on the intellectual level, and moral and ethical values on the spiritual level; and finally, undertake careful planning which takes into consideration the factor of time and the need for a realistic attitude.[64]

Based on the precedents of the Prophet, Ghannoushi distinguishes two phases for the achievement of the restitution of Islam. The first is the reconstruction of the Islamic society through the socialization of the individual members, a process that eventually is to encompass society as a whole. Influenced by the revivalist themes of Sayyid Qutb, he compares this phase to the Meccan phase of the Prophet's life, during which he focused on refuting false doctrines, addressing the moral corruption and social ills of society, and spreading the Islamic values of justice, freedom, and equality. Like the Prophet in this period, Ghannoushi urges his followers to endure all sorts of repression and to avoid the use of violence in any form. This orientation, Ghannoushi argues, would reflect the movement's belief in the freedom of thought, preempt any further escalation of violence, and generate the sympathy of the population with the members of the movement and their message.

The second phase is the establishment of the Islamic order. It would come as a result of the fruition of the first phase of socializing the members of society. If the people responded to the message of Islam, Ghannoushi believes, they would accept the supremacy of its rules, and, hence, the Islamic state would be established. The new Islamic state would have to carry out God's rules, spread justice, and prevent the oppression and exploitation of its people.[65]

In his book, *Public Freedoms in the Islamic State,*[66] Ghannoushi elaborates on the specific structure and the institutions of the Islamic state. Based on an exhaustive examination of classic and modern Islamic political thought, he provides a detailed blueprint of the philosophical basis and characteristics of the Islamic system of government with a particular emphasis on public freedoms and the rights of the people. Ghannoushi acknowledges that several political concepts in Islam, such as *shura* and political parties, have not been successfully turned into stable institutions for administering differences in society. This was masterfully achieved in the West, which established various mechanisms for popular representation and controlled government. This realization affects Ghannoushi's perception of the Islamic state as he attempts to devise a very systematic and institutionalized design. He begins with the concept of freedom, which permeates most of his recent writings. Ghannoushi adopts a dynamic perspective of freedom. In his view, "Human beings are not born free; they make themselves free."[67] They should always strive to achieve and maintain their freedom on all levels: belief, self, economic, cultural, and political. Freedom, therefore, is a must and not a right granted by others. He even equates freedom with faith; it is part of the faith and therefore, should not be surrendered to any one.[68]

Ghannoushi delineates the nature of authority in the Islamic state. Political authority is necessary in Islam in order to achieve justice and uphold religion. The nature of this authority is civic and not divine. The reason is simply because the source of this authority is not God but the people. Political authority in Islam is based on *bay`a*, a contract between the members of the Muslim community and the ruler. As initiators (first party) of this contract, it is the right of the people to abrogate this *bay`a* and depose their ruler whenever they wish. Because political authority is Islamic, it has to be based on two sources: the *shari`a* (Islamic laws), which is the source of its legitimacy, and *shura* (consultation and rule of the people in accordance with the *shari`a*). The *shura*, which represents for Ghannoushi the real empowerment of the members of society, takes place at various levels. It could be exercised in a direct form (referendum and public elections), through parliamentary representation and through councils of scholars and experts specialized in their fields.

To avoid the historical mistakes that institutionalized tyranny in Muslim societies under the name of religion in the past and democracy at present, Ghannoushi warns that rulers should not be the guarantors of popular representation and public freedoms. He outlines several concepts that should be instilled in the people's consciousness, and institutions that represent actual checks on the power of the government. First, the Muslim nation and not an individual ruler, a group, or a single institution, is the source of political authority. Second, the *bay`a* (contract) that the people grant to their representatives at any level hold public officials responsible and accountable before the nation which has every right to change them. Third, the people should have access to the rulers, who cannot combine political authority and economic or financial influence. Fourth, the economic system of the Islamic state should prevent the accumulation of wealth in the hands of a few and guarantee its equitable distribution among the different segments of society. Fifth, the social system of the Islamic state should limit the control of the state over the economy and ensure the independence of society from the state through respecting the right of private ownership and individual initiative. Sixth, the civil society should be strengthened by an educational system that provides access to knowledge and lift the fear of the coercive authority of the state off the minds and consciousness of the people. In this regard, the mosques should be independent from the control of the state and become centers for popular education. Seventh, a pluralistic party system should be established to mobilize and recruit the people, articulate their demands, and ensure the peaceful transfer of power. Eighth, the Islamic state should have a decentralized local and provincial system that operates on the basis of *shura* and the involvement of the people in administering their affairs and exercising direct control over the government. Finally, while the judicial power must maintain its independence, the Islamic system allows for either the separation between the executive and legislative branches or their integration. Ghannoushi, however, advocates their benign separation, while maintaining a cooperative relation that would avoid conflict between the two branches.[69]

In discussing the characteristics of the economic system in the Islamic state, Ghannoushi views this issue as part of a general political, social, and educational process. Therefore, the economic policies should be closely linked with the Islamic doctrines which mold all the institutions of the state.[70] He proposes general principles which do not deviate from the traditional Islamic perception and the contributions of other Muslim intellectuals in this regard. Ghannoushi emphasizes the idea that God has delegated the Muslim community with the authority to accumulate and allocate capital. The community in turn can transfer this authority to individuals who enjoy the right of private ownership, as long as it does not contradict the public interest. Otherwise, the community can impose restrictions and even confiscate private property. The economic ills of society are addressed through moral measures that stress the concept of justice, in terms of distribution, cooperation, the prevention of usury, exploitation, monopoly, and the emergence of a financially privileged class.[71] The Constitution of the al-Nahda Movement stated as economic objectives:

- To build a strong and cohesive national economy based on our resources, self-reliant, meeting the basic needs of the people; guarantee equality between the regions; and contribute to more collective cooperation on the Maghrib, Arab, and Islamic levels.
- To accomplish cohesion and coordination between the private and the public sectors in order to serve the national interest.
- To emphasize the importance of work as the condition for acquiring wealth and progress, as both a right and an obligation; and strive for a more humanistic economic system based on the principle: from each man according to his abilities, to each man according to his needs. This means that every individual has the right to benefit from his work within the societal needs, and every individual has the right to fulfill his basic needs in every case.[72]

The perception of change for the FIS takes a different course. Due to FIS's unique political experience, Madani's perspectives on change and the Islamic model takes place at two levels: intellectual and practical. The intellectual is articulated in Madani's writings and numerous statements, while the practical manifests itself in the fact that the FIS has been the only Islamic party in North Africa which has been legalized. Prior to the formation of FIS, Madani drew the intellectual blueprints of an Islamic solution that would evade the problems inherent in modern thought and furnish an ideological framework for the political formation of the Islamists. In his book, *The Crisis of Modern Thought*, Madani attempts to demonstrate the inability of liberal and Marxist ideologies in resolving the problems of modern man and provides intellectual justifications for the need for an Islamic solution. This solution is based on the functional integration of religion, philosophy, and science. He realizes that the combination of these three fields may raise criticism as they appear contradictory. Madani stresses, however, that the contradiction is apparent and not real. It does not stem from the objectives of each field, which are compatible as they all seek the truth and better understanding of reality, but from the modern perception of religion, philosophy, and science.[73]

When discussing the process of change, Madani makes a distinction between the human being and his environment. Whereas most ideologies, liberal or Marxist, focus on the environment and try to change it to improve the condition of the human being, Madani considers the human being as the central unit and the primary step in the process of change. He raises the issue of freedom as the prerequisite for human will to change on the individual and the collective levels. He considers the solutions offered by liberal or Marxist ideologies insufficient as they conceal the contradictions between individual and public freedoms and interests. These theories mitigated the conflict either through alleviating the conditions of the less fortunate segments of society while maintaining political power and influence in the hands of the rich, as is the case of liberal societies, or by suppressing individual freedoms for the sake of society, as was the case in the communist countries. Madani explains:

> Democracy in the US, in a liberal and pragmatic sense, has upheld freedom, but it has given more rights to personal freedoms at the expense of the group. It has given more rights to the powerful and less to the weak. This is freedom at the expense of social and economic justice...Democracy in the Marxist sense, as defined by Karl Marx, Engles, Prudhomme Tuttle and others, on the other hand, is a restriction of freedom. This system has limited personal freedoms by using the rights of the group and society as an excuse. Their fundamentalism in this way is at the expense of freedom and the spirit of enterprise which limits their political longevity. Liberal democracy is not free of contradictions, nor is socialist democracy free of oppression and injustice. So what is the way to freedom?

The answer to Madani's rhetorical question lies, in his view, in an Islamic alternative that while guaranteeing freedom, emphasizes the concept of justice. Madani maintains that:

> The Islamic alternative provides the kind of freedom wherein individual and societal freedoms do not oppose each other. It provides for rights that are not opposed to obligations, such that duty becomes a right and right becomes a duty, as two faces of a single coin. In realizing justice

and freedom without contradictions, the Islamic *shari`a*, or jurisprudence, has gone beyond democracy and has achieved something not achieved in liberal or socialistic democracy. Islam then meets the level of our needs and provides a model to confront the ideological crises that civilization is living in today."[74]

What are then the characteristics of the Islamic alternative that Madani is proposing? According to Madani, this model is based on two main sources: the Qur'an and the Sunna. These sources guarantee the soundness of its ideological approach.[75] This does not mean that differences would not arise, but they would be over details and not on the validity of the sources themselves. Madani delineates his model with regards to the man and the state of the caliphate, in both religious and political terms. Its basic components include the restoration of human dignity through freedom which is not absolute but restricted by ability and justice; the acceptance of the divine source behind humanity in order to define loyalty and the nature of authority; the recognition of the sovereignty of God that prevents the conflict of interests; the protection of the dignity of the human being and his property; the freedom of opinion, belief, thought, and opposition of tyranny; the right of the people to nominate, elect, and change its political leadership and hold them accountable; the enjoyment of equal opportunities, education, and care.[76] As it is based on the concept and exercise of *shura*, the political system in Islam is characterized by "collective leadership and the collective responsibility of society to guarantee unity that permits pluralism and individual initiative."[77]

Politically, Madani has demonstrated consistency between his intellectual ideas and the political practices of FIS under his leadership. The FIS has chosen political participation within the system as a means to effect change in society. Prior to its electoral victory in the 1990 local elections Madani expressed his expectations of the regime and the other political forces in the country. He contends, "We adopt the concept of *shura*. Democracy represents the base of agreement between the FIS and the other political forces in society. We expect them to be committed to their values, that is, democracy, while we do not expect them to abide by ours."[78] When the FIS won these elections with an overwhelming majority and FIS's position on pluralism was questioned, Madani firmly stated, "We are human and make mistakes, and we are not prepared to impose ourselves on our people even when we are wrong. Never. We exist whenever legitimacy exists, and where there is no legitimacy, we do not exist. Therefore, pluralism must be allowed, because there is opposition...Pluralism is a guarantee of cultural wealth, and diversity is needed for any development."[79]

To set the groundwork for seeking the restoration of Islamic values through political activism, Yassin, like Ghannoushi and Madani, attempts to draw a theoretical framework in order to clarify the solutions offered within the guidelines of Islamic teachings. He raises the historical issue of the caliphate, whose restoration on the basis of justice, consultation, and benevolence, in his view, is the ultimate objective of Islamic political action. On the level of internal politics, he argues for the need to replace the despotic regimes with a just regime conducive to consultative rule and the social transformation of the present Muslim community. This should take into account the divine principles included in the teachings of the Qur'an.[80] As Yassin puts it, "With no single exception, all systems in *dar al-Islam* (Land of Islam) today are systems of terrorism, coercion, and suppression."[81] As such, he formulates the groundwork for bringing about economic, political, and military liberation. As Yassin points out, "The caliphate cannot be established on unsound political, economic, social, military, and administrative bases."[82]

As observed, the revival of Islam is based on the notion of socializing the individual members of society, a process that would eventually encompass society as a whole. It then would be concerned with reaching out to revive Islam throughout the political, economic, cultural, and administrative structures of the country. This is a process that, according to Yassin, would involve a crisis on two levels: the crisis of leadership; and the crisis of devising and implementing an appropriate paradigm.[83]

On the level of leadership, Yassin argues that historically the Islamic nation as well as the state were founded on the basis of the *da`wa* (here, Islamic doctrines). Over the years, the *dawla* (the state) has subdued the *da`wa*, rendering it an instrument for the justification of its unjust policies and authoritarian rule. This process in Yassin's view has been responsible for the degeneration of Muslims. To redress this situation and avoid further deviation from the principles of the Qur'an, the *da`wa* must remain independent of the politics of the regime, yet retain a dominant role in shaping the lives of the Muslim community. In fact, the *da`wa* opposing the secular policies of the Westernized elite has already disappeared. This calls for the establishment of separate institutions for the *da`wa*, which, in the context of restoring Islamic values, would be a decisive public apparatus for dispensing justice. These institutions would be responsible for the socialization of the nation, overseeing the conduct of the state, and controlling the affairs of the Muslim community. The regime would need to conform to the new body of Islamic scholars, who would be represented in a council of learned men.[84]

The establishment of institutions for the *da`wa* would pave the way for the restoration of Islamic values through *jihad*. Although Yassin divides this into two broad categories, *jihad da`wa* (intellectual struggle) and *jihad bina'* (restructuring struggle), he identifies a total of eleven different kinds of *jihad*. Some are related to the education and socialization of the Muslim individual in his relation with God, himself, and the nation. Some deal with the vanguard community (*jama`a*) during its socialization process. Others deal with it before, while, and after taking over power. What they have in common is that they are *jihad*-s of social transformation: *jihad* of the soul; of capital; of education; of enjoining the good and forbidding evil; of word and proof; of mobilization and restructuring; and of addressing political and social problems.[85] In general terms, the use of *jihad* as a strategy for social change should set the stage for the removal of the dominant sociopolitical mentality of the regime, which fosters blind submission to its system and laws; the socialization and reawakening of the Muslim population and encouragement of mass participation in running the affairs of the state; the removal of corrupt elements at higher levels of the bureaucracy; and the rectification of the economic institutions of the state.

The Prophetic Paradigm

What Yassin sets out to propose, if a revival of Islamic values is to occur, is a comprehensive process of socialization and mobilization that involves disobedience and opposition to dictatorship. At a time when the state has managed to use its resources to subdue the *da`wa*, a reconciliation of the state and the *da`wa* must come about through the implementation of the prophetic paradigm. As Yassin puts it, "It is a paradigm for a *jihadi* socialization and organization to prepare for the establishment of the Islamic caliphate. The Muslims are under dictatorships at present, which has deprived the state institutions, media, and education of the true meaning of Islam."[86]

Indeed, unlike many Islamic activists and thinkers who believe that the establishment of the Islamic state should be given priority over the development of a theoretical framework for such a state, Yassin is strongly convinced that a clear theoretical blueprint for Islamic action should be available and should precede the attempts to found an Islamic state. For this purpose, Yassin has almost wholly concentrated his efforts since 1972 on drawing the outlines of the Prophetic Paradigm. It is derived from the principles of the Qur'an, the traditions of the Prophet, the experience of past and present Islamic movements, Yassin's own experience with Sufism, and his own *ijtihad*. He has continued to revise it since it was first devised, maintaining its basic components while elaborating on its details and dynamics.

He proposes ten components of the Prophetic Paradigm that should be understood and implemented to redress the conditions of *fitna* (disorder) and achieve the proper socialization and active mobilization of the Muslim community. The terminology used in the paradigm and the values recommended reflect Sufi influences on Yassin. He nevertheless succeeds in giving them new meanings and usage to relate to the social and political conditions of the country and the objectives of his thought. Aware of this fact, he notes that, "the Prophetic Paradigm involves moral and spiritual elements...Putting them in this form will definitely shock those who are used to material terminology."[87]

The first three components deal with the organization of the community of believers. These are *al-suhba wa al-jama'a* (companionship and community), *al-dhikr* (recitation), and *al-sidq* (sincerity). As the unified entity of a leadership and a community, companionship leads to the reformation of the behavior of the Muslim through the values and regulations adhered to by the rest of the community. He asserts that the community (*al-jama'a*) is a step ahead and is different from the concept of society (*mujtama'*). It is an organic entity tied horizontally by the attachment and affection between its members; and vertically by the obedience and advice to its leader. By *dhikr*, Yassin refers to adherence to the principles of the Qur'an and prayer, with all its ritual and organizational implications such as assembly, collective action, and the restoration of the mosque (in schools, factories, administrations, etc.) as a nucleus and center for daily mobilization. He considers that sincerity (*sidq*) complements the first two and is a requirement for revealing the quality of the Muslims and the level of their willingness to change the existing order.

The remaining six components are applications of the first three just mentioned. Thus the fourth of these components is *al-badhl* (sacrifice), which is the practical proof of a sincere commitment to the causes of the

Muslim community. The fifth is *al-'ilm* (knowledge), by which one learns about the acquisition of power, the regulation of the society and economy, and the achievement of complete mobilization. The sixth is *al-'amal* (action), which means moving towards a comprehensive mobilization to change the structures of society from one controlled and squeezed by a well-to-do class to one that is an independent community under a strong and legitimate Islamic leadership. The seventh is *al-samat* (behavior), a process that involves the development of a distinct and attractive culture to achieve the universalism of Islam. The eighth is *al-ta'uda* (moderation), which rejects extremism and violence as means for achieving any objectives. The ninth is *al-iqtisad* (economy), which is associated with power, austerity, and rejection of the consumerist mentality. The last component is *al-jihad*, which can not be achieved without an organized community, whose members are willing to sacrifice money and themselves.[88]

Yassin goes on to expound on the nature and method of political action considered necessary to bring about the implementation of the Prophetic Paradigm, and, hence, the establishment of the Islamic state. In 1974, he presented his paradigm to the king, hoping that a Muslim leader such as Hassan would endorse it and put it into effect. Instead of receiving encouragement, however, Yassin received three years of imprisonment. In the late 1970s and early 1980s, he republished this paradigm in his journal *al-Jama'a* and introduced some improvements to it. Instead of having a reformed leader as the focal point of his plan, Yassin now places more emphasis on the organization of believers, which he calls *jund Allah* (soldiers of God), as the nucleus for the establishment of an Islamic state. The tasks of these activists include the establishment of a regional community (*jama'a*) of Muslims, the socialization and organization of its members, the establishment of a regional Islamic state, the unification of Islamic countries, and the restoration of the caliphate.[89] Another indication of the evolution of Yassin's thinking is that whereas in his early writings, he criticized the multi-party system as divisive and un-Islamic, in the new version, he accepts participation in the democratic process. This change is due, no doubt, to necessity but also to the hope of embarrassing the regime and demonstrating its insincerity in implementing democracy (he referred to the precedents of al-Nahda Movement Tunisia in this regard).

He perceives three alternative means for inducing change and the establishment of the Islamic state. The first is through the party system and elections, a process that is expected to end the regime's marginalization and containment of the Islamic movement, and, at the same time, enable the movement to compete for public support and expose the hypocrisy of the official Islam of the regime and that of the other political parties. This process would also necessitate public action, flexibility of strategy and program, and persistence. The second channel is through political violence, which Yassin firmly rejects as he considers it suicidal for the movement. The final option is a popular Khomeini-like revolution, which would come as a result of the maturation of the first alternative following the full preparation of the Islamic party and the involvement of the population in the transformation process.[90] Yassin presents these alternatives for the consideration of Islamists without advocating any of them. However, as was mentioned above, since 1983, he has been applying for the establishment of a political party, which must be seen as preference for the first alternative.

Yassin provides brief and general ideas on the characteristics of the political and economic systems of the Islamic state. He envisions the Islamic government to be a religio-political one, which would be divine in legislation (*tashri`*) but human in the implementation of policies (*tanfidh*). It would combine the functions of the *da`wa* and the *dawla*, yet would have their separate and independent institutions. The former would be the decision-making body of the Islamic state, charged with the tasks of socializing and mobilizing the Muslim community and checking the executive branch. The latter would be the executive branch of the state, which would carry out all the functions of the government. For Yassin, the establishment of the state of the caliphate would mean, on the internal front, the replacement of tyrannical rule by a consultative one; and on the external front, the emergence of an Islamic nation, independent of the Western and Eastern blocs.[91]

What Yassin presents concerning the political institutions of the Islamic states falls short of being clear or satisfactory. Though he provides a detailed blueprint for the organization, structure, dynamics, activities, and socialization of the movement that would carry out the task of mobilization and then the establishment of the Islamic order,[92] he does not speak specifically of the political structures of the Islamic state and its political institutions. For example, he describes the Islamic political system as a consultative one, but he never describes the political form or institutions through which the process of consultation would be exercised, nor the criteria by which the people who would practice this right would be chosen.[93] He also seems to empower the head of the Islamic states with considerable executive authority.

With regard to the economic system of the Islamic state, Yassin points to the need to undergo an economic transformation. The great task of restructuring is a prerequisite to the foundation of a just economic system. In rejecting the liberal and socialist models of economic development, he presents a model that is based on the following moral and practical principles: the distribution of rights and duties in order to prevent the accumulation of wealth among a minority class; the reallocation of national resources to achieve the general prosperity and welfare of the nation; the elimination of social injustice and poverty; and the full mobilization of the nation's resources and potentialities.

Yassin considers the elimination of class differences as the most important difficulty that would confront the Islamic solution. He expects the concept of Islamic moderation (*rifq*) to replace class struggle, which is devastating to the welfare of the nation.[94] It is the pivotal task to replace the socioeconomic conditions inherited from *fitna* with a sound Islamic reality, without destroying the economic institutions of the country or resorting to radical measures. As Yassin states, "the Islamic solution for the problem of distribution is the achievement of justice; for the problem of productivity, it is reliance on individual initiative; for the contradiction between just distribution and sufficiency, it is nationalization, not as a rule but as a possible means."[95]

This raises the issue of preparing the necessary groundwork for developing an Islamic economy in order to resolve the persistent problem of underdevelopment as brought about by the Westernized elite through its deficient modernization schemes. Yassin sums up the pressing need to overcome the problems of underdeveloped economies by fulfilling the following requirements:

1. the full mobilization of national resources, while respecting private property, in order to reach the level of self-sufficiency;
2. the liberation of the labor force of the country from capital control;
3. the encouragement of private initiative, which should be well integrated within the general framework and objectives of the national economy;
4. the establishment of Islamic industrial cooperatives to divert capital from non-productive investments and fixed assets;
5. the nationalization of banks and their gradual transformation to interest-free institutions in order to stimulate productivity;

6. the nationalization of the major industrial means of production that are related to the public interest;

7. the formulation of a development plan that would enable the state to direct, encourage, and organize the production process of the country without impeding private initiatives by state bureaucracy;

8. the implementation of labor intensive techniques that would provide benefits to the workers, while realizing the need for capital intensive techniques for heavy industry and the armed forces;

9. the training of the necessary technical cadres and the initiation of prompt educational reforms to rectify the problems of brain-drain;

10. the creation of a domestic market for products of Islamic countries by enhancing the purchasing power of the impoverished population and curbing the wealthy from squandering the surplus of domestic investment returns in foreign markets;

11. the implementation of land reform;

12. the expansion of a market for Islamic products by establishing an economic coalition between the Islamic countries, regardless of the types of their regimes; and

13. the provision of patterns of technology, planning, production, and consumption appropriate to Islamic values in order to liberate Muslims from the *jahili* model.[96]

Similar to Ghannoushi, Yassin recommends that the members of the Islamic movement should align themselves with the *mustad`afin* (the disinherited). During the transformation period, the national resources of the Muslim community should be directed towards achieving overall national development, self-sufficiency, food security, and economic and military security. During this phase, it may be necessary to rely on the available patterns of technology, planning, production, and consumption until different ones are developed. More importantly, he argues that the Islamic economy cannot be truly established in a non-Islamic society. The process of production and distribution of wealth cannot work in isolation of the total process of renewing religion and faith.[97] In arguing thusly, Yassin relies on the implementation of *ijtihad* in order to reformulate the *shari`a* into applicable rules and practices that address the problems of modern society.[98]

Conclusion

As lay intellectuals, Ghannoushi, Madani, and Yassin, who lack the traditional popularity and legitimacy of the religious scholars, rely on traditionalist ideas while in fact reinterpreting them to accommodate the modern issues of their societies. This was clearly observed in the Prophetic Paradigm of Yassin's writings. In presenting the concept of change and an Islamic model, we see *ijtihad* actively at work as a social tool calling for collective awareness and unity of consciousness in addressing issues of national significance. The restoration of Islamic values is not automatic, but requires an appreciation of the way in which Qur'anic principles and modern conditions can be reconciled in the eyes and minds of the Muslim constituency. Ghannoushi, Madani, and Yassin tackle that task by turning away from both the excessive submission of the traditional `ulama' and the excessive Westernization of the elite. In effect, they are deliberately seeking to give rise to a more vital civilization—an orientation that is clearly positive and world-affirming. The three intellectuals are not revolutionaries. They do not call for violent and radical means for the transformation of their societies. Rather, they take a careful, gradualist stance with regard to advocating pro-Islamic social change and economic reforms. The pitfall of such a cautious policy is that it falls short of bringing about a fundamental change in the immediate future and, thereby, risks losing the popular support of its growing constituency. On the other hand, the burgeoning quest for Islamic solutions to the massive socioeconomic problems and lack of free political expression is likely to motivate the regimes to preempt the perceived threat of the Islamic movements by appropriating some of their demands.

Notes

1. Rashed al-Ghannoushi, "Baramij al-Falsafa wa Jil al-Daya`'" [Philosophy Programs and the Generation of Loss], *al-Ma`rifa*, No. 10, 1973, reprinted in Rashed al-Ghannoushi, *Maqalat* (Paris: Dar al-Karawan, 1984), p. 12.

2. Ghannoushi, "Baramij al-Falsafa," p. 13.

3. Ghannoushi, "Baramij al-Falsafa," p. 9.

4. Rashed al-Ghannoushi, "al-Tatawur = Ihtifadh + Tajawuz" [Evolution = Preservation and Transcendence], in Ghannoushi, *Maqalat*, pp. 15-25.

5. Rashed al-Ghannoushi, "al-Adab wa al-Akhlaq" [Literature and Ethics], *al-Ma`rifa*, Vol. 2, No. 6, 1974.

6. The contributions of North African reformers and intellectuals like Khayr Eddin al-Tunsi, Abdel Aziz al-Tha`alibi, and al-Taher Haddad in Tunisia; Abdel Hamid Ben Badis, al-Bashir al-Ibrahimi, and Malik Ben Nabi in Algeria; and Mukhtar al-Soussi, Abdel Karim al-Khattabi and Allal al-Fassi in Morocco could be viewed within this context.

7. Rashed al-Ghannoushi, "Min Jadid Nahnu wa al-Gharb" [Once More: We and the West], *al-Ma`rifa*, Vol. 4, No. 9, August 1, 1978, p. 3.

8. For an example of books which raised these issues, see Shakeeb Arslan, *Limadha Ta'akhar al-Muslimun wa Taqaddam Ghayrahum* [Why Were the Muslims Set Back While Others Advanced], (Cairo, 1939-1940) and Ahmed Fathi Zaghlul, *Sir Taqaddum al-Inkiliz al-Saksuniyyin* [The Secret for the Advancement of the Anglo-Saxons], (Cairo, 1911-12).

9. On the different responses of the Arab intellectuals, see Albert Hourani, *Arabic Thought in The Liberal Age: 1798-1939* (London: Oxford University Press, 1970), Majid Khadduri, *Political Trends in the Arab World: The Role of Ideas and Ideals in Politics* (Baltimore: The Johns Hopkins University Press, 1970), Hisham Sharabi, *Arab Intellectuals and the West: The Formative Years, 1875-1914* (Baltimore: The Johns Hopkins University Press, 1970), and Ibrahim Abu-Lughod, *Arab Rediscovery of Europe: A Study in Cultural Encounters* (New Jersey: Princeton University Press, 1963).

10. Rashed al-Ghannoushi, "Min Jadid," part one, *al-Ma`rifa*, Vol. 4, No. 9, August 1, 1978, pp. 4-5.

11. Rashed al-Ghannoushi, "Min Jadid," part two, *al-Ma`rifa*, Vol. 4, No. 10, October 1, 1978, p. 9.

12. Ghannoushi, "Min Jadid," part two, *al-Ma`rifa*, Vol. 4, No. 10, October 1, 1978, pp. 10-12.

13. Ghannoushi, *Maqalat*, pp. 59-61.

14. Abbasi Madani, *Azmat al-Fikr al-Hadith wa Mubarirat al-Hal al-Islami* [The Crisis of Modern Thought and the Justifications for an Islamic Solution] (Mecca: Maktabat al-Manar, 1989), pp. 16-18.

15. Abdel Salam Yassin, "al-Minhaj al-Nabawi" [The Prophetic Paradigm], *al-Jama`a*, No. 10, 1982, p. 93.

16. Abdel Salam Yassin, *al-Islam Ghadan* [Islam Tomorrow] (Casablanca: Maktabat al-Najah, 1973), p. 147.

17. *Al-Jama`a*, No. 4, 1980, p. 103.

18. Abdel Salam Yassin, *La Révolution à l'Heure de l'Islam* (Gignac-La-Nerthe: Borel and Feraud SA, 1981), p. 11. On Qutb's idea of *jahiliyya*, see Sayyid Qutb, *Milestones* (International Islamic Federation of Students Organizations, 1978). See also Yvonne Haddad, "The Qur'anic Justification for an Islamic Revolution: The Views of Sayyid Qutb," *The Middle East Journal*, Vol. 37, No. 1, Winter 1983; Yvonne Haddad, "Sayyid Qutb: Ideologue of Islamic Revival," in John Esposito (ed.), *Voices of Resurgent Islam* (New York:

Oxford University Press, 1983), pp. 85-7; and Tariq and Jacqueline Ismael, *Governments and Politics in Islam* (New York: St. Martin's Press, 1985), pp. 110-13.

19. Yassin, *al-Islam Ghadan*, p. 693.

20. Yassin, *al-Islam Ghadan*, p. 763.

21. Abdel Salam Yassin, *al-Islam Bayn al-Da`wa wa al-Dawla* [Islam Between the Call and the State] (Casablanca: Maktabat al-Najah, 1972), p. 104.

22. Yassin, *al-Islam Ghadan*, p. 20.

23. Rashed al-Ghannoushi, "al-Taghreeb wa Hatmiyyat al-Dictatoriyya" [Westernization: an Imperative to Dictatorship] in Ghannoushi, *Maqalat*, pp. 167-170.

24. Ghannoushi, "al-Taghreeb wa Hatmiyyat al-Dictatoriyya," p. 168.

25. Al-Hashmi, "Mahattat ma`a al-Shaykh Rashed al-Ghannoushi" [Pauses with Shaykh Rashed al-Ghannoushi], *al-I`lan*, No. 496, April 4, 1986.

26. Ghannoushi, *Maqalat*, p. 168.

27. Ghannoushi, *Maqalat*, pp. 77-82.

28. Ghannoushi, *Maqalat*, pp. 168-69.

29. Ghannoushi, *Maqalat*, p. 169.

30. Rashed al-Ghannoushi and Hassan al-Turabi, *al-Haraka al-Islamiyya wa al-Tahdith* [The Islamic Movement and Modernization] (Beirut: Dar al-Jil, 1980), p. 35.

31. Abbasi Madani, *Mushkilat Tarbawiyya fi al-Bilad al-Islamiyya* [Educational Problems in the Muslim Countries] (Mecca: Maktabat al-Manar, 1989), pp. 8-9.

32. Madani, *Mushkilat Tarbawiyya*, pp., 123-35 and 148-49.

33. Yassin, *al-Islam aw al-Tufan*, pp. 12-3.

34. Yassin, *al-Islam aw al-Tufan*, p.14.

35. Yassin, *al-Islam aw al-Tufan*, p. 57.

36. Yassin, *al-Islam aw al-Tufan*, p. 19.

37. *Al-Jama`a*, No. 4, 1980, p. 103.

38. Yassin, *al-Islam aw al-Tufan*, p. 13.

39. Yassin, *al-Islam aw al-Tufan*, pp. 107-12.

40. Abdel Salam Yassin, *al-Islam wa al-Qawmiyya al-`Almaniyya* [Islam and Secular Nationalism] (Casablanca: Matba`at al-Najah, 1989), pp. 28-9. See also Emad Eldin Shahin, "Secularism and Nationalism: The Political Discourse of Abd al-Salam Yassin," in John Ruedy (ed.), *Islamism and Secularism in North Africa* (New York: St. Martin's Press, 1994), pp. 167-85.

41. Abdel Salam Yassin, *Hiwar ma`a al-Fudala' al-Dimuqratiyyin* [Dialogue with the Virtuous Democrats] (Casablanca: Matba`at al-Ufuq, 1994), p. 58.

42. Yassin, *Hiwar ma`a al-Fudala' al-Dimuqratiyyin*, pp. 68-9.

43. Yassin, *Hiwar ma`a al-Fudala' al-Dimuqratiyyin*, p. 59.

44. Rashed al-Ghannoushi, *al-Fikr al-Islami bayn al-Mithaliyya wa al-Waqi`iyya* [Islamic Thought Between Idealism and Reality] (Tunis: n.p., n.d.), p. 4.

45. "Nobody's Man," p. 20.

46. Madani, *Mushkilat Tarbawiyya*, p. 89.

47. Madani, *Mushkilat Tarbawiyya*, pp. 90-4.

48. Madani, *Mushkilat Tarbawiyya*, pp. 95.

49. Abdel Salam Yassin, "al-Jihad Tandhiman wa Zahfan" [Jihad: Organization and March], *al-Jama`a*, No. 11, May 1983, p. 51.

50. Yassin, "al-Jihad Tandhiman wa Zahfan," Ibid., pp. 54-5.

51. Abdel Salam Yassin, "Iftitahiya wa Istiftah" [Prologue], *al-Jama`a*, Vol. 1, No. 1, March-April-May 1979, p. 12.

52. Rashed al-Ghannoushi, "Baramij al-Falsafa," and "al-Adab wa al-Akhlaq."

53. Madani, *Mushkilat Tarbawiyya*, p. 32.

54. Madani, *Mushkilat Tarbawiyya*, p. 37.

55. Madani, *Mushkilat Tarbawiyya*.

56. Yassin, *al-Islam Ghadan*, pp. 722 and 727.

57. Yassin, *al-Islam Ghadan*, pp. 685-95, 707-28, and 739-68. See also, Abdel Salam Yassin, *Hiwar ma`a al-Fudala' al-Dimuqratiyyin*, pp. 120-207.

58. Rashed al-Ghannoushi, "al-Islam wa al-`Unf" [Islam and Violence], in *Maqalat*, p. 173.

59. Ghannoushi, *al-Haraka al-Islamiyya wa al-Tahdith*, p. 21.

60. Ghannoushi, *al-Haraka al-Islamiyya wa al-Tahdith*, pp. 19-24.

61. Rashed al-Ghannoushi, "al-`Alam al-Islami wa al-Isti`mar al-Hadith" [The Islamic World and Neo-Imperialism], in Ghannoushi, *Maqalat*, p. 163-4.

62. Rashed al-Ghannoushi, "Qadat al-Haraka al-Islamiyya al-Mu`asira" [The Leaders of the Contemporary Islamic Movement], *al-Ma`rifa*, Vol. 5, No. 4, April 1, 1979, p. 14.

63. Rashed al-Ghannoushi, "al-Fikr al-Islami la Yanhazim fi Ma`raka Nadhifa" [Islamic Thought Cannot Be Defeated in a Clean Battle], *al-Musawar*, December 20-27, 1985.

64. Rashed al-Ghannoushi, *al-Haraka al-Islamiyya wa al-Tahdith*, pp. 32-8.

65. Rashed al-Ghannoushi, "al-Islam wa al-`Unf," p. 176.

66. This book was originally a Ph.D. dissertation that Ghannoushi prepared for submission to the Faculty of Shari`a in Tunis. Due to his political condition he was unable to obtain the doctoral degree.

67. Rashed al-Ghannoushi, *al-Huriyyat al-`Amma fi al-Dawla al-Islamiyya* [Public Freedoms in the Islamic State] (Beirut: Markaz Dirasat al-Wihda al-Arabiyya, 1993), p. 319.

68. Ghannoushi, *al-Huriyyat al-`Amma*, pp. 42-68.

69. Ghannoushi, *al-Huriyyat al-`Amma*, pp. 326-28.

70. Ghannoushi, *al-Huriyyat al-`Amma*, pp. 190-95.

71. Rashed al-Ghannoushi, *Haykal `am li al-Iqtisad al-Islami* [A General Framework for the Islamic Economy] (Tunis: n.p., n.d). See also Ghannoushi's article with the same title in *al-Furqan*, No. 13, Rajab-Sha`ban 1408, pp. 20-4.

72. "Constitution of the Renaissance Party," in *The Renaissance Party in Tunisia: The Quest for Freedom and Democracy* (Washington, D.C.: American Muslim Council, 1991), p. 184.

73. Madani, *Azmat al-Fikr al-Hadith*, p. 26-8.

74. Transcript of a video interview with Abbasi Madani, Summer 1990, pp. 4-5.

75. Madani, *Azmat al-Fikr al-Hadith*, p. 55.

76. Madani, *Azmat al-Fikr al-Hadith*, pp. 58-88.

77. Madani, *Azmat al-Fikr al-Hadith*, p. 95.

78. *Al-Bashir*, No. 2, April 1990, p. 5.

79. *FBIS*-NES-90-124, June 27, 1990.

80. Abdel Salam Yassin, *Nadharat fi al-Fiqh wa al-Tarikh* [Views on Jurisprudence and History] (Al-Muhammadiyya: Matba`at Fadala, 1989), p. 82.

81. Yassin, *al-Islam Ghadan*, p. 923.

82. Yassin, "al-Jihad: Tandhiman wa Zahfan," p. 76

83. *Al-Jama`a*, No. 5, 1980, p. 47.

84. Abdel Salam Yassin, *al-Islam bayn al-Da`wa wa al-Dawla*, pp. 26-7. See also *al-Jama`a*, No. 11, May, 1983, pp. 73-82 and *Nadharat fi al-Fiqh*, pp. 82-85.

85. Yassin, *al-Minhaj al-Nabawi* [The Prophetic Paradigm] (Morocco: n.p., 1989), pp. 360-438.

86. Abdel Salam Yassin, "al-Minhaj al-Nabawi," *al-Jama`a*, No. 8, 1981, p. 8.

87. Yassin, *al-Islam Ghadan*, p. 43.

88. Yassin, *al-Islam aw al-Tufan*, pp. 85-100.

89. *Al-Jama`a*, No. 8, 1981, pp. 20-2.

90. *Al-Jama`a*, No. 11, 1983, pp. 44-50.

91. Ibid., pp. 77-82.

92. Abdel Salam Yassin, "al-Minhaj al-Nabawi: Tarbiyyatan wa Tandhiman wa Zahfan" [The Prophetic Paradigm: Socialization, Organization, and March], *al-Jama`a*, No. 8, June 1981, p. 6.

93. In fact, in *al-Jama`a*, No. 11, Yassin mentioned that he would explain in details the political characteristics of the Islamic state in future issues. *Al-Jama`a*, however, was suspended after this issue.

94. Yassin, *al-Islam aw al-Tufan*, p. 109-10.

95. *Al-Jama`a*, No. 2, 1979, p. 66.

96. Abdel Salam Yassin, "al-Minhaj al-Nabawi," *al-Jama`a*, No. 10, 1982, pp. 98-101.

97. Yassin, "al-Minhaj al-Nabawi," *al-Jama`a*, No. 10, 1982, pp. 101-5.
98. Yassin, "al-Minhaj al-Nabawi," *al-Jama`a*, No. 10, 1982, pp. 66-73.

7

General Conclusion

This work, by focusing on the local and particular dimensions of Tunisia, Algeria, and Morocco, sought to investigate the phenomenon of Islamic resurgence, its nature, evolution, and dynamics. It is clear that the nature of the phenomenon of political Islam is a complex one. The Islamic movements are intrinsically related to the issue of social change. Their objective is not based on accelerating the process of development, nor on a desire to block ongoing changes taking place in society. On the contrary, they aim at redirecting the political orientation of their respective countries from secularism to Islamism. In this respect, it would be inaccurate to term them radical or revolutionary. Unlike revolutionary movements that seek to advocate the absolute removal of existing values in order to impose a new set of values, the Islamic revival movements take a reformist stance. They aim at bringing about social reforms by advocating social change within the limits of existing values. They may seek to challenge the legitimacy of the regime on a political level, but by the same token, what they espouse may in turn be interpreted as having clear moral values on the practicing faith of the members of society. As such, the members of the Islamic movements may consider themselves a political entity, but their interaction vis-à-vis the regime may be perceived as clearly religious.

It is evident that Islam is bound to play an increasing role in the social development and political process of the three countries. The emergence of Islamic protest movements is not an isolated phenomenon in the history of Muslim societies. Islam has always taken different manifestations as a source for national identity, political legitimacy, overall reform, popular mobilization, and resistance against internal and external challenges. In the post-colonial state, Islam ceased to play an equal role and was subordinated to the institutions of the state in order to sanction its secular-inspired policies, in what became known as official Islam. The formation and expansion of the Islamic movements, since the late 1960s, came as a response to the marginalization of Islam in state and society and to a perceived failure of imported models of development to resolve the socioeconomic and political problems in society or incorporate the indigenous belief system of the Muslim population into a general plan of social transformation. The continuation of these conditions will assist the Islamic opposition movements to preserve their status in society and expand their base of support by proposing an alternative political discourse.

The closure of the traditional centers of education and the nationalization of religion in Tunisia, Algeria, and Morocco enabled the government to impose a general secular model of education. The secularization of the educational system, in turn, brought about a new generation of Muslim intellectuals, who sided neither with the conservative religious scholars nor with the Westernized elite that ran the country. These new intellectuals are well-educated Muslims who have a strong sense of national identity and, at the same time, believe that local conditions can be improved by implementing Islamic values on the social level, and that, on the international level, a degree of independence, solidarity, and unity of the Muslim world can be brought about.

This new intellectual elite has emerged as a political counterweight to the Westernized elite. By questioning the credibility of the co-opted scholars and presenting a modernist vision of Islam, it has dissociated itself from official Islam, proposing, instead, a populist Islam that seeks to achieve a comprehensive socialization and mobilization of the people. At the same time, in challenging the authenticity of the ruling Westernized elite, questioning the validity of its imported programs, and demanding an agenda of national development which would improve the socioeconomic lot of the population, this new intellectual elite is in a favorable position to win approval and support from the masses. The Islamic movements, due to the totality of their ideology and the religious nature of their message, attract adherents from all social classes rather than from one particular class. This counter-elite has no stack in maintaining the status-quo so it cannot be co-opted by the Westernized elite the way the traditional scholars were.

The ideology of the Islamic revival movements challenges the mandate of the Westernized elite by questioning its secular orientation, while at the same time condemning the submission of the traditional scholars to the regime. Lay intellectuals such as Rashed al-Ghannoushi, Abbasi Madani, and Abdel Salam Yassin, in light of the futility of official Islam, have expressed a different ideological content and attempted to put forth an Islamic approach to social transformation, which relies on traditional ideas while reinterpreting them to suit modern requirements. To mobilize mass support, Ghannoushi, Madani, and Yassin unleashed a scathing condemnation of the Westernized elites of Tunisia, Algeria, and Morocco for undertaking secular policies, neglecting the socioeconomic grievances of the masses, imposing authoritarian measures, and discarding traditional values. The rearticulation of intellectual themes of Islam enables these intellectuals to acquire some degree of legitimacy for their program of change. This new intellectual orientation is bound to strengthen the revivalists' claim and their challenge in drawing mass support.

It is important to note that political pluralism in society and that society's perception of the Islamic movements affect the level of cohesion and behavior of the Islamic opposition. In the case of Tunisia, which lacks real pluralism, it is clear that al-Nahda tends to be anti-regime, but not necessarily violent. The source of al-Nahda's strength lies in its ability to present itself as a viable alternative to the regime. This image has been enhanced particularly by the increasing monopolization of power by the state and its official party, as manifested in the regime's intolerance of public dissent and the results of recent presidential, local, and parliamentary elections. Political pluralism in Algeria before 1992 reflected itself in the diversity of the Islamic movements there. The FIS, however, succeeded in gaining popularity in a relatively short time due to the support it received from the historic religious scholars, its ability to project itself as an umbrella national movement open to all Algerians, and to the tactic of appealing directly to the streets to press for demands.

A number of conclusions can be drawn by examining the fortunes of these movements. When the movement is perceived as constructive and moderate, it resorts to a set of rational tactics to draw the support of the social forces in society and the recognition of the government. This has been the case of several major Islamic movements in Tunisia, Algeria, and Morocco. As an Islamic movement rapidly grows in size and influence, its prominence is likely to dictate a strategy of moderation. This is clearly observed in the case of the main movements, al-Nahda in Tunisia, the FIS, Hamas, and al-Nahda in Algeria, and al-'Adl wa al-Ihsan and HATM in Morocco, where they have adopted a policy of moderation in order to preserve their organization, protect their constituency, and advance their objectives.

The case of the Islamic movements in Morocco clearly reflects a lack of coherent formation and adequate expansion due to the fragmentation of the movement. This is because the Moroccan society provides various channels of political expression and discourse. At the same time, it divides the potential constituency of the different groups, which makes it hard for a single Islamic group to draw a large constituency. In brief, the more the new counter-elite is concerned with differences of opinion and strategies of social transformation, the greater the intellectual and organizational factionalism of the Islamic opposition. This factionalism is a liability when facing an incumbent elite that is united in preserving the status quo.

It is clear in Morocco that the Islamic movements face a tremendous obstacle in challenging a regime whose support is derived principally from historical and Islamic sources of legitimacy. They thus tend to be reformist rather than explicitly anti-regime when challenging the Islamic policies of a king whose lineage is religiously important. The case is particularly daunting when the king takes every opportunity to present himself as a fervent follower of Islam. In the case of Tunisia, on the other hand, the Islamic opposition movements have challenged a regime whose support has been derived primarily from secular sources. In such a case, it is clear that the movements may tend to be anti-regime, though not necessarily violent in tactics and strategy.

When an Islamic movement is perceived as radical and dogmatic, the movement is likely to resort to a strategy of violence and dissent. As observed in the case of Morocco in the mid-seventies, the Moroccan Islamic Youth Association and the various splinter groups resorted at times to extremist acts to express their disapproval of the regime of King Hassan. The purpose of such violent tactics is not to win the approval of the population but to reiterate a dogmatic stance on the objectives of the movement. On the other hand, as observed previously, when an Islamic movement rapidly grows in size and influence, its prominence is likely to dictate a strategy of moderation. This is observed clearly in the case of al-Nahda which adopted a policy of moderation during and after the Bourguiba era in order to legitimize its organization and protect its expanding constituency.

Finally, as the regime deploys a policy of repression against an Islamic movement, the opposition group is weakened in the short term, yet gains sympathy to its cause in the long run. As observed in the case of Tunisia and Algeria, where members of the mainstream Islamic movement were repeatedly detained and imprisoned, the movement appeared to lose its momentum. On the other hand, these repressive measures, which were viewed as exceeding any violations committed by al-Nahda or the FIS, strengthened the long-term position and credibility of the movement as an opposition group and justified its demands. This is borne out by the two movements' ability to broaden their base of coalition with other political forces in society. Conversely, as shown in the case of pre-coup Algeria, when the regime attempts to appease the members of an Islamic movement, the movement gains a large constituency but remains within the bounds of government authority. In the case of post-coup Algeria, on the other hand, it is clear that when the regime seeks the persecution and liquidation of a group, the Islamic movement breaks down into smaller but more cohesive—and generally more radical—splinter groups.

It thus appears that the Islamic movements in Tunisia, Algeria, and Morocco are a complex, diverse, and persistent force of change. The regime might go to great lengths to deny a particular Islamic movement access to legitimate channels of active political participation and public forums. No matter how the regime may attempt to isolate an Islamic movement and oppress its members, however, this policy is offset by the nature of activism and the ideological appeal of the Islamic movement. The general membership of the Islamic movements is a collectivity of people with diverse interests and personal needs expressed under an umbrella of common goals and shared values. This provides a sense of security or a reservoir based on the notion that these movements are not operating in a political or social vacuum. Al-Nahda, due to its commitment to non-violence and rational behavior, on one hand, and the increasing control of the regime, on the other, is bound to play an effective role in the future to counter the excessiveness of the regime and support other groups currently undergoing similar types of political testing. While the Algerian regime is becoming increasingly isolated and relying more on repression than political consensus, the FIS has succeeded in broadening its base of political alliance. This has been achieved through coordination and forging common grounds with other political forces in society, a process that generated the Rome Accord and a legitimate bloc of opposition to the continuation of the military-backed elite. The Islamic groups in Morocco, due to their fragmentation and the nature of the regime they are confronting, are in no position, at the present, to pose a threat to the stability of King Hassan's regime.

Selected Bibliography

Books and Articles in English and French

Abdallah, Rafik. "Bourguiba et l'Islam." (Mémoire pour le Diplôme d'Etudes Supérieures de Sciences Politiques, Université de Paris, 1973).

Abu-Lughod, Ibrahim. *Arab Rediscovery of Europe: A Study in Cultural Encounters* (New Jersey: Princeton University Press, 1963).

Abun-Nasr, Jamil. *A History of the Maghrib in the Islamic Period* (London: Cambridge University Press, 1975).

------."The Salafiyya Movement in Morocco: The Religious Base of the Moroccan Nationalist Movement," *St. Anthony's Papers*, No. 16, Middle East Affairs, No. 3 (London: Chatto and Wind, 1963).

Ajami, Fouad. *The Arab Predicament: Arab Political Thought and Practice Since 1967* (Cambridge: Cambridge University Press, 1981).

------. "The Arab Road," *Foreign Policy*, No. 47 (Summer 1982).

El-Alami, Raja. "La Nuit du Destin: Cette Année en Tunisie," *Dialogue*, No. 108 (September 27, 1976).

Arkoun, Mohammad. "Algeria," in Shireen Hunter, ed., *The Politics of Islamic Revivalism: Diversity and Unity* (Indianapolis: Indiana University Press, 1989).

Barakat, Halim, ed. *Contemporary North Africa: Issues of Development and Integration* (Washington, D.C.: Center for Contemporary Arab Studies, Georgetown University, 1985).

Barrada, Hamid. "De Rabat à la Mecque," *Jeune Afrique*, Nos. 990-1 (December 26, 1979 and January 2, 1980).

Belaid, Sadok. "Role of Religious Institutions in Support of the State," in I. William Zartman and Adeed Dawisha, eds., *Beyond Coercion* (London: Croom Helm, 1988).

Belhassan, S. "Femmes Tunisiennes Islamistes," in Christiane Souriau, et al. *Le Maghreb Musulman en 1979* (Paris: Centre National de la Recherche Scientifique, 1981).

Ben Achour, Yadh. *L'Etat Nouveau et la Philosophie Politique et Juridique Occidentale* (Tunis: 1980).

Ben Achour, Yadh. "Islam Perdu, Islam Retrouvé," in Christiane Souriau, et al. *Le Maghreb Musulman en 1979* (Paris: Centre National de la Recherche Scientifique, 1981).

Ben Nabi, Malik. "Sociologie de l'Indépendence," *Humanisme Musulman*, No. 5 (May 1965).

Benomar, Jamal. "The Monarchy, the Islamist Movement and Religious Discourse in Morocco," *Third World Quarterly*, Vol. 10, No. 2 (April 1988).

Ben Salah, Hafedh. "Système Politique et Système Religieux en Tunisie," (Memoire pour le Diplôme d'Etudes Supérieures de Sciences Politiques, Université de Tunis, Faculté de Droit et des Sciences Politiques et Economiques, Tunis, 1973-74).

Bouhamza, Moustapha. "L'Opposition Islamique en Algérie ," *La Cause*, Vol. 3, No. 24 (July 29-August 4, 1995).

Boulars, Habib. *L'Islam: La Peur et l'Espérance* (Paris: J.-C. Lattes, 1983).

Boulby, Marion. "The Islamic Challenge: Tunisia since Independence," *Third World Quarterly*, Vol. 10, No. 2 (April 1988).

Bowen, Donna Lee. "The Paradoxical Linkage of the `Ulama' and Monarch in Morocco," *The Maghrib Review*, Vol. 10, No. 1 (1985).

Brown, Leon Carl, ed. *State and Society in Modern North Africa* (Washington, D.C.: The Middle East Institute, 1966).

------. "The Islamic Reformist Movement in North Africa," *Journal of Modern African Studies*, Vol. 2, No. 1 (March 1964).

Burgat, François. *L'Islamisme au Maghreb: La Voix du Sud* (Paris: Karthala, 1988).

Burgat, François. "L'Algerie: de la Laïcité Islamique à l'Islamisme," *Maghreb-Machrek*, No. 121 (July-September 1988).

------. "Islamistes en Tunisie: La Crise?," *Grand Maghreb*, No. 44 (November 11, 1985).

------. "Intégristes: La Voie Tunisienne?," *Grand Maghreb*, Nos. 33-4 (October 1984).

Burgat, François and William Dowell. *The Islamic Movement in North Africa* (Texas: Center for Middle Eastern Studies, University of Texas in Austin, 1993).

Burke, Edmund, III and Ira M. Lapidus, eds. *Islam, Politics, and Social Movements* (Berkeley: University of California Press, 1988).

Chaouachi, Alya. "L'Islam et les Tunisiens," *Dialogue*, No. 108 (September 27, 1976).

Chaoui, Mohamed. "Islam et Politique au Maroc," *Lamalif*, No. 121, (December 1980).

Clement, Jean-François. "Morocco's Bourgeoisie: Monarchy, State, and Owning Class," *Middle East Report*, Vol. 16, No. 142 (September-October 1986).

Cody, Edward. "Dissidents' Trial Tests Tunisia," *Washington Post* (September 26, 1987).

Davis, James. "Towards a Theory of Revolution," *American Sociological Review*, No. 27 (1962).

Dekmejian, R. Hrair. *Islam in Revolution: Fundamentalism in the Arab World* (New York: Syracuse University Press, 1985).

------. "The Islamic Revival in the Middle East and North Africa," *Current History* (April 1980).

Delaney, Paul. "Uneasy Lies the Head that Wears Two Crowns," *New York Times* (December 25, 1987).

Denny, Frederick Mathewson. *An Introduction to Islam* (New York: Macmillan Publishing Company, 1994).

Dessouki, Ali E. Hilal, ed. *Islamic Resurgence in the Arab World* (New York: Praeger Publishers, 1982).

Disey, Nigel. "The Working Class Revolt in Tunisia," *MERIP* Report, Vol. 8, No. 4 (May 1978).

Duteil, Mireille. "L'Intégrisme Islamique au Maghreb: La Pause?", *Grand Maghreb*, No. 24, (October 3, 1983), and No. 26 (November 14, 1983).

Eedle, Paul. "Top-Level Algerian Plot Is Alleged," *Philadelphia Inquirer* (July 28, 1992).

El-Effendi, Abdelwahab. "The Long March Forward," *Inquiry*, Vol. 4, No. 10 (October 1987).

Eickelman, Dale. "Religion in Polity and Society," in I. William Zartman, ed., *The Political Economy of Morocco* (New York: Praeger Publishers, 1987).

Eldeman, Murray. *The Symbolic Uses of Politics* (Urbana: University of Illinois Press, 1967).

Enayat, Hamid. "The Resurgence of Islam," *History Today*, No. 30 (February 1980).

Entelis, John. "Political Islam in Algeria: The Nonviolent Dimension," *Current History*, Vol. 94, No. 588 (January 1995).

------. *Algeria: The Revolution Institutionalized* (Boulder: Westview Press, 1986).

------. "The Political Economy of North African Relations: Cooperation or Conflict?," in Halim Barakat, ed., *Contemporary North Africa: Issues of Development and Integration* (Washington, D.C.: Center for Contemporary Arab Studies, Georgetown University, 1985).

------. *Comparative Politics of North Africa: Algeria, Morocco, and Tunisia* New York: Syracuse University Press, 1980).

Esposito, John. "Islamic Revivalism," *The Muslim World Today*, Occasional Paper, No. 3, (July 1985).

------. *Islam and Politics* (New York: Syracuse University Press, 1984).

Esposito, John, ed. *Voices of Resurgent Islam* (New York: Oxford University Press, 1983).

Esposito, John L. and John J. Donohue, eds. *Islam in Transition* (New York: Oxford University Press, 1982).

Esposito, John and James Piscatori. "Democratization and Islam," *Middle East Journal*, Vol. 45, No. 3 (Summer 1991).

Feuer, Lewis. *The Conflict of Generations* (New York: Basic Books, 1969).

Al-Ghannoushi, Rashed. "The Battle Against Islam," paper presented at the Symposium on Islam and Democracy in the Arab Maghreb, London School of Economics (February 29, 1992).

Gellner, Ernest, et al. *Islam et Politique au Maghreb* (Paris: CNRS, 1981).

Green, Arnold. "A Comparative Historical Analysis of the `Ulama' and the State in Egypt and Tunisia," *Revue de L'Occident Musulman et de la Méditerranée*, No. 29 (1980).

Greenhouse, Steven. "Radicals Seen as New Peril for Tunisians," *New York Times* (October 1, 1987).

Gurr, Ted. *Why Men Rebel* (Princeton: Princeton University Press, 1970).

Gusfield, Joseph, ed. *Protest, Reform and Revolt: A Reader in Social Movements* (New York: John Wiley & Sons, Inc., 1970).

Haddad, Yvonne Y. "Sayyid Qutb: Ideologue of Islamic Revival," in John Esposito, ed., *Voices of Resurgent Islam* (New York: Oxford University Press, 1983).

------. "The Qur'anic Justification for an Islamic Revolution: The Views of Sayyid Qutb," *The Middle East Journal*, Vol. 37, No. 1 (Winter 1983).

------. *Contemporary Islam and the Challenge of History* (New York: State University of New York, 1982).

------. "The Islamic Alternative," *The Link*, Vol. 15, No. 4 (September-October 1982).

Heper, Metin and Raphael Israeli. *Islam and Politics In the Middle East* (London: Croom Helm, 1984).

Hermassi, Mohamed Elbaki. "La Société Tunisienne au Miroir Islamiste," *Maghreb-Machrek*, No. 103 (January-February-March 1984).

------. *Leadership and National Development in North Africa: A Comparative Study* (Berkeley: University of California Press, 1972).

Hoffer, Eric. *The True Believer* (New York: Holt, Rinehart and Winston, 1951).

Hourani, Albert. *Arabic Thought in The Liberal Age: 1798-1939* (London: Oxford University Press, 1970).

Hunter, Shireen, ed. *The Politics of Islamic Revivalism: Diversity and Unity* (Indianapolis: Indiana University Press, 1989).

Ibrahim, Saad Eddin. "Anatomy of Egypt's Militant Islamic Groups: Methodological Note and Preliminary Findings," *International Journal of Middle East Studies*, Vol. 12 (December 1980).

Ingram, Simon. "Why Ben Ali Ousted His President," *Middle East International*, No. 313 (November 21, 1987).

Ismael, Tareq Y. and Jacqueline S. Ismael. *Government and Politics in Islam* (New York: St. Martin's Press, 1985).

Jansen, G.H. *Militant Islam* (New York: Harper and Row, 1979).

Khadduri, Majid. *Political Trends in the Arab World: The Role of Ideas and Ideals in Politics* (Baltimore: The Johns Hopkins University Press, 1970).

Kowalwski, David. "The Protest Uses of Symbolic Politics: The Mobilization Functions of Protest Symbolic Resources," *Social Science Quarterly*, Vol. 81, No. 1 (June 1980).

LaFranchi, Howard. "Algerians Test Support for Islam in a Free Vote," *Christian Science Monitor* (June 7, 1990).

Leca, Jean and Jean-Claude Vatin. *L'Algérie Politique* (Paris: Presses de la Fondation Nationale des Sciences Politiques, 1975).

Lewis, Bernard. "The Return of Islam," *Commentary*, Vol. 61 (January 1976).

Lipset, Seymour Martin and Philip Altbach, eds. *Students in Revolt* (Boston: Hougfhton Mifflin Co., 1969).

Marshall, Susan E. "Islamic Revival in the Maghreb: The Utility of Tradition for Modernizing Elites," *Studies in Comparative International Development*, No. 14 (Summer 1979).

McCarthy, John and Mayer Zald. "Resource and Mobilization and Social Movements: A Partial Theory," *American Journal of Sociology*, Vol. 6, No. 82 (1977).

Medimegh, Aziza and Elbaki Hermassi. *Essais pour une Socilogie Religieuse* (Tunis: Centre de Perspective Sociale, 1983).

Memmi, Albert. *The Colonizer and the Colonized* (Boston: Beacon Press, 1965).

Moore, Clement Henry. *Tunisia Since Independence* (Berkeley: University of California Press, 1965).

Morello, Carol. "City and Resort Show Two Sides of Algeria," *Philadelphia Inquirer* (January 20, 1992).

Mortimer, Edward. *Faith and Power: The Politics of Islam* (New York: Random House, 1982).

Munson, Henry. *Islam and Revolution in the Middle East* (New Haven: Yale University Press, 1988).

------. "The Social Base of Islamic Militancy in Morocco," *The Middle East Journal*, Vol. 40, No. 21 (Spring 1986).

------. "The Islamic Revival in Morocco and Tunisia," *Muslim World*, Vol. 76, Nos. 3-4 (July-October 1986).

Al-Naifar, Hemida. "How can a Muslim live in this era?," interview by François Burgat (translated by Linda Jones), *Middle East Report* (July-August 1988).

Naccache, Gilbert. "Idéologie et Projet de Société: L'Inéquation Tunisienne," *Le Mensuel*, No. 3 (October 1984).

Nassib, Selim. "Manipulation Intégriste: Tunis," *Liberation* (March 27, 1987).

Nolan, Riall. "Tunisia's Time of Transition," *Current History*, Vol. 80, No. 470 (December 1980).

Parker, Richard. *North Africa: Regional Tensions and Strategic Concerns* (New York: Praeger Publishers, 1984).

Paul, Jim. "States of Emergency: The Riots in Tunisia and Morocco," *MERIP Reports*, Vol. 14, No. 8 (October 1984).

Perkins, Kenneth. *Tunisia: Crossroads of the Islamic and European Worlds* (Boulder: Westview Press, 1986).

Pipes, Daniel. *In the Path of God: Islam and Political Power* (New York: Basic Books Publishers, Inc., 1983).

------. "Oil Wealth and the Islamic Resurgence," in Ali E. Hilal Dessouki, ed., *Islamic Resurgence in the Arab World* (New York: Praeger Publishers, 1982).

Piscatori, James. *Islam in a World of Nation-States* (Cambridge University Press, 1986).

Piscatori, James, ed. *Islam in the Political Process* (London: Cambridge University Press, 1983).

Plath, David. "Modernization and its Discontents: Japan's Little Utopias," in Joseph Gusfield, ed., *Protest, Reform and Revolt: A Reader in Social Movements* (New York: John Wiley & Sons, Inc., 1970).

Promise Unfulfilled: Human Rights in Tunisia Since 1987 (New York: Lawyers Committee for Human Rights, October 1993).

Quandt, William. *Revolution and Political Leadership: Algeria, 1954-1968* (Cambridge, MA: MIT Press, 1969).

Qutb, Sayyid. *Milestones* (International Islamic Federation of Muslim Students Organizations, 1978).

The Renaissance Party in Tunisia: The Quest for Freedom and Democracy (Washington, D.C.: American Muslim Council, 1991).

Robertson, Ian. *Sociology* (New York: Worth Publisher, Inc., 1981).

Rosenthal, Erwin. *Islam in the Modern National State* (London: Cambridge University Press, 1965).

Ruedy, John. *Modern Algeria: The Origins and Development of a Nation* (Indianapolis: Indiana University Press, 1992).

Ruedy, John , ed. *Islamism and Secularism in North Africa* (New York: St. Martin's Press, 1994).

Ruthven, Malise. *Islam in the World* (New York: Oxford University Press, 1984).

Sa`af, Abdullah. "Middle Class and State in Morocco," unpublished Paper Delivered at Morocco's Day at the Johns Hopkins University School of Advanced International Studies (Washington, D.C.: April 12, 1985).

Salem, Nora. *Habib Bourguiba, Islam, and the Creation of Tunisia* (London: Croom Helm, 1984).

Schemm, Paul. "Algeria's Return to its Past: Can the FIS Break the Vicious Cycle of History?," *Middle East Insight*, Vol. 11, No. 2 (January-February 1995).

------. "Hope for Algeria?" *Middle East Insight*, Vol. 10, No. 6 (September-October 1994).

Seddon, David. "Winter of Discontent: Economic Crisis in Tunisia and Morocco," *MERIP Reports*, Vol. 14, No. 8 (October 1984).

Seibert, Sam, et al. "The Worst Has Been Avoided," *Newsweek* (October 12, 1987).

Shahin, Emad Eldin. "Muhammad Rashid Rida," *The Oxford Encyclopedia of The Modern Islamic World*, Vol. 3 (New York: Oxford University Press, 1995).

------. "Salafiyah," *The Oxford Encyclopedia of The Modern Islamic World*, Vol. 4 (New York: Oxford University Press, 1995).

------. "Tunisia's Renaissance Party: The Rise and Repression of an Islamic Movement," *Middle East Insight*, Vol. 11, No. 2 (January-February 1995).

------. "Under the Shadow of the Imam: Morocco's Diverse Islamic Movements," *Middle East Insight*, Vol. 11, No. 2 (January-February 1995).

------. "Secularism and Nationalism: The Political Discourse of Abd al-Salam Yassin," in John Ruedy, ed., *Islamism and Secularism in North Africa* (New York: St. Martin's Press, 1994).

------. "Algeria: The Limits to Democracy," *Middle East Insight*, Vol. 8, No. 6 (July-October, 1992).

Sharabi, Hisham. *Arab Intellectuals and the West: The Formative Years, 1875-1914* (Baltimore: The Johns Hopkins University Press, 1970).

Shehadi, Philip. "'Islamic Communes' Set about Cleaning up Algeria," *New York Times* (November 11, 1990).

Sivan, Emmanuel. *Radical Islam: Medieval Theology and Modern Politics* (New Haven: Yale University Press, 1985).

Smesler, Neil. *Theory of Collective Behavior* (New York: Free Press, 1962).

Sorel, Georges. *Reflections on Violence* (Glencoe: The Free Press, 1950).

Soudan, François, "Verdict Pondere en Tunisie," *Jeune Afrique*, No. 1396 (October 7, 1987).

Souriau, Christiane, et al. *Le Maghreb Musulman en 1979* (Paris: Centre National de la Recherche Scientifique, 1981).

Taleb, Ahmed. "Réflexions sur la Décolonisation Culturelle en Algérie," *Humanisme Musulman*, Nos. 6 and 7 (June-July 1965).

Taylor, Alan R. *The Islamic Question in Middle East Politics* (Boulder: Westview Press, 1988).

Tessler, Mark. "Image and Reality in Moroccan Political Economy," in I. William Zartman, ed., *The Political Economy of Morocco* (New York: Praeger Publishers, 1987).

------. "Tunisia at the Crossroads," *Current History*, Vol. 84, No. 502 (May 1985).

------. "Morocco: Institutional Pluralism and Monarchical Dominance," in I. William Zartman, ed., *Political Elites in Arab North Africa* (London: Longman, 1982).

------. "Social Change and the Islamic Revival in Tunisia," *The Maghreb Review*, Vol. 5, No. 1 (January-February 1980).

Tidjani, El-Hachemi. "Les Composants de Notre Personnalité," *Humanisme Musulman*, No. 8 (August 1965).

Tozy, Muhammad. "Champ et Contre Champ Politico-Religieux au Maroc," (Thèse pour le Doctorat d'Etat en Sciences Politiques, Faculte de Droit et de Sciences Politiques d'Aix, Marseille, 1984).

------. "Champ Politique et Champ Religieux au Maroc: Croisement ou Hiérarchisation," (Mémoire pour l'Obtention du Diplôme d'Etudes Supérieures de Sciences Politiques, Faculté de Sciences Juridiques, Economiques, et Sociales, Université Hassan II, Casablanca, 1980).

------. "Monopolisation de la Production Symbolique et Hiérarchisation du Champ Politico-Religieux au Maroc," in Christiane Souriau, et al., *Le Maghreb Musulman en 1979* (Paris: CNRS, 1981).

Tozy, Mohamed and B. Etienne. "La Da`wa au Maroc: Prolegomenes Theoritico-Historique," in Oliver Carr and Paul Dumont, eds., *Radicalismes Islamiques: Maroc, Pakistan, Inde, Yougoslavie, Mali*. Vol. 2 (Paris: L'Hartmattan, 1986).

Vatin, Jean Claude. "Popular Puritanism versus State Reformism," in James Piscatori, ed., *Islam in the Political Process* (London: Cambridge University Press, 1983).

------. "Revival in the Maghreb: Islam as an Alternative Political Language," in Ali E. Hilal Dessouki, ed., *Islamic Resurgence in the Arab World* (New York: Praeger Publishers, 1982).

Voll, John. *Islam: Continuity and Change in the Modern World* (Boulder: Westview Press, 1985).

Waltz, Susan. "Islamist Appeal in Tunisia," *The Middle East Journal*, Vol. 40, No. 4 (Autumn 1986).

Ware, Lewis B. "Ben Ali's Constitutional Coup in Tunisia," *Middle East Journal*, Vol. 42, No. 4 (Autumn 1988).

Waterbury, John. *The Commander of the Faithful: The Moroccan Political Elite* (New York: Columbia University Press, 1970).

Wilkinson, Paul. *Social Movement* (New York: Praeger Publishers, 1971).

Wilson, John. *Introduction to Social Movements* (New York: Basic Books, 1973).

Yassin, Abdel Salam. *La Révolution à l'Heure de l'Islam* (Gignac-La-Nerthe: Borel and Feraud SA, 1981).

Zald, Mayer and John McCarthy, eds. *The Dynamics of Social Movements* (Cambridge: Winthrop, 1979).

Zald, Mayer and John McCarthy. "Resource Mobilization and Social Movements: A Partial Theory," *American Journal of Sociology*, Vol. 6, No. 82 (1977).

Zartman, I. William. "The Opposition as Support of the State," in I. William Zartman and Adeed Dawisha, eds., *Beyond Coercion* (London: Croom Helm, 1988).

Zartman, I. William, ed. *The Political Economy of Morocco* (New York: Praeger Publishers, 1987).

------. "King Hassan's New Morocco," in I. William Zartman, ed., *The Political Economy of Morocco* (New York: Praeger Publishers, 1987).

------. "Political Dynamics in the Maghreb: The Cultural Dialectic," in Halim Barakat, ed., *Contemporary North Africa: Issues of Development and Integration* (Washington, D.C.: Center for Contemporary Arab Studies, Georgetown University, 1985).

------, ed. *Political Elites in Arab North Africa* (London: Longman, 1982).

Zartman, I. William and Adeed Dawisha, eds. *Beyond Coercion* (London: Croom Helm, 1988).

Ziadeh, Nicola A. *Origins of Nationalism in Tunisia* (Beirut: The American University in Beirut, 1962).

Books and Articles in Arabic

Al-Akhdar, G. "Al-Shaykh Abdel Latif Sultani" *al-Mujtama`*, No. 672 (May 22, 1984).

Al-Amari, Ibrahim. *Al-Tanmiyya wa al-Takhaluf fi al-Mantiqa al-`Arabiyya al-Islamiyya* [Development and Underdevelopment in the Arab-Muslim Region] (Tunis: Matba`at Tunis, 1985).

Al-Amin, Fadeel. "Algeria's Democracy at Crossroads," *al-Amal*, No. 162 (August-September 1991).

Al-Aqqad, Moustapha. *Al-Maghrib al-Arabi* [The Arab Maghrib] (Cairo: Maktabat al-Anglo al-Masriyya, 1993).

Arslan, Shakeeb. *Limadha Ta'akhar al-Muslimun wa Taqadam Ghayrahum* [Why Were the Muslims Set Back While Others Advanced?] (Cairo: 1939-40).

Ayachi, Ihmeda. *Al-Haraka al-Islamiyya fi al-Jaza'ir: al-Juzur, al-Rumuz, al-Masar* [The Islamic Movement in Algeria: Roots, Symbols, and Path] (Casablanca: Ouyoun al-Maqalat, 1993).

Balgheeth, Fatheya. "Al-Haraka al-Islamiyya fi Tunis min Khilal Sahifat al-`Amal: 1979" [The Islamic Movement in Tunisia Through al-`Amal Newspaper] (Unpublished Dissertation, Institute of Press and Media, Tunis, 1979).

Belhaj, Ali. *Fasl al-Kalam fi Muwajahat Dhulm al-Hukkam* [The Decisive Statement on Confronting the Aggression of Rulers] (The Islamic Salvation Front, December 21, 1992).

Bekhtir, Salaman, et al. "Nahwa al-Bahth `an Kharita Thaqafiyya wa Idiulujiyya" [Toward a Search for a Cultural and Ideological Map]. (Unpublished Dissertation, Faculty of Literature and Humanities, Muhammad V University, Rabat, 1979-1980).

Ben Aziza, al-Mukhtar. "Risala min Dakhil al-Itijah" [A Message from Within the Islamic Tendency], *al-Mawqif*, No. 21 (October 6, 1984).

Ben Nabi, Malik. *Shurut al-Nahda* [The Conditions of Renaissance] (Damascus: Dar al-Fikr, 3rd ed., 1969).

Blassi, Nabil A. *Al-Itijah al-Arabi al-Islami wa Dawrahu fi Tahrir al-Jaza'ir* [The Arabo-Islamic Trend and Its Role in the Liberation of Algeria] (Cairo: al-Hay'a al-Masriyya al-Amma li al-Kitab, 1990).

Boularas, Abdel Hai. "Hiwar ma`a Hizb al-Tahrir" [Dialogue with the Islamic Liberation Party], *al-Mawqif*, No. 42 (March 19, 1985).

Bouraoui, Ali. "Halaqa Muhimma fi Tarikh al-Haraka al-Islamiyya bi al-Jaza'ir" [A Significant Link in the History of the Islamic Movement in Algeria], *al-`Alam*, No. 426 (April 11, 1992).

Bourguiba, Habib. *Khutab Mawlidiyya* [Speeches on the Occasion of the Prophet's Anniversary] (Tunis: The Ministry of Information, 1979).

------. *Khutab* [Speeches] (Tunis: The Ministry of Information, 1957-1982).

Boutizoua, Moustapha and Abdel Rahim Gannouhi. "Al-Haraka al-Islamiyya fi al-Maghrib: Harakat al-Islah wa al-Tajdid Namudhajan" [The Islamic Movement in Morocco: HATM as a Model] (Unpublished Thesis, Faculty of Literature and Human Sciences, Ibn Zuhr University, Agadir, 1991-1992).

The Charter, Jam`iyyat al-Jama`a al-Islamiyya al-Maghribiyya (Casablanca: Dar Qurtuba, 1989).

Darif, Muhammad. *Al-Islam al-Siyasi fi al-Jaza'ir* [Political Islam in Algeria] (Casablanca: Manshurat al-Majalla al-Maghribiyya li-`Ilm al-Ijtima` al-Siyasi, 1994).

------. *Al-Islam al-Siyasi fi al-Maghrib: Muqaraba Watha'iqiyya* [Political Islam in Morocco: A Documentary Approach] (Casablanca: Manshurat al-Majalla al-Maghribiyya li-`Ilm al-Ijtima` al-Siyasi, 1992).

Al-Darwish, Qusai Saleh. "Algeria: The Possible and Impossible Dialogue," *al-Majalla*, No. 759 (August 28-September 3, 1994).

Al-Dimni. "Na`am li al-Hiwar al-Fikri" [Yes to Intellectual Dialogue], *al-Ra'i*, No. 334 (August 16, 1985).

Al-Fassi, Allal. *Al-Naqd al-Dhati* [Self-Criticism (Rabat: Lajnat Nashr Turath Za`im al-Tahrir, 1979).

Al-Furati, Abdel Latif. "`Ala Hamish al-Ahkam" [On the Surroundings of the Sentences], *al-Majalla*, No. 187 (September 10-16, 1983).

Al-Ghannoushi, Rashed. *Al-Huriyyat al-`Amma fi al-Dawla al-Islamiyya* [Public Freedoms in the Islamic State] (Beirut: Markaz Dirasat al-Wihda al-Arabiyya, 1993).

Al-Ghannoushi, Rashed. Interview, *Kayhan al-Arabi*, No. 955 (December 12, 1987).

------. "Al-Fikr al-Islami la Yanhazim fi Ma`raka Nadhifa," [Islamic Thought Cannot be Defeated in a Clean Battle], *al-Musawar* (December 20-27, 1985).

------. *Maqalat* [Articles] (Paris: Dar al-Karawan, 1984).

------. "Al-'Alam al-Islami wa al-Isti`mar al-Hadith" [The Islamic World and Neo-Imperialism], in Rashed al-Ghannoushi, *Maqalat* (Paris: Dar Karawan, 1984).

------. "Al-Islam wa al-'Unf" [Islam and Violence], in Rashed al-Ghannoushi, *Maqalat* (Paris: Dar Karawan, 1984).

------. "Al-Taghreeb wa Hatmiyyat al-Dictatoriyya" [Westernization: an Imperative to Dictatorship], in Rashed al-Ghannoushi, *Maqalat* (Paris: Dar Karawan, 1984).

------. "Al-Tatawur: Ihtifadh + Tajawuz" [Evolution: Preservation and Transcendence], in Rashed al-Ghannoushi, *Maqalat* (Paris: Dar Karawan, 1984).

------ [Rushdi Abdel Sabour, pseud.]. *Al-'Uruba wa al-Islam* [Arabism and Islam] (Tunis: Matba`at Tunis: 1983).

------. "Al-'Amal al-Islami wa Quta` al-Turuq" [Islamic Action and the Bandits], *al-Ma`rifa*, Vol. 5, No. 5 (May 15, 1979).

------. "Qadat al-Haraka al-Islamiyya al-Mu`asira" [The Leaders of the Contemporary Islamic Movement], *al-Ma`rifa*, Vol. 5, No. 4 (April 1, 1979).

------. "Al-Thawra al-Iraniyya Thawra Islamiyya" [The Iranian Revolution Is an Islamic Revolution], *al-Ma`rifa*, Vol. 5, No. 3 (February 12, 1979).

------. "Min Jadid: Nahnu wa al-Gharb" [Once More: We and the West], *al-Ma`rifa*, Vol. 4, No. 9 (August 1, 1978); Vol. 4, No. 10 (October 1978); and Vol. 5, No. 1 (November 20, 1978).

------. "Da`wa ila al-Rushd" [A Call to Guidance], *al-Ma`rifa*, Vol. 5, No. 2 (January 1, 1978).

------. "Al-Adab wa al-Akhlaq" [Literature and Ethics], *al-Ma`rifa*, Vol. 2, No. 6 (1974).

------. "Baramij al-Falsafa wa Jil al-Daya`" [Philosophy Programs and The Generation of Loss], *al-Ma`rifa*, No. 10 (1973).

Al-Ghannoushi, Rashed. *Haykal `am li al-Iqtisad al-Islami* [A General Frame for the Islamic Economic System] (Tunis: n.p., n.d).

------. *Al-Fikr al-Islami bayn al-Mithaliyya wa al-Waqi`iyya* [Islamic Thought Between Idealism and Reality] (Tunis: n.p., n.d.).

Al-Ghannoushi, Rashed and Hassan al-Turabi. *Al-Haraka al-Islamiyya wa al-Tahdith* [The Islamic Movement and Modernization] (Beirut: Dar al-Jil, 1980).

Al-Ghozzi, Kamal. "Al-'Awamel al-Maudu`iyya li al-Inti`asha al-Islamiyya bi al-Sahil al-Tunisi" [The Objective Factors Behind the Revival of the Islamic Movement in the Tunisian Sahel] (Unpublished Dissertation, Faculty of Literature and Social Sciences, Sociology Department, Tunis, 1984).

Al-Hamdi, Muhammad al-Hashmi. *Al-Ru'ya al-Fikriyya wa al-Manhaj al-Usuli li-Harakat al-Itijah al-Islami* [The Ideological Perception and the Fundamentalist Paradigm of the MTI] (London: Dar al-Sahwa, 1987).

Haqa'iq Hawl Harakat al-Itijah al-Islami [Facts on the Movement of Islamic Tendency] (Tunis: MTI, 1983).

Harbi, Muhammad. *Al-Thawra al-Jaza'iriyya: Sanawat al-Makhad* [The Algerian Revolution: Years of Deliverance] (Muhammadiya: Matba`at Fadala, 1988).

Harakat al-Itijah al-Islami: al-Dhikra al-Thalitha, 1981-1984 [The Islamic Tendency Movement: The Third Anniversary 1981-1984] (Tunis: n.p., 1984).

Al-Harras, Abdel Salam. "Mulahadhat Hawl al-Tarbiyya al-Islamiyya" [Remarks on Islamic Education], *al-Huda*, Vol. 3, No. 10 (November-December 1984).

Al-Hermassi, Abdel Latif. *Al-Haraka al-Islamiyya fi Tunis: al-Yasar al-Ishtiraki, al-Islam, wa al-Haraka al-Islamiyya* [The Islamic Movement in Tunisia: The Socialist Left, Islam, and the Islamic Movement] (Tunis: Bayram li al-Nashr, 1985).

Al-Jabri, Muhammad Abid. *Al-Ta`lim fi al-Maghrib al-`Arabi* [Education in the Arab Maghrib] (Casablanca: Dar al-Nashr al-Maghribiyya, 1989).

Jama`at al-`Adl wa al-Ihsan: Rijal, Ahdath wa Minhaj [The Association of al-Adl wa al-Ihsan: Men, Events, and Approach], a newsletter published by the association (March 1992).

Al-Jourshi, Salah Eddin. "Mubadarat Mourou Fursa Jadida Law" [Mourou's Initiative Is a New Opportunity, If], *Realities*, No. 295 (May 2, 1991).

------. "Al-Ittijah al-Islami Tahawal ila Haraka Fa`ila" [The Islamic Tendency Turned into an Effective Movement], *al-Muslimun* (April 14, 1989).

------. *Al-Haraka al-Islamiyya fi al-Dawwama* [The Islamic Movement in the Whirlpool] (Tunis: Dar al-Buraq li al-Nashr, 1985).

------. "Limadha al-Fikr al-Islami al-Mustaqbali?" [Why Is the Futuristic Islamic Thought?], *15/21*, No. 2 (January 1983).

------. "In`ikasat al-Thawra al-Iraniyya" [The Repercussions of the Iranian Revolution], *al-Ma`rifa*, Vol. 5, No. 4 (April 1, 1979).

------. *Tajrubat al-Islah* [The Experience of Reform] (Dar al-Raya li al-Nashr, 1978).

------, et al. *Min ajl Tashih al-Wa`i bi al-Dhat* [For Reforming Self-Consciousness] (Tunis: Maktabat al-Jadid, 1985).

------, ed. *Jawanib min al-Mas'ala al-Ijtima`iyya* [Aspects of the Social Issue] (Tunis: Maktabat al-Jadid, n.d.).

Al-Jourshi, Salah Eddin, Muhammad al-Quomai, and Abdel Aziz al-Tamimi, *Al-Muqadimat al-Nadhariyya li al-Islamiyyin al-Taqadumiyyin* [The Theoretical Basis of the Progressive Islamists] (Tunis: Dar al-Buraq li al-Nashr, 1989).

Ju`ait, Hisham. *Al-Shakhsiyya al-`Arabiyya al-Islamiyya wa al-Masir al-`Arabi* [The Arab-Muslim Personality and Arab Fate] (Beirut: Dar al-Tali`a, 1984).

Al-Ka`bi, al-Monji. "al-Zaytouna fi Mira't al-Damir al-Tunisi" [The Zaytouna in the Tunisian Conscience], *al-Marji`*, Vol. 1, No. 2 (October 1982).

Al-Kandahlawi, Muhammad Youssef. *Hayat al-Sahaba* [The Biography of the Companions] (Damascus: Dar al-Qalam, 1987).

Khashana, Rasheed. "Qadiyyat Hizb al-Tahrir al-Islami" [The Case of the Islamic Liberation Party], *al-Maghrib*, No. 65 (August 20, 1983).

Khashojgui, Jamal Ahmed. "Mushahadat min Dakhil al-Haraka al-Islamiyya" [Scenes From Inside the Islamic Movement], *al-Liwa'* (June 20, 1990).

King Hassan's Directives to the Civil Servants, *Da'wat al-Haqq*, No. 238 (July 1984).

King Hassan's speech to the Scholars in the Supreme Scientific Council, *Da'wat al-Haqq*, No. 235 (April 1984).

King Hassan's speech to the Scholars in the Concluding Session of the Supreme Council, *Da'wat al-Haqq*, No. 224 (August 1982).

King Hassan's speech to the scholars, *Da'wat al-Haqq*, Vol. 21, No. 1 (March 1980).

Kouroum, Hassanin. "Madha Wara' al-Ahkam" [What is Behind the Sentences], *al-Wafd*, October 1, 1987.

Madani, Abbasi. *Azmat al-Fikr al-Hadith wa Mubarirat al-Hal al-Islami* [The Crisis of Modern Thought and the Justifications for an Islamic Solution] (Mecca: Maktabat al-Manar, 1989).

------. *Mushkilat Tarbawiyya fi al-Bilad al-Islamiyya* [Educational Problems in the Muslim Countries] (Mecca: Maktabat al-Manar, 1989).

Mashru` al-Barnamaj al-Siyasi li al-Jabha al-Islamiyya li al-Inqadh, manuscript (March 1989).

Al-Mili, Muhsin. *Dhahirat al-Yasar al-Islami* [The Phenomenon of the Islamic Left] (Tunis: Matba`at Tunis, 1983).

Mourou, Abdel Fattah. Interview in *al-Ma'rifa*, Vol. 5, No. 5 (May 15, 1979).

Mouti`, Abdel Karim. *Al-Thawra al-Islamiyya: Qadar al-Maghrib al-Rahin* [The Islamic Revolution: The Current Fate of Morocco] (Holland: n.p., 1984).

Mrimish, Aziz. "Al-Jabha al-Islamiyya li al-Inqadh," *Adwa'*, No. 436 (June 25, 1992).

Al-Mu'amara `ala Harakat al-Shabiba al-Islamiyya [The Conspiracy against the Islamic Youth Association] (Holland: n.p., 1984).

Al-Nabahani, Taqi Eddin. *Nidham al-Islam* [The Islamic System] (Jerusalem: Manshurat Hizb al-Tahrir, 1953).

Al-Nidham al-Bourguibi [The Bourguibi System] (Beirut: Dar Ibn Khaldoun, 1980).

"Qadiyyat al-Muntasibin li al-Itijah al-Islami" [The Trial of the Members of the MTI], *al-Sabah* (September 1-4, 1981).

The Royal Decree of April 18, 1981. *Da'wat al-Haqq*, Vol. 22, No. 4 (June-July 1981).

Sa`dallah, Abu al-Qasim. *Al-Haraka al-Wataniyya al-Jaza'iriyya: 1900-1930* [The Algerian National Movement: 1900-1930] (Beirut: Dar al-Adab, 1969).

Al-Sagheer, Abu Bakr. "Al-Ifraj `an Qiyadat al-Ittijah al-Islami" [The Release of the Leaders of the MTI], *al-Ra'i* (August 10, 1984).

"Al-Shaykh Rashed al-Ghannoushi Uhakim Sajjanih" [Shaykh Rashed al-Ghannoushi Tries his Captives], *al-Tali`a al-Islamiyya*, Vol. 5, No. 31 (October 1987).

Shrit, Abdullah and Muhammad al-Mili. *Al-Jaza'ir fi Mir'at al-Tarikh* [Algeria in the Mirror of History] (Algeria: Maktabat al-Ba`th, 1965).

Al-Tahiri, Nour Eddin. *Al-Jaza'ir Bayn al-Khiyar al-Islami wa al-Khiyar al-`Askari* [Algeria Between the Islamic Alternative and the Military Alternative] (Casablanca: Dar Qurtuba, 1992).

Al-Tarzi, Kamal. "Innana Nad`u ila Islam al-I`tidal" [We Call for a Moderate Islam], interview in *Haqa'iq*, No. 31 (June 1, 1984).

Tazghart, Othman. "Algeria: The Hardliners in the Military," *al-Majalla*, No. 770 (November 13-19, 1994).

------. "Assassinations in Algeria," *al-Majalla*, No. 687 (April 7-13, 1993).

Al-Tha`alibi, Muhammad al-Hajawi. "Al-Majalis al-`Ilmiyya al-Iqlimiyya" [The Regional Scientific Councils], *Da`wat al-Haqq*, Vol. 22, No. 6 (October 1981).

Al-Tunsi, Las`ad. "Al-Islamiyyun wa al-Haraka al-Niqabiyya" [The Islamists and the Union Movement], *al-Anwar* (September 9, 1984).

Al-Tuwati, Moustapha. *Al-Ta`bir al-Dini `an al-Sira` al-Ijtima`i fi al-Islam* [The Religious Expression of the Social Conflict in Islam] (Tunis: Dar al-Nashr li al-Maghrib al-`Arabi, n.d.).

Abd al-Salam Yassin, *Hiwar ma`a al-Fudala' al-Dimuqratiyyin* [Dialogue with the Virtuous Democrats] (Casablanca: Matba`at al-Ufuq, 1994).

------. *Al-Islam wa al-Qawmiyya al-`Almaniyya* [Islam and Secular Nationalism] (Casablanca: Matba`at al-Najah, 1989).

------ *Al-Minhaj al-Nabawi: Tarbiyyatan wa Tandhiman wa Zahfan* [The Prophetic Paradigm: Socialization, Organization, and March] (Morocco: n.p., 1989).

------. *Nadharat fi al-Fiqh wa al-Tarikh* [Views on Jurisprudence and History] (Al-Muhammadiyya: Matba`at Fadala, 1989).

------. "Al-Jihad: Tandhiman wa Zahfan" [Jihad: Organization and March], *al-Jama`a*, Vol. 4, No. 11 (May 1983).

------. "Al-Minhaj al-Nabawi" [The Prophetic Paradigm], *al-Jama`a*, No. 10 (1982).

------. "Al-Minhaj al-Nabawi: Tarbiyyatan wa Tandhiman wa Zahfan" [The Prophetic Paradigm: Socialization, Organization, and March], *al-Jama`a*, No. 8 (June 1981).

------. "`Unwan li `Amalina" [A Title for our Action], *al-Jama`a*, No. 1 (March-May 1979).

------. "Iftitahiyya wa Istiftah" [Prologue], *al-Jama`a*, Vol. 1, No. 1 (March-May 1979).

------. *Al-Islam aw al-Tufan* [Islam or the Deluge] (Marrakech: n.p., 1974).

------. *Al-Islam Ghadan* [Islam Tomorrow](Casablanca: Maktabat al-Najah, 1973).

------. *Al-Islam Bayn al-Da`wa wa al-Dawla* [Islam Between the Call and the State] (Casablanca: Maktabat al-Najah, 1972).

Zaghlul, Ahmad Fathi. *Sir Taqadum al-Inkiliz al-Saksuniyyin* [The Secret for the Advancement of the Anglo-Saxons] (Cairo, 1911-12).

Interviews

Baha, Abdullah, HATM vice-president, Rabat, November 27, 1994.

Ferjani, Sayyid, London-based Nahda Official, Virginia, June 8 and July 10, 1995.

Gassouss, Muhammad, Professor of Sociology at Muhammad V University, Rabat, April 5, 9, and 12, 1986.

Al-Ghannoushi, Rashed, the leader of the MTI, Tunis, February 14, 1986.

Haddam, Anwar, President of FIS Parliamentary Delegation in Europe and the United States, Washington, D.C., July 1994.

Al-Jourshi, Salah Eddin, Journalist and Co-founder of the MTI and the MTPI, Tunis, December 28, 1985; January 5, 10, and 13, 1986.

Al-Naifar, Shaykh Muhammad Saleh, Zaytouna Scholar, Tunis, December 19, 24, and 26, 1985 and January 1, 1986.

Al-Naifar, Shaykh Hemida, Professor at the Zaytouna University, Tunis, January 11, 1986.

Newspapers, Periodicals, Magazines, Newsservices

L'Action.
Adwa'.
Al-`Alam.
Al-`Alam al-Islami.
Al-`Amal.
Al-Anwar.
Al-`Aqida.
Arabia.
Asharq al-Awsat.
Al-Batal.
Christian Science Monitor.
Da`wat al-Haqq.
Democratie.
Dialogue.

15/21.
Haqa'iq.
Al-Hayat.
Al-Hidaya.
Al-Huda.
Al-I`lan.
Al-Iman.
Al-Jama`a.
Juene Afrique.
Kayhan al-`Arabi.
Lamalif.
Liberation.
Al--Liwa'.
Al-Maghrib.
Al-Majala.
Al-Ma`rifa.
Al-Marji`.
Al-Mawqif.
Al-Mithaq.
Le Monde.
Al-Mujahid.
Al-Mujtama`.
Al-Muslimun.
Al-Mustaqbal.
Newsweek.
New York Times.
Al-Nour.
La Presse.
Al-Ra'i.
Al-Sabah.
Al-Salam
Al-Sayyad.
Al-Tali`a al-Islamiyya.
Al-Wafd.
Wall Street Journal.
Al-Wasat.
Washington Post.
Al-Watan al-`Arabi.
Al-Wihda.

About the Book and Author

Islamic movements in North Africa have historically been distinguished from their counterparts in other parts of the Arab world because they have demonstrated a marked willingness to work within the political system and have at times even been officially recognized and allowed to participate in local and national elections. As a result, Islamic thinkers from the Maghrib have produced important writing about the role of Islam and the state, democracy, and nonviolent change. In this book, Emad Shahin offers a comparative analysis of the Islamic movements in Algeria, Tunisia, and Morocco, exploring the roots of their development, the nature of their dynamics, and the tenets of their ideology. He argues that the formation and expansion of Islamic movements since the late 1960s has come in response to the marginalization of Islam in state and society and to a perceived failure of imported models of development to resolve socioeconomic problems or to incorporate the Muslim belief system into a workable plan for social transformation.

Emad Eldin Shahin is an assistant professor at Al Akhawayn University in Ifrane, Morocco.

Index